Shaker Furniture Projects

BY GLEN D. HUEY & THE EDITORS OF POPULAR WOODWORKING

POPULAR WOODWORKING BOOKS
CINCINNATI, OHIO
www.popularwoodworking.com

Contents

Introduction

When I first became interested in building furniture, I searched through books and antiques-based newspapers to find images and descriptions of Shaker furniture. If you asked me to go into the shop to build whatever I wanted, I would immediately begin on something, anything, Shaker – the first two major pieces I built were a pair of shaker cupboards originally built in a New York Shaker community. For me, furniture with straight lines and understated elegance – which is what Shaker design and craftsmanship is all about – is the perfect first step into furnituremaking.

As it turns out I'm not alone in my way of thinking. Many woodworkers jump into furniture construction through the Shaker furniture porthole. Not only are the designs pleasing to the eye, the construction methods – especially joinery – are time-honored techniques that appear in pieces built by the Shakers as well as other top-notch craftsmen. If you learn techniques or methods of work as you build the furniture shown in this book, you'll use those techniques and methods over and over throughout your woodworking life.

What makes this particular book a great addition to your collection of Shaker projects is the wide range of pieces available. You'll find projects to fit in many areas of your home, including projects for the beginning woodworker as well as those that challenge woodworkers with years of experience. As a result, as you build projects from this book, your growth as a woodworker grows, too.

Included within these pages are a number of projects that are recognized as quintessential Shaker furniture designs. In fact, a few of the projects I've built many times. The Press Cupboard found in chapter 15 is a project that I retired during my woodworking days. I've built so many of those cupboards I could mill the lumber and cut the parts without the aid of a cut sheet. That was the point when I reached the decision to turn away orders. That piece alone, in my opinion, is worth your investment in this book.

Also inside you'll find other iconic Shaker furniture designs, such as the candlestand, drop-leaf table and blanket chest. There are tall clocks, wall clocks and chairs, both straight and of the rocking variety. There's even a woodbox and stepstool. And if you need to start at the beginning, we've included a Shaker workbench for your shop.

If you have any interest in Shaker furniture from an educational perspective (learning construction techniques), or actually building projects for yourself or others, this book is invaluable.

— GLEN D. HUEY

1

Tables

Trestle Desk

BY GLEN D. HUEY

Part of the job requirement of being a self-employed custom woodworker is self-promotion. Word of mouth works well, but starting the word can sometimes be a challenge. That's where competitions come into play. There are a number of woodworking shows every year throughout the country where I set up my booth and sell my wares. Many of them also have some type of woodworking competition. The competition can be organized so woodworkers compete in a certain category (professional, amateur, intarsia, turning). But it was a slightly different competition that brought me to the table pictured here. It's called a "side-by-side," and the idea is that an original piece, usually an antique of some note or reputation, is chosen by the event's organizers, and the competitors build a reproduction to mimic the piece.

The table shown is attributed to the Shaker community at Harvard, Mass., and is believed to have been used as a work table, side table or writing desk. The table is a wee bit wobbly, and the drawer may have been added at a later time. On the original, the drawer is maple, while the rest of the table is cherry. My desk is also cherry and maple, but the finish is done so it's hardly obvious.

As mentioned above, the reproduction (like the original) is a little unsteady. My recommendation for your piece is to make the stretcher between the legs considerably wider (6" or more), perhaps even cutting a decorative arch in the stretcher to lighten the look. Depending on how you plan to use the table, you may want to take that into account.

The Wood

This is a fairly simple table with some basic mortise-and-tenon construction, so contrary to Shaker philosophy I wanted to adorn the heck out of this thing with some amazing flame cherry. Quite honestly, I'm not allowed to tell you where I got it, and I don't know if I'll ever get any like this again. Suffice it to say you should look for some nicely figured cherry, then follow the cutting list to rough the material to the sizes given.

The Joints

The legs are made from three boards that are joined together with mortise-and-tenon joints and then shaped. It's easier to make the mortises in a square piece of wood, so I cut the mortises on the feet and top cross braces before shaping them. I used my drill press to cut the $3/8$" x 2" x $1\frac{1}{8}$"-deep mortise on the feet because the $7\frac{3}{8}$"-wide board wouldn't fit in my benchtop mortiser. However, my mortiser worked fine for the $3/8$" x 2" through-mortises in the top braces.

Cut the tenons on the leg pieces (which go between the feet and top cross braces) on the table saw. First define the shoulder of the tenon by setting the rip fence for the tenon length and set your blade height for $1/4$". Cut the shoulders on the two wide sides of the legs using the miter gauge, then raise your blade height to $13/16$" and define the shoulders on the two edges. Reset the fence for the length of the other tenon and repeat the process.

Now set your table saw fence to $5/8$", set the blade height to match the lengths of the tenon and run the leg upright to define the cheeks. Set the fence for $2\frac{13}{16}$" and cut the other cheeks. Check the fit on your joints and make any necessary adjustments.

After drilling out the mortises in the feet using my drill press, I cleaned up the mortise and squared the corners with a chisel. I'm glad they shot this picture because I don't use hand tools too often.

With the mortise-and-tenon joints complete, I transferred the shape of the legs from the template to the pieces. Band saw the shape, then sand the edges smooth. You might note that the grain orientation on the feet isn't really the best, as it makes a weak support. But when making a reproduction....

The legs and stretcher are held together with an edge-lap joint. The legs are notched through the mortise-and-tenon joint (left), and a mating notch is cut in the stretcher (above).

Shaping the Legs

With the leg pieces dry-assembled, transfer the leg shape from the scaled template on the next page to the legs. Then use your band saw to cut the legs to shape and sand the edges. I've found an oscillating spindle sander works well for this task, but if you can't spend the money, a drum sander attachment for your drill press is an economical option.

Glue up the legs, and while the glue is drying, cut out the stretcher. The stretcher fits over the legs using an edge lap joint, interlocking the legs and the stretcher. Cut two $^{7}/_{8}$"-wide x $^{13}/_{16}$" notches, $2^{3}/_{8}$" in from either end of the stretch-

er. The band saw works fairly well for this, with a little chisel clean up. When the glue is dry, cut the duplicate notches in the center of the cross braces, cutting into the through-tenon on the leg. Check the fit and make any necessary adjustment. When the fit is good, add a screw to the joints to make it a little stronger.

Make the Drawer

The drawer is made with traditional dovetail joinery. I used hand-cut half-blind dovetails on the drawer front and sides, and through-dovetails on the back. The drawer bottom fits into a $^{1}/_{8}$"-deep x $^{3}/_{16}$" groove in the sides and back, held

up $^{3}/_{16}$" from the bottom of the sides. Another $^{3}/_{16}$"- deep x $^{1}/_{4}$"-wide groove is cut on the outside of the drawer sides, $^{3}/_{16}$" down from the top edge to serve as part of the drawer runner.

Attaching the Legs and Drawer

The drawer is hung on the legs using two drawer runners screwed to the inside of each leg. Adjust the location of the runners to allow the drawer to slide freely. Conveniently, this table design allows you to adjust the drawer's fit before the top is attached. Use screws and elongated holes drilled in the top cross braces to attach the top to the legs.

Trestle Desk

NO.	ITEM	DIMENSIONS (INCHES)			MATERIAL	COMMENTS
		T	W	L		
1	Top	$^{9}/_{16}$	$17^{1}/_{2}$	29	Cherry	
2	Legs	$^{7}/_{8}$	$3^{5}/_{8}$	$20^{1}/_{8}$	Cherry	TBE*
2	Feet	$^{7}/_{8}$	$7^{3}/_{8}$	$16^{1}/_{4}$	Cherry	
2	Top cross braces	$^{7}/_{8}$	$1^{5}/_{8}$	$16^{7}/_{8}$	Cherry	
1	Stretcher	1	$1^{5}/_{8}$	$28^{3}/_{4}$	Cherry	
2	Drawer runners	$^{1}/_{4}$	$^{7}/_{16}$	7	Poplar	
1	Drawer front	$^{7}/_{16}$	$2^{1}/_{4}$	$21^{3}/_{4}$	Maple	
2	Drawer sides	$^{7}/_{16}$	$2^{1}/_{4}$	$7^{1}/_{8}$	Poplar	
1	Drawer back	$^{7}/_{16}$	$1^{3}/_{4}$	$21^{3}/_{4}$	Poplar	
1	Drawer bottom**	$^{1}/_{4}$	$7^{1}/_{8}$	$21^{1}/_{8}$	Poplar	
*TBE=tenons both ends; ** chamfer edges to fit in groove						

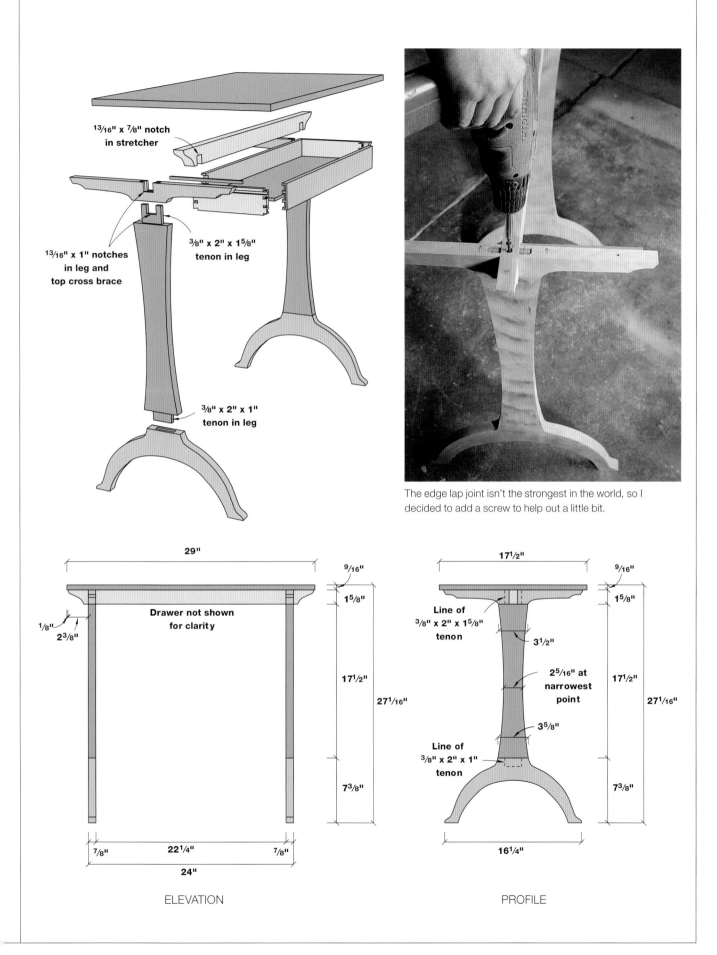

$^{13}/_{16}$" x $^{7}/_{8}$" notch
in stretcher

$^{13}/_{16}$" x 1" notches
in leg and
top cross brace

$^{3}/_{8}$" x 2" x 1$^{5}/_{8}$"
tenon in leg

$^{3}/_{8}$" x 2" x 1"
tenon in leg

The edge lap joint isn't the strongest in the world, so I decided to add a screw to help out a little bit.

29"

$^{9}/_{16}$"

1$^{5}/_{8}$"

Drawer not shown
for clarity

$^{1}/_{8}$"

2$^{3}/_{8}$"

17$^{1}/_{2}$"

27$^{1}/_{16}$"

7$^{3}/_{8}$"

$^{7}/_{8}$"

22$^{1}/_{4}$"

$^{7}/_{8}$"

24"

ELEVATION

17$^{1}/_{2}$"

$^{9}/_{16}$"

1$^{5}/_{8}$"

Line of
$^{3}/_{8}$" x 2" x 1$^{5}/_{8}$"
tenon

3$^{1}/_{2}$"

2$^{5}/_{16}$" at
narrowest
point

3$^{5}/_{8}$"

Line of
$^{3}/_{8}$" x 2" x 1"
tenon

17$^{1}/_{2}$"

27$^{1}/_{16}$"

7$^{3}/_{8}$"

16$^{1}/_{4}$"

PROFILE

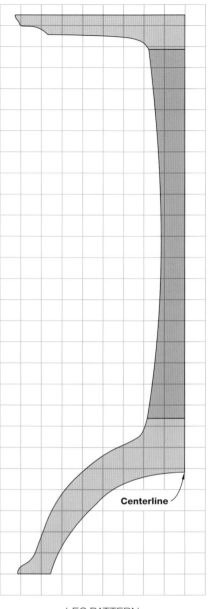

When attaching the top to the leg assembly, use elongated holes drilled in the cross braces to allow for wood movement due to changes in humidity.

LEG PATTERN
One square = 1"

After everything fits well, remove the top and sand all the pieces in preparation for finishing. I used a water-base aniline dye (Moser's Dark Antique Cherry, Woodworker's Supply, 800-645-9292) to color the piece. I then followed the dye with a ragged-on coat of boiled linseed oil, a coat of clear shellac to seal the oil and then a final top coat of clear lacquer.

You may not be looking to drum up word of mouth about your woodworking to help your business, by I guarantee this piece will stir up word of mouth about your skills among your friends and family.

A groove in the top edge of the drawer sides slips over the drawer runners that are attached to the ends for a simple, but very efficient, drawer slide.

Classic Candlestand

BY MALCOLM HUEY

Built by members of the Mount Lebanon community in New York during the first half of the 19th century, this recognizable Shaker form is actually their stylish interpretation of earlier forms. The legs are a derivation of a Sheraton design. The Shakers referred to the leg design as "umbrella" or "spider feet." I first found this table in John Kassay's "The Book of Shaker Furniture." The original shown in the book is part of the J.J.G. McCue collection, and resides in the Museum of Fine Arts in Boston. A very similar cherry table is also in the collection of the Metropolitan Museum of Art in New York City.

Forgiving Form

While I've included detailed patterns for both the pedestal and the legs on this table, the form is actually forgiving. If your turning ends up a little thinner in one area, or the legs end up a hair thinner at the bottom, it's OK. It's a nice-looking project that will allow you to practice your skills and end up with a great-looking table.

Everything about the table connects to the pedestal, so let's begin there. I've included a pattern that gives the diameter of the pedestal all along its length. While the turning skills required for the piece aren't taxing, it also isn't something to attempt your first time at the lathe. Some basic knowledge of turning is required. Start with a 12/4 maple turning blank

Turning the pedestal is a great way to practice your lathe skills. While there is a pattern to follow, the lines are fluid enough to allow for personalization, slight miscalculations or both.

that is about 20" long. Turn the entire piece to round, finishing out at about $2^7/8$". That is the largest diameter dimension used on the pattern, but if you end up with less than that, adjust the rest of the dimensions to match that difference. Turn the rest of the pedestal according to the pattern, leaving a 1"-diameter x $3/4$"-long stub on both ends.

When you're done with the pedestal, the next step is to cut the three sliding dovetail grooves for the legs on the base of the pedestal. The legs are oriented at 120° around the base of the pedestal. You need to mark the locations accurately, but to cut the grooves themselves I've borrowed from a few different books to make a router jig that makes it nearly foolproof. The jig is made from shop scraps and holds the two stubs of the pedestal in place and uses a screw to hold the pedestal oriented correctly to cut each groove. Use two different bits to cut the grooves. Start with a $1/2$" straight bit to remove most of the wood, then follow up with an 8° dovetail bit. Stop the groove at the shoulder, $3^1/2$" up from the base of the pedestal.

The next step is to rough out the legs by milling three pieces to $7/8$" x 4" x 15".

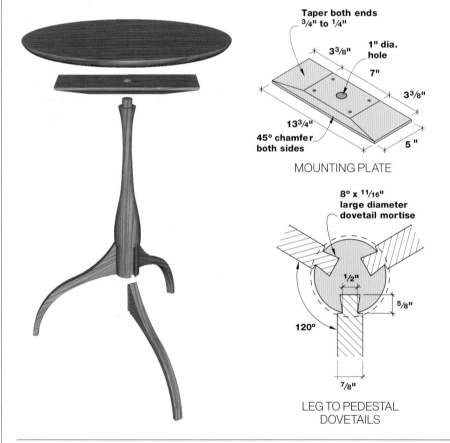

MOUNTING PLATE

Taper both ends $3/4$" to $1/4$"
$3^3/8$"
1" dia. hole
7"
$3^3/8$"
$13^3/4$"
45° chamfer both sides
5 "

8° x $11/16$" large diameter dovetail mortise
$1/2$"
$5/8$"
120°
$7/8$"

LEG TO PEDESTAL DOVETAILS

Clasic Candlestand

NO.	ITEM	DIMENSIONS (INCHES)			MATERIAL
		T	W	L	
1	Top	$3/4$	$19^7/8$ dia.		Maple
1	Mounting plate	$3/4$	5	$13^3/4$	Maple
3	Legs	$7/8$	$3^9/16$	$14^5/8$	Maple
1	Pedestal	3 dia.	20		Maple
4	Wood screws	#9	$1^1/4$	FH	Steel

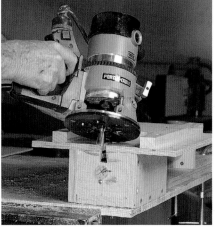

The dovetailing jig makes it fairly simple to place the leg, run the groove, then rotate the leg to the next position. Note the screw in the diagram and photo that's used to hold the pedestal in the appropriate position.

Then use the provided scaled pattern to lay out the shape of the legs in pencil on the pieces. Make sure the grain runs the length of the leg, or your legs could snap. Determine the location of the dovetail pin on each leg and cut the corner from the leg blank at that point. Before shaping the rest of the leg, it's easier to cut the dovetail pin first.

Set up your dovetail bit in a router table. Attach an auxiliary fence to allow you to hold the leg upright against the fence. Run a test piece on some scrap to see if your offset is correct. You want the fit to be tight at this point. You'll hand-fit each joint later. When the test piece fits to your satisfaction, run each side of the leg past the bit, shaping the pins.

With this important joint complete on all three leg pieces, head for the band saw and rough cut the legs to shape. Then use a spindle sander (or spokeshave) and finish shaping the legs to finished size. On the original Shaker piece, the legs are also tapered slightly in thickness down to the feet. You can achieve this authentic look with a bench plane and some care.

The next step is to fit each leg to the pedestal. I re-use part of my router jig as a stop on my bench to hold the pedestal in place while I carefully pare away material with a chisel until each leg slides in place with a snug fit.

Once satisfied, trim the lower stub off the pedestal, finish sand the legs and post, and glue the legs in place. If your joint is well-made, you shouldn't need any clamping pressure. The Shakers used metal plates across the base of the pedestal to hold the legs in place, but our glues are more reliable. Allow the glue to cure and move on to the top.

You now have a table base. The last two parts are actually the easiest. If you can find a piece of maple that is 20" wide, use it for the top. That's what the Shakers did, and it looks great. If you can't find a board that wide, look for a thicker piece, cut it in half along the width on your band saw and make the top bookmatched. While you're scrounging for

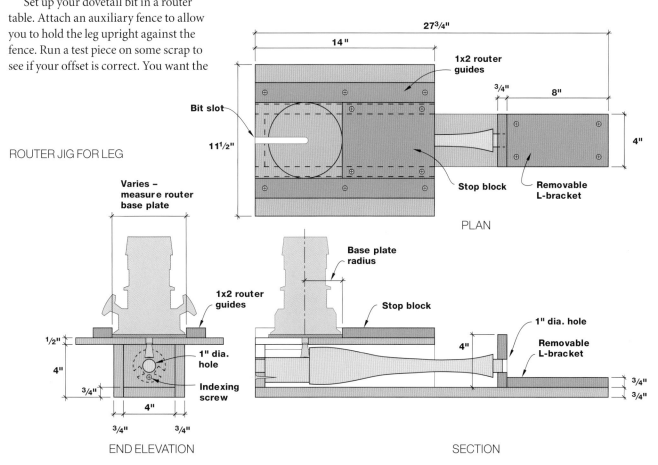

ROUTER JIG FOR LEG

PLAN

END ELEVATION

SECTION

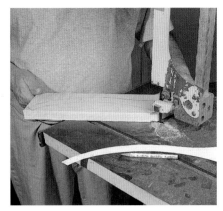

To cut the mating pins for the sliding dovetails, a router table works best. By using an auxiliary fence clamped above the table, first one side of the leg is run (left), then the leg is turned around and the opposite side is run (right).

The leg shape is created by making a full-size template from the included scaled pattern, then transferring that to the leg blanks. A band saw makes quick work of the roughed-out shapes.

wood, grab a piece that's 5" x 13¾" to use as the mounting plate.

To shape the top, I use a simple circle-cutting jig that mounts to my router. With the center of the jig attached to the underside of the top, cut the 19⅞"-diameter shape using a spiral bit, taking the cut in three or four passes. When the top is round, chuck a ½" roundover bit in your router and round over the bottom edge of the top. Then do the same to the top edge with a 1⁄16" roundover bit (or break the edge with sandpaper).

The mounting plate is simple, except that to keep it like the original, both ends of the plate taper to ¼" thick within the first 3⅜" of each end. There are a couple

of ways to do this, but I still think the safest way is to use a band saw to cut the taper, then use a sander to clean up the surface.

With the plate tapered, cut a 3⁄16" roundover on all four edges and drill a 1"-diameter hole in the center of the plate. Then drill a few more mounting holes for attaching the top. You're now ready to finish sand the piece.

To attach the base to the mounting plate, cut a saw kerf across the width of the top stub on the pedestal, running the kerf with the grain. Slip the mounting plate over the top of the stub, then add glue and drive a wedge into the saw kerf to lock the plate in place. When the glue

is dry, cut the tenon and stub flush to the top of the mounting plate.

All that's left is to attach the top and add the finish. I use a water-based aniline dye made by Moser that's available from Woodworker's Supply (800-645-9292). Traditionally, in my shop we dilute the dye more than the manufacturer recommends. Be sure to make some sample boards to find a color that you like. Next, I follow that with a couple coats of orange shellac. I level that with 360-grit sandpaper and then apply a brown glazing stain over the shellac. After I allow that to dry overnight, a few coats of lacquer finish the job.

A spindle sander makes what could be a daunting task reasonably painless. By using double-sided tape to hold the legs together, all three can be sanded at the same time, reducing work and ensuring uniform shapes.

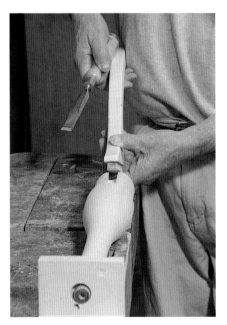

No matter how accurate your machining, there needs to be some hand-fitting to make the legs just right. A sharp chisel can make a big difference here. Don't make the joint too tight, but not too loose, either.

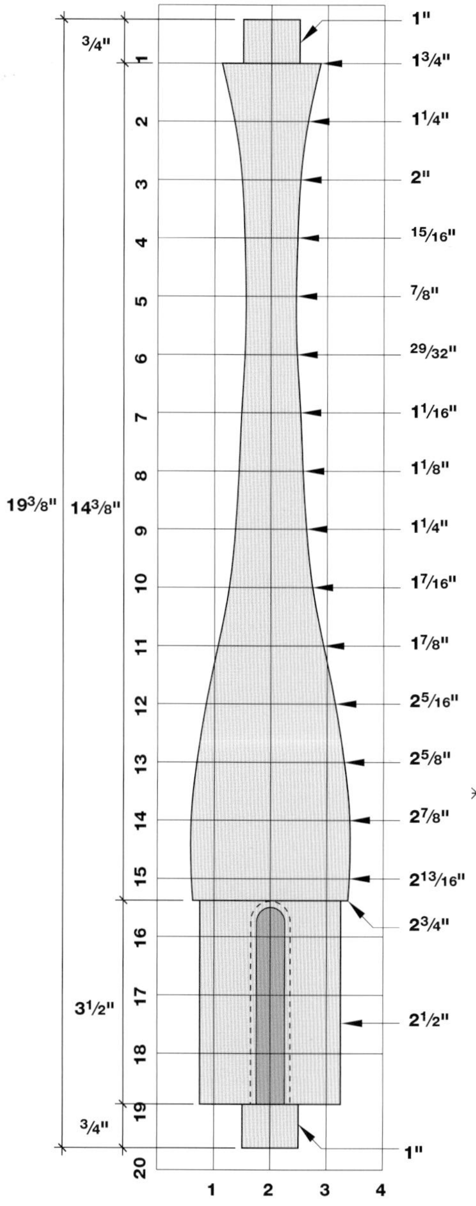
1"
1 3/4"
1 1/4"
2"
15/16"
7/8"
29/32"
1 1/16"
1 1/8"
1 1/4"
1 7/16"
1 7/8"
2 5/16"
2 5/8"
2 7/8"
2 13/16"
2 3/4"
2 1/2"
1"
3/4"
19 3/8"
14 3/8"
3 1/2"
3/4"

PEDESTAL TURNING
& DOVETAIL MORTISE

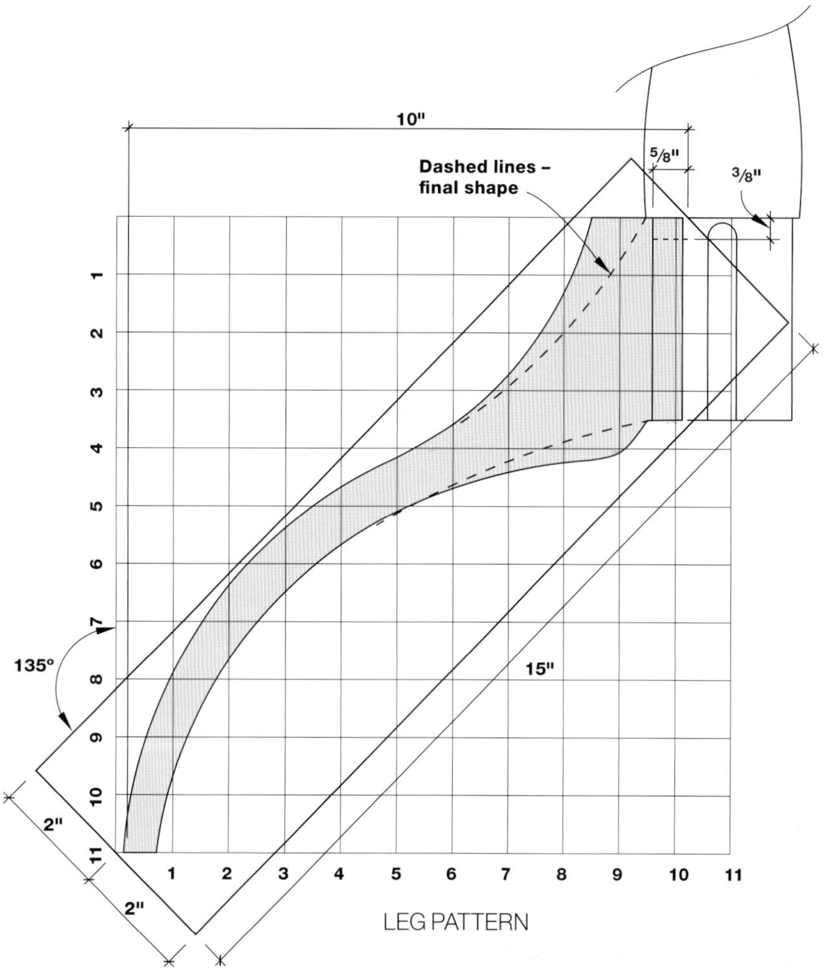
10"
Dashed lines –
final shape
5/8"
3/8"
135°
15"
2"
2"

LEG PATTERN

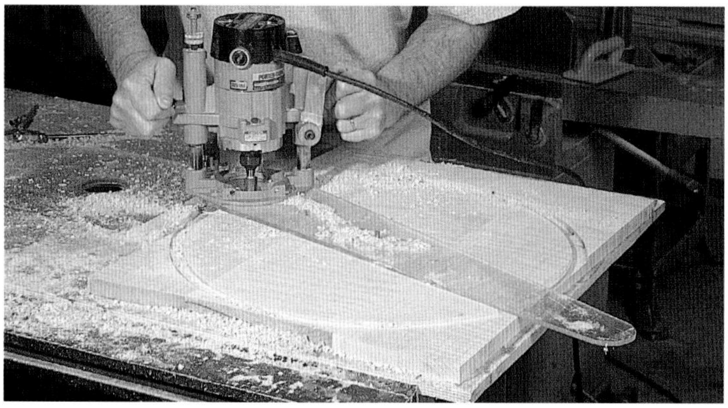

A circle-cutting jig attached to my router lets me make a true circle. Take increasingly deeper passes around the perimeter of the top to complete the cut.

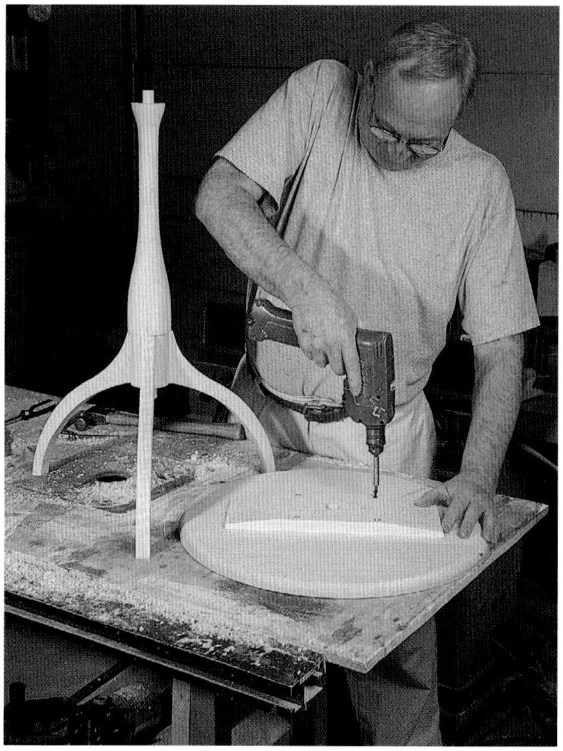

It's a good idea to drill clearance holes in the mounting plate before gluing the mounting plate to the base. It screws on much easier the second time.

Trestle Table

BY GLEN D. HUEY

Nibbling away the mortise locations on the leg halves can be accomplished with a flat-tooth rip blade or a dado stack.

I've built a number of trestle tables in the Shaker style over the years, usually following the style of an original table from one Shaker collection or another. But when I decided to do a trestle table for *Popular Woodworking* readers, I took a second look at some of the designs and decided I could add a feature and come up with a stronger table without sacrificing the simple Shaker lines.

The one shown here is a standard two-pedestal table with a single stretcher tying the bases together. One of the concerns I've always had with this design was the stability of the joint at the stretcher. Anyone who has been to a family dinner at my house knows that a sturdy table is important when everyone starts hungrily reaching for platters of food. To solve the stability concern I doubled-up the hardware from another sturdy piece of furniture – the bed. By using a pair of bed bolts at each joint, this table becomes amazingly stout.

Save Money on Wood

If you've seen my other furniture (woodworkersedge.com), you know I'm addicted to figured maple. Though they've tried to get me into treatment, I haven't yet accepted that I have a problem.

But when it came to choosing the wood for this table, even I had to admit that with such a simple piece, adding busy figure to the base would be gilding the lily. So I saved the good stuff for the

top and chose to use painted poplar to build the base.

Half a Foot, not Six Inches

Construction on the base begins with the feet blanks. The feet actually are two "half-feet" that you face-glue together. This allows you to conserve lumber (no sense trying to find 3" x 3" wood for a painted base) and you can make the mortise for the leg post before gluing the halves together. Mill out the two halves for each foot, then clamp the pairs together and lay out the two notches that will form the $1\frac{1}{2}$" x $2\frac{1}{4}$" mortise for the post tenon.

There are many ways to remove the waste material from the notches, but I'm a table-saw guy, so that's where I headed. Use your miter gauge and make repeated passes across the blade to nibble away the waste area on all four pieces, as shown above.

With the notches cut, it's time to make the halves a whole. When gluing the two halves together, the last thing you want are the pieces to "creep," or slide on the glue, which will cause misalignment. My solution is to mount a 1" section of a #6 finish nail into one half by drilling a small hole and gluing in the nail piece with the point out. As you glue the two halves, align the two sections and press them together. The nails "bite" into the wood and prevent creeping. Go ahead and clamp the pieces securely and set

them aside to dry.

While the feet could be left flat at the floor, it's not as attractive as shaping them to leave "pads" at either end. It also helps the table to sit flat on uneven floors. To form the pads, clamp the two assembled feet together with the bottoms facing the same direction. Mark the pads on the feet according to the illustrations, then drill a $\frac{3}{8}$" hole at the transition point at either end. The hole itself will create the small radius for the transition. After making the two holes per foot, head to the band saw to cut away the portion between the radius cuts to finish the pad shapes.

Some simple shaping using a couple of saws will give the feet an even more graceful look. First cut a 7° bevel on the ends of the feet using the table saw. Next, make a mark $\frac{3}{4}$" down from the top edge at the ends of each foot. Make another mark $10\frac{1}{2}$" in toward the mortise at the top of the leg. Connect the two marks and you have the slope for the top of each foot. Head to the band saw and cut the slopes. To finish the feet, sand the surfaces and round all the edges with a $\frac{3}{16}$" radius bit in your router.

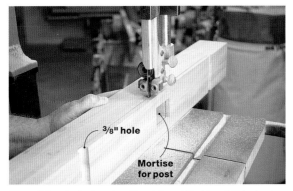

After gluing the halves together, I first drilled two 3/8" holes to define the foot pad and then connected the dots. The rest was simple band saw work.

With the post cut to shape, the first step in forming the tenon is to define the shoulder on all four sides. The miter gauge (hidden behind the work) on my saw works well, while the rip fence allows you to set the shoulder location.

Going Vertical

The next step is the 2⅞" x 2⅞" posts. As with the feet, there's a good chance you'll need to glue up thinner pieces to form the posts.

Once assembled and milled to the size given in the cutting list, it's time to form the tenons to match the mortises in the feet. Start cutting the tenons by first defining the shoulder on the table saw with the posts flat on the saw's table. Then reset the table saw and run the posts upright to form the cheeks. Cut two cheeks, then adjust the fence and cut the other two. Make the tenons slightly oversize and then trim them to achieve a snug fit.

At the tops of the posts, cut out a notch the width of the post to hold the cross braces. Lay out this notch using the photos above to locate them. Note that the notches aren't centered in the posts – rather, they're offset by ¼" to one side. An easy method to remove the 4" of waste is to hog the majority out with a band saw, then chisel away the remain-

I use a high-sided shop-made tenoning jig to cut the cheeks on the tenon. You could also nibble away the waste á la the foot mortise if you don't have, or want to build, a tenoning jig.

The top of the post is notched 4" deep, so the table saw won't cut it (pun intended). The band saw will and I use staggered cuts to remove much of the wood, then chisel out the excess. Notice the notch isn't centered on the post, but offset by ¼" to one side.

ing waste. To finish off the posts, use a chamfer bit in your router to make decorative cuts on each edge, stopping ⅞" from the joinery at each end.

Visible Means of Support

The part of the leg that actually supports the top is the cross brace. Mill the stock

for the cross braces, then use the table saw to nibble away the shallow notches (as you did on the feet halves) on the two opposing sides of each brace. These notches will fit into the 4"-deep notches at the tops of the leg posts, so test the fit to make sure it's snug, but not too tight.

While the cross braces are mostly hid-

Trestle Table

NO.	ITEM	DIMENSIONS (INCHES)			MATERIAL
		T	W	L	
4	Feet halves	1¹¹⁄₁₆	3	30	Poplar
2	Cross braces	1½	4	30	Poplar
2	Posts	2⅞	2⅞	29⅜	Poplar
1	Center brace	1½	2	28	Poplar
1	Stretcher	1½	6	43¼	Poplar
1	Top	⅞	36	71	Cherry
2	Breadboard ends	⅞	1½	38*	Cherry
10	Top fasteners	¾	⅞	2¼	Cherry
*Finished size is 36" long.					

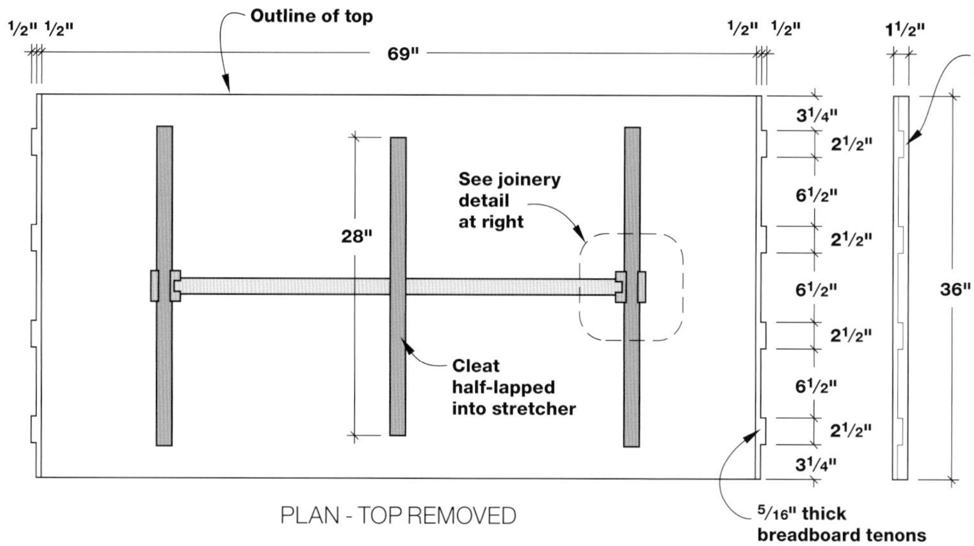

1/2" 1/2"
Outline of top
1/2" 1/2"
69"
1 1/2"
Breadboard ends - two required
3 1/4"
2 1/2"
6 1/2"
2 1/2"
6 1/2"
2 1/2"
6 1/2"
2 1/2"
3 1/4"
28"
36"
See joinery detail at right
Cleat half-lapped into stretcher
5/16" thick breadboard tenons

PLAN - TOP REMOVED

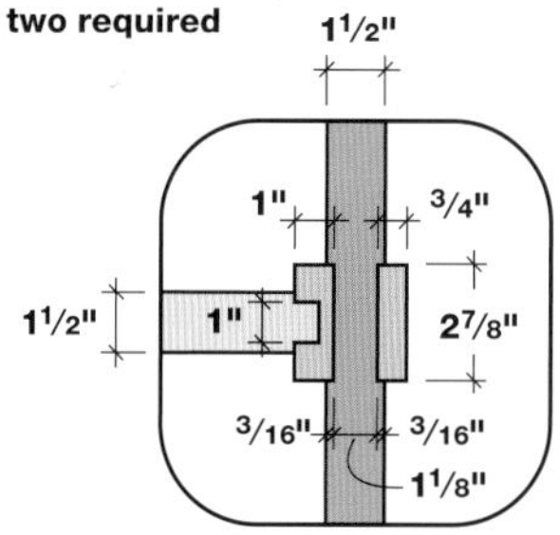

1 1/2"
1"
3/4"
1 1/2"
1"
2 7/8"
3/16"
3/16"
1 1/8"

POST TOP
W/CROSS-BRACE DETAIL

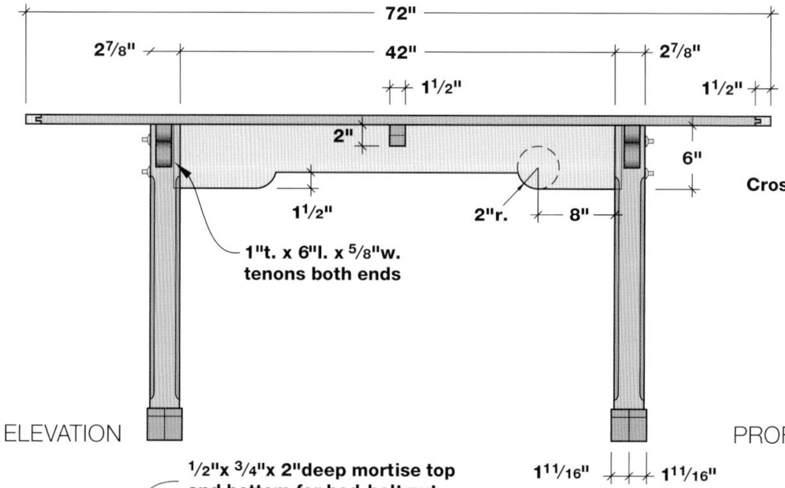

72"
2 7/8"
42"
2 7/8"
1 1/2"
1 1/2"
2"
6"
1 1/2"
2"r.
8"
1"t. x 6"l. x 5/8"w.
tenons both ends
1 11/16"
1 11/16"

ELEVATION

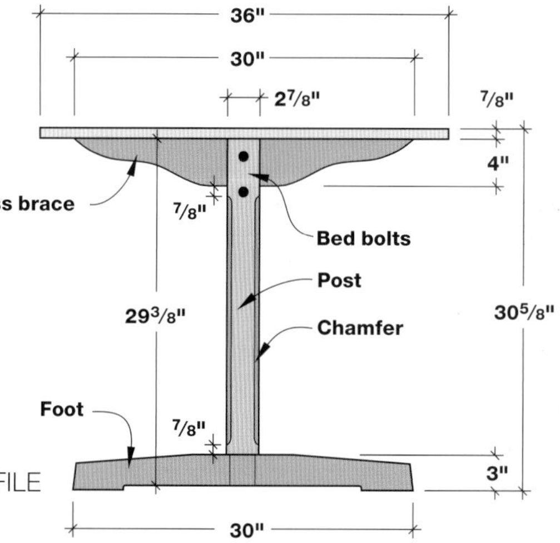

36"
30"
2 7/8"
7/8"
4"
Cross brace
7/8"
Bed bolts
Post
29 3/8"
Chamfer
30 5/8"
Foot
7/8"
3"
30"

PROFILE

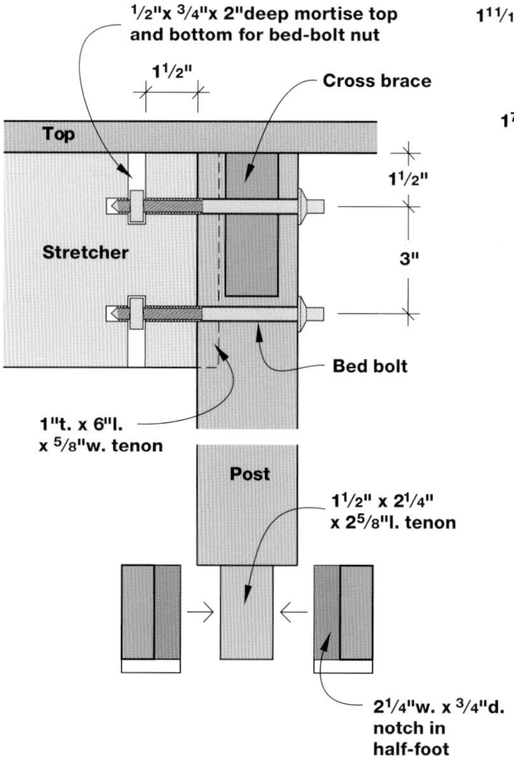

1/2"x 3/4"x 2"deep mortise top
and bottom for bed-bolt nut
1 1/2"
Cross brace
Top
1 1/2"
Stretcher
3"
Bed bolt
1"t. x 6"l.
x 5/8"w. tenon
Post
1 1/2" x 2 1/4"
x 2 5/8"l. tenon
2 1/4"w. x 3/4"d.
notch in
half-foot

SECTION THROUGH POST

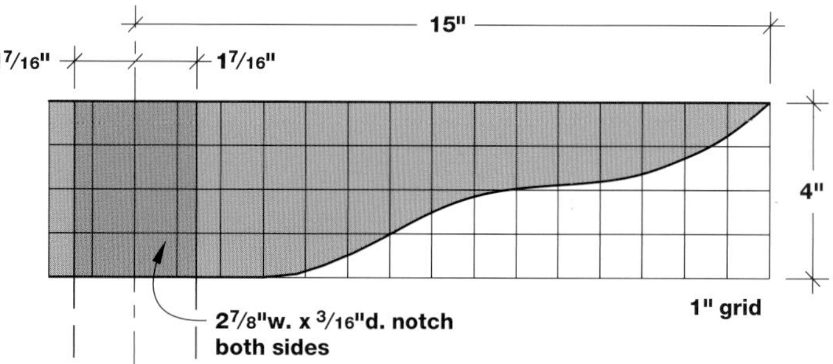

15"
1 7/16"
1 7/16"
4"
1" grid
2 7/8"w. x 3/16"d. notch
both sides

CROSS-BRACE LAYOUT

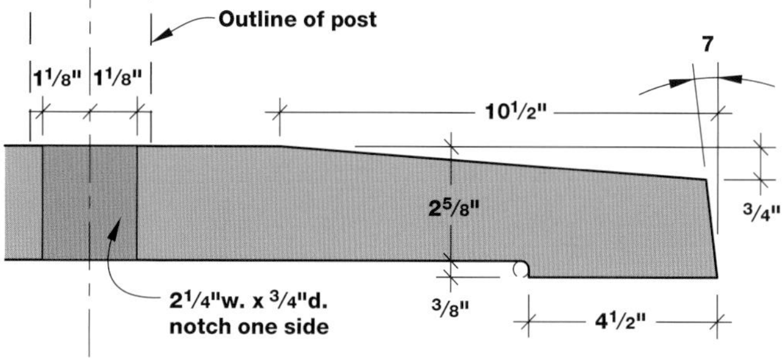

Outline of post
7
1 1/8"
1 1/8"
10 1/2"
2 5/8"
3/4"
2 1/4"w. x 3/4"d.
notch one side
3/8"
4 1/2"

HALF-FOOT LAYOUT

den under the tabletop, they can be seen at times and therefore there's no sense leaving them square and chunky. Use the pattern (on p. 21) to trace or mark the curved shape on the pieces themselves. Then use the band saw to cut out the shape on the braces, cutting wide of the line and then smoothing the curve with sandpaper.

Now glue the foot and cross brace to each post. To add a bit more strength after the glue has dried, drill two $^7/_{16}$" holes (on opposite sides of the leg) in each joint and pin the joint with dowels. Make sure to stagger the pins on each side so they don't run into each other. Using a knife or sandpaper, taper one end of each peg a bit to make it easier to insert in its hole. After tapping the dowels in place, cut the extra length nearly flush to the leg surface and sand it smooth.

Bridging the Gap

With the ends assembled it's time to attach the stretcher to tie everything together. This is the joint where you need all the strength you can muster. As I mentioned earlier, I used bed bolts here, but I started with the traditional method of cutting mortises in the legs and tenons on both ends of the stretcher. Start by cutting the 1" x 6"-long x $^5/_8$"-deep mortises on the thicker side of each assembly. I used a Forstner bit to make most of the mortise (see below) then chiseled out the waste to square everything up, but you could use a router with a straight bit. To create the short tenons on the stretcher, I used a rabbeting bit in a router to cut rabbets on opposite faces of the stretcher.

If you haven't used bed bolts before, they're essentially heavy-duty bolts that screw into a square nut buried in a mortise in the other piece. After cutting the rabbets on the stretcher, make two $^1/_2$" x

$^3/_4$" x 2"-deep mortises at each end of the stretcher, one in the top edge and one in the bottom edge, to hold the bed-bolt nuts.

To add more stability to the table, a third center brace is half-lapped into the center top of the stretcher. Mill the stock for this part and use one of the finished cross braces as a pattern to shape the center brace. Next, use the illustration to lay out the decorative cut on the bottom edge of the stretcher. Then use the table saw and miter gauge to cut the half-lap joint for the center brace. This piece is attached with glue and a 2" wood screw, but don't attach it until you're done installing the bed bolts.

Use a drill press to make the holes in the trestle legs for the bed bolts. The holes are $^7/_{16}$" in diameter and are in the center of the stretcher mortises, $1^1/_2$" from both the top edge and bottom edge of the mortise. To finish making the hole

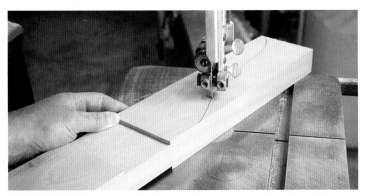

Sculpting a shape on the cross braces isn't necessary to keep the table sturdy, but it does keep it from looking clunky. After transferring the pattern onto the brace, I cut wide of the line on the band saw, then used a spindle sander to smooth the shape.

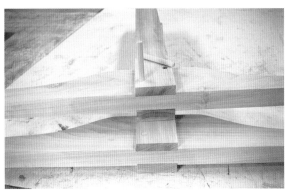

With the cross braces glued to the posts, they are pegged in position. Clamp them tight and check for square between the post and brace. Note that the pegs are at opposite corners of the joint. This allows room for the mortise (in the next step).

Here's the mortise for the stretcher. I removed most of the waste with a Forstner bit, then chiseled the mortise square.

Getting the holes for the bed bolts straight is important. And the best tool for that task is the drill press. The two $^7/_{16}$" holes are located in $1^1/_2$" from the top and bottom edges of the mortise.

for the bed bolt, slip a stretcher tenon into the end section, clamping the two pieces firmly. Use a long $^7/_{16}$" drill bit to finish the hole through the end of the stretcher and into the mortise area created for the bed-bolt nut. The straight hole at the drill press acts as a guide to drill the remainder of the hole straight. Clean out any waste from the hole, place the nuts into the mortises, slide the bolt into the hole, and attach it to the nut. Tighten the connection with a wrench.

Holding the Top in Place

I use wooden clips to hold the top in place on the base. The clips have a rabbet cut on one end that slips into slots cut into the cross braces on the base. I use a biscuit cutter set to make a cut for a #20 biscuit and start the slot $^1/_2$" down from the top of the brace. Because the tenon on the clip is almost $^1/_4$" thick, make two cuts with the biscuit joiner, lowering the cutter to finish the cut at $^1/_4$" wide. Place two slots on each inside of the cross braces and one on either side of the center brace.

Rather than trying to cut rabbets on the ends of the little wooden clips, start with a 5"-6" wide piece of wood that is $4^5/_8$" long and $^3/_4$" thick. Cut a $^1/_2$" x $^1/_2$" rabbet along the end grain leaving a $^1/_4$" tongue. Then rip the piece into $^7/_8$"-wide strips and crosscut the ends to $2^1/_4$"-long pieces.

Pre-drill clearance holes in the wooden clips you've just made to accept a #8 x $1^1/_4$" wood screw.

With a Cherry on Top

Again, trying to avoid admitting I have a curly maple addiction, I chose cherry for the top. Cut and glue the slab to the finished size given in the cutting list.

Appropriately, the Shakers used breadboard ends (traditionally called a "clamp") on their tops to hide the end grain and to help keep the top flat. The breadboard requires a tongue on each end of the top for the breadboard to fit over. I created the $^5/_{16}$"-thick x 1"-long tongue on the top using a straightedge to guide my router and a $^3/_4$" pattern bit.

Use a marking gauge at each edge to locate the tongue depth and align the straightedge to the mark. Set your bit to cut just behind the mark on the bottom side and just covering the mark on the top side to ensure the breadboards will fit snugly against the tabletop on the top side.

After the tongue is made, draw another line on it $^1/_2$" from the end, running the entire width of the top. At four equally spaced locations on the tongue, mark locations for the $2^1/_2$"-wide tenons. Trim the tongue around the tenons, leav-

Supplies

Ball and Ball

800-257-3711 or ballandball.com

4 • 6" bed bolts
    #U60-076, $7.03 each

Horton Brasses

800-754-9127 or horton-brasses.com

4 • 6" bed bolts
    #H-73, $4.50 each

Olde Century Colors

oldecenturycolors.com

1 • pint of lamp black acrylic
    latex paint
    #2022, $14.20

Rockler

800-279-4441 or rockler.com

1 • pint of Sam Maloof
    Oil/Wax Finish
    #58669, $20.99

10 • #8 x 1¼" slotted screws

Prices correct as of publication deadline.

After clamping the stretcher between the legs and drilling the bed bolt holes into the stretcher I simply dropped the nut into the previously cut mortises and bolted the base together.

Double-wide #20 biscuit slots in the braces work well to hold the wooden top fasteners (shown in the inset photo).

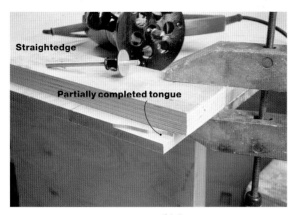

Straightedge

Partially completed tongue

With the top milled to size, mark a $^5/_{16}$"-thick x 1"-wide tongue on each end with your marking gauge. Then use a straightedge and a $^3/_4$" pattern bit to shape the tongue on both sides of the top.

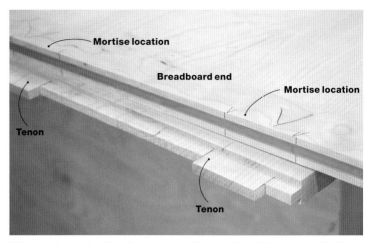

Mortise location

Breadboard end

Mortise location

Tenon

Tenon

After marking and cutting the tenons on the breadboard tongue, use the finished tenons to locate the mortises in the already-grooved breadboard ends.

ing them extending the full 1". This is where the breadboards and top will be pinned.

Cut the two breadboard ends and plow the $^1/_2$"-deep groove the length of the ends for the tongue. Then lay out the areas that match up with the extended tongues and cut the $^1/_2$"-deep mortises in the bottom of the grooves.

Fit the breadboard ends to the top and clamp. At each extended tongue, drill a $^1/_4$" hole for the pin. Use a scrap piece on the underside to prevent "blowout."

Remove the ends and elongate the holes to accommodate wood movement. Apply glue to only the middle 4" of the tongue, reinstall the ends, then drive the pins into the holes and apply glue to only the top edge of the hole. Trim the pins and the extra length of the breadboards flush.

Finishing Touches

Sand the top with #150 grit sandpaper and rout the edges, top and bottom, with a $^3/_{16}$" roundover bit. Final sand to #180 grit and apply three to four coats of an

oil/varnish blend following the product directions, then add a top coat of furniture wax.

After following the instructions in "Painting the Base" below to paint and age your base, attach the top to the base with the wooden clips and #8 x 1$^1/_4$" wood screws.

You and your table are now ready for years of family dinners with no concerns about sliding the ham or vegetables onto the floor because of a banquet table that's less than sturdy.

Painting the Base

A simple coat of paint on the base may suffice for many, but it looked too new and shiny for my taste, so I added an antique finish to the piece.

Begin by staining the piece and applying two coats of shellac. Sand the finish.

Next, mix Olde Century Colors lampblack acrylic paint with fine sawdust particles and paint the mixture onto the base. As the paint dries, wipe with a very wet rag. The wiping will remove paint and dislodge some of the sawdust pieces leaving a "worn" surface.

Once the paint is dry, apply a coat of Maloof's Oil/Wax finish. Simply brush it on and wipe with a clean rag. This step provides a dull sheen to the paint, adding the look of years of polish.

A simple coat of paint looks too new and shiny for a traditional Shaker piece of furniture.

Here I've wiped the piece with a very wet cloth as the paint dried, which removed some of the paint, creating an antique finish.

Pleasant Hill 'Saturday' Table

BY KERRY PIERCE

Last summer I had the pleasure of visiting the Shaker Village at Pleasant Hill in Harrodsburg, Ky. During my stay there, the volunteer who showed me around explained that this piece is an example of something called a "Saturday table" – a table made on Saturday from bits of wood left over from the workshop's weekday labors.

I like to work in the presence of a certain amount of aesthetic risk. While I do use jigs and fixtures, I also try to preserve the need for manual skill and an educated eye. In the case of this particular piece, my original intention was to execute the legs as a high-wire act, forming their eight-tapered swelling facets completely by hand using a drawknife. However, after experimenting, I realized that – although I could produce clean surfaces with a drawknife – I might not be able to define the underlying form of each leg with enough clarity using only that one tool.

That's when I decided to build a cradle that would allow me to use the band saw to rough in the eight surfaces of each leg, surfaces I would then finish with planes, chisels and sandpaper.

First Things First

Begin by carefully prepping the lumber for the top and apron. Glue up the top, set it aside and turn your attention to the legs.

After milling leg blanks that finish out $1^3/4$" on a side, turn your attention to the band saw cradle (see next page). This doesn't have to be anything fancy. All you need is something that will hold the blank above the band saw table at a great enough height to allow it to be rotated on its centers.

Once the cradle is made, drill a $1/8$" hole through each of the cradle's end pieces. These holes will mark the legs' axes of rotation. On the inside surface of

one of the cradle's end pieces (which I'll call the headstock end), draw a square $1^3/4$" on a side centered on the legs' axes of rotation with its bottom line parallel to the bottom of the cradle. Then draw a second square exactly the same size and also centered on the legs' axes of rotation that is rotated 45° from the first square. Finally draw a square on the inside surface of the cradle's tailstock end that is centered on the legs' axes of rotation and parallel to the bottom of the cradle. These squares will allow you to align the leg blanks for the sawing of each leg's eight faces.

Then drill an extra hole through the end piece on the headstock end. This hole should be placed so that it is apart from the center hole and still inside each of the two squares you drew on the inside of the headstock end piece. The screw you turn into this extra hole will hold the blank in the proper alignment for each pass over the band saw.

Find the center of each end of each leg blank and mark it with a pencil. Then drill a shallow hole in the centers of each leg ($1/2$" deep, $1/8$" in diameter).

Turn a $1^1/4$" #6 drywall screw through all three of the cradle end piece holes so that the points of each screw can just barely be felt on the inside surfaces of cradle's end pieces.

Hold a leg blank in place so that its centers are positioned directly in line with the center points you marked on the inside of the cradle's end pieces. Then turn the drywall screws on each end of the cradle into the centers of each end of the leg. With the leg blank positioned so that it aligns with the single square you drew on the inside of the tailstock end of the cradle, turn the extra screw on the headstock end of the cradle into the end grain of the blank. This third screw – the set screw – will hold the blank in the correct rotational alignment for cutting the

first of the leg's eight facets.

Next, you need to make a flexible pattern for marking the leg's facets. I made mine from $1/4$" birch plywood, but stiff cardboard would work just as well. The pattern should be as long as the full length of the leg's lower section – $20^7/8$" – and the full width of the blank – $1^3/4$". The taper you mark must retain enough of the leg's thickness so that after you've made the band saw cuts, you can plane away the saw marks without removing any of the leg's finished thickness. After some experimentation, I settled on a width of $1^1/4$" at the foot of the pattern.

Lay the pattern on the blank so that its straight side aligns with one side of the leg blank and the narrow end of the pattern aligns with the foot of the blank. Then draw a line along the taper.

Place the cradle (with the leg blank attached) on the band saw and cut the first taper. Place the cradle back on the bench, back off the set screw enough so that the leg can be rotated, then rotate the blank 90° (using the squares drawn on the cradle's headstock end piece as your guide), then turn the set screw into this new position to lock the blank in place. Use your pattern to mark the next taper, return the cradle to the band saw and saw this next facet. Repeat until the first four facets are sawn.

Then remove the blank from the cradle, plane the four sawn tapers until they're smooth, and reinstall the blank in the cradle.

Before you go any further, take a close look at the drawing of the leg and the photo of the finished table. Notice that the facets you've already cut are simply tapering extensions of the four sides of the leg's upper, apron section. Notice also the next four facets – those you're about to cut – begin at shoulders which are cut in a way that connects adjacent faces of the table's square apron section.

'Saturday' Table

NO.	ITEM	DIMENSIONS (INCHES)			MATERIAL
		T	W	L	
1	Top	$7/8$	17	$19^3/4$	Walnut
4	Legs	$1^3/4$	$1^3/4$	$27^1/8$	Walnut
2	Short aprons	1	$4^5/8$	$11^1/4$	Walnut
2	Long aprons	1	$4^5/8$	14	Walnut

If you haven't already done so, with your try square and a pencil, mark the bottom of the leg's four-sided apron section. Then mark a location ³⁄₈" in from each end of each of these lines on the leg blank. This will be a total of eight marks, two on each side of the apron section of the leg. Next, with a fine-toothed backsaw, cut the shoulders marking the top of the leg's other four facets. Each saw cut should connect two marks, each ³⁄₈" from the outside edges on two of the leg's adjacent faces. Be sure to cut shy of the shoulder's finished location so that you'll have material you can pare away in order to produce a finished end-grain surface.

The foot of the leg should now be a finished square measuring something in the area of 1" on a side. If it's a little more or a little less, that's fine. Make a mark ¼" from the outside of each side of the foot. Here, too, there should be eight marks.

Working by Eye

Working freehand, draw a line connecting the mark (¼" from the outside) at the foot with the mark (³⁄₈" from the outside) at the bottom of the apron section of the leg. The cut along that line will form the next facet of the leg. Remember that you're going to further define this line with a plane, so don't worry if it's not absolutely perfect.

Position the blank so that the top section aligns with the second square you marked on the headstock end of the cradle. Turn the set screw into the end grain of the leg blank. Working from the middle of the marked taper, saw toward both ends of the cut.

Repeat this process until the other four sides of the octagon have been roughed in.

Remove the blank from the cradle and plane this second set of facets smooth. Holding the blank in your bench vise, use a couple of your favorite planes – and a good paring chisel up under the sawn shoulders – to fine-tune the tapers on the four legs.

If possible, resist the temptation to reach for a measuring tool. This process works best if the only measurements are those made by your unassisted eye. Take a shaving or two from a facet that seems a little thin. (Remember that when you take a shaving, you actually increase the width of the facet.) Then rotate the blank in your vise. Take another shaving from another facet if you think you need to.

In the 15 years I've been writing for woodworking magazines, I've had the pleasure of visiting the shops of some of this country's greatest craftsmen, and every single one routinely demonstrated the ability to find the right line – not only by measuring – but also by working with tools that were guided by the unassisted human eye. This isn't a skill they'd had since birth. This was a skill they developed over the course of many years of practice, and it is, I believe, the most important tool in their woodworking arsenal. If a line looks right, it probably is right, even if your rule shows you could make it little righter by taking off one more shaving.

Mark and cut the mortises for each of the apron tenons. (This time you should measure.)

Making the Apron

The apron sections of the Pleasant Hill original were made, I suspect, from material left over from other jobs. One apron section is 1" thick. Another is 1¹⁄₈" thick, and all four sections taper in thickness. I decided to make my aprons a consistent 1" thick.

Create the tenon thickness with a

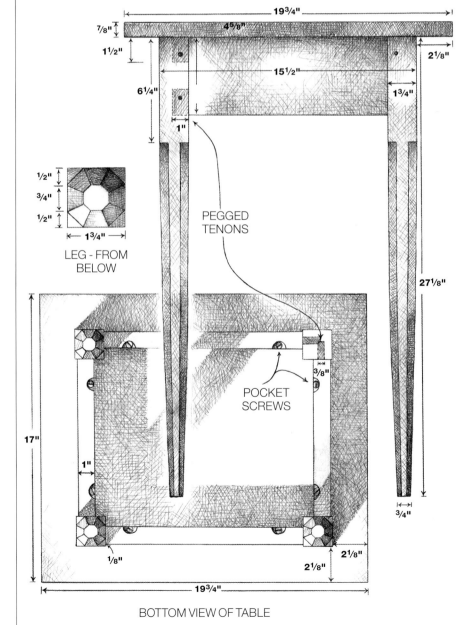

LEG - FROM BELOW

PEGGED TENONS

POCKET SCREWS

BOTTOM VIEW OF TABLE

Making the Tapered Octagonal Legs

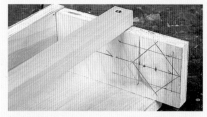

The eight sides of the tapered legs are cut on the band saw using a cradle (which can be seen in its entirety below). On one end, the headstock end, draw two squares 1¾" on a side. Each should have the same center point. One should have its bottom side parallel to the bottom of the cradle. The other is canted 45° from the first.

The leg blank is held in place by turning a screw into the center point of each end of the leg blank. The second screw on the headstock end keeps the blank in the same rotational position.

Use a pattern to draw in the first four tapers.

Cut those first four tapers by passing the cradle past the band saw blade.

After the first four tapers have been cut, fix the untapered apron section of the leg blank in your vise. Then plane away the saw marks on the taper.

After defining the shoulders of the other four facets with a backsaw, sketch in the next set of tapers freehand.

Working both ways from the middle, saw each of these facets by passing the cradle past the band saw blade.

This photo shows the leg blank in the cradle after the second set of four facets have been sawn. Notice that the top of the leg blank is aligned with the second of the two squares I drew on the inside of the headstock end piece.

The top section of each of the second set of facets can't be reached with a plane. Clean up these saw marks with a sharp paring chisel.

The two legs in front have been finished. The one immediately behind them has had the second set of facets sawn but not planed. The leg at the rear has had only the first set of facets sawn and planed, although the shoulders for the second set have been defined by a backsaw cut.

couple of passes of each apron section over a stack of dado cutters on your table saw. Then on the band saw cut away the waste to separate the two tenons on each end of each apron section.

The tenons should come off the table saw a little thicker than needed so you have some material to plane away during the final fit. Fit each tenon to each mortise.

The screw pockets on the inside of the apron should be cut before you assemble the table. These can be made on the drill press using a Forstner bit, but I chose to use chisels and gouges as the Pleasant Hill maker had done.

I started by drawing lines on the inside face of the apron sections 1" from the top edge. I then made two marks along each of these lines 1" from the shoulders. I used the intersection of these marks as the center points for 1"-diameter half circles I scribed with a compass. I used a paring chisel to cut the flat area at the top of each pocket. This flat was tilted about 70° from the outside surface of the apron. I made the round half circle with a couple of carving gouges. You don't need to get fancy with these pockets. The ones on the original table were pretty crudely executed.

Finish each pocket by drilling a through $^3/_{16}$" hole in the center of each pocket's flat spot at an angle about 90° from the surface of the pocket's flat. This will create an angle that will keep the hole from breaking out on the outside face of the apron and allow you to use 2" #6 drywall screws (coarse threaded) to hold the $^7/_8$"-thick top in place without breaking through the top and marring the surface.

Gluing it Up
The apron sections are fairly narrow, and if your material is thoroughly dry, I think there is little chance of any cracking in response to seasonal changes in humidity, even for a table housed in a home with forced-air heat.

Nevertheless, I did take one precaution to account for any possibility of shrinkage. I undercut by $^1/_8$" the middle edges of each tenon (the edges adjacent to the waste you removed between the tenons). This provides a little breathing room if the apron does begin to shrink

The tenons can be fine-tuned with a shoulder plane or a rabbet plane.

across its width.

Then swab a little glue into each mortise and on each tenon and assemble the base.

Check the frame for square (when viewed from above) by measuring the diagonals of the frame. If the measurements aren't identical, apply a little pressure along the longer diagonal.

Each tenon is then further secured via a round peg tapped into a drilled hole that passes through the post and through the tenon.

These pegs are best riven, splitting them out with a chisel and paring them to approximate size. They should taper from a diameter of a bit less than $^1/_4$" on one end to a bit more than $^1/_4$" on the other. The peg holes on the original were bored – I suspect – without measuring because there was a fair amount of variation in their placement. I bored mine in measured locations: $^1/_2$" from the tenon shoulder and $^3/_4$" from the top and bottom of each apron section.

Split out the pegs. Then shave them to size with a paring chisel.

Paring chisels will cut the flat in each screw pocket. The rounded excavation can be made with a gouge.

Put a dab of glue on the thinner end of your peg and tap the peg – thinner end first – into the hole until it is firmly seated.

The holes on the original were bored clear through the post so that one end of the peg pokes through on the inside. I decided that mine would go in only $^7/_8$".

Invert the top on your bench protecting it with a towel or blanket. Then center the undercarriage and join the two parts with eight 2" #6 drywall screws. Sand and finish to suit.

Just One More Thing
If you ever get the chance to measure a piece of 18th- or early 19th-century furniture, you'll notice that – despite the solid engineering and execution you will likely see – there is far less of the obsessive perfectionism that is characteristic of some modern work and some modern woodworkers. Each side of each dovetail might slant at different angles. Each section of a table's apron might be a different thickness. Cabinet backs of even magnificent high-style work might consist of unplaned boards of random widths simply nailed into a rabbet.

In part, such imperfections are simply a reflection of the craftsman's need to get work out the door so he could get paid. But more often than not, I think, they result from the craftsman's knowledge that their clients didn't evaluate their work with a ruler and a set of dividers. They knew their clients would judge the beauty of the work with their eyes. It's not surprising, then, that often the craftsman did too.

Drop-leaf Table

BY STEVE SHANESY

Just about every woodworker will agree that any project with angles other than 90° makes things more challenging. This handsome Shaker-style table with splayed, or angled, legs is no exception. But don't be put off, because it's not as difficult as it looks.

First, keep in mind that virtually all the angles are 4°. Simple enough. As for making the leg-to-apron mortise-and-tenon joint, breathe easy because it's almost as simple as making 90° joints.

All the Angles

Before we start, here's a list of the angle cuts: All apron ends and long edges, including the top edge of the drop-leaf support arm; both ends of the legs; and the cleats for attaching the top. That's it!

There's not a lot of material required for this project, so go ahead and mill the pieces to size, leaving some length for trimming later. Be sure you have some extra pieces to use for setups. I used 1"-thick material for the aprons, but ¾" works equally well (just change the tenon thickness to ⅜").

Before preparing the stock for the legs, see "Legs: It's All in the Growth Rings"

article on page 46. I used this technique with excellent results. Keep the leg stock square (don't taper it until after the mortises are cut) and, when cutting to length, cut the 5½° angle on the ends.

Use a V-block to simplify the angle cutting, as shown in the photo above. To determine which corner is up, first mark the mortise locations on the legs. To cut the angle, bevel the miter saw 5½° to the right and position the leg to the left of the blade with its inside corner (where you will cut the mortises) facing up. Make your cut. To cut to final length, measure and turn the leg so the inside corner is down. Save a short angled scrap from the leg – it will be useful when mortising.

Lay out the mortise locations on a test piece with the angle cut on the top edge. I used an ⅛" setback for the apron to the leg.

The mortise starts 1" down and is 3¼" long. The depth is ¾". Now turn to the poster section in the center of this issue and follow the mortising steps.

After mortising, complete the legs by cutting tapers on their two inside faces (the faces with mortises). The taper begins 1" down from the bottom edge of

the apron. Mark this point. The leg tapers to ¾" x ¾" at the floor – which is one-half its thickness. Mark your taper lines on all four legs. Cut the tapers on the band saw wide of the line and clean up the cut using a hand plane or jointer. Except for sanding, the legs are now complete.

Angled Tenons

Next work on the aprons. Cut them to length as shown in the illustration on page 45 – don't forget the 4° angle on the ends.

Before ripping the angles on the top and bottom edges of the apron, determine which face will be outside and mark it. When done, the longer edge of the apron is the bottom edge. To cut the angles, bevel the table saw blade 4°. Now set the fence and place the apron on the saw so the less-acute angle will be the outside. (This depends on whether your saw tilts right or left.) Reset the fence and cut the complementary angle on the bottom edge.

Clamp a V-block to a miter saw and bevel the blade to the right 5½°. With what will be the inside corner of the leg facing up, make the cut for the top of the leg. Turn the leg 180° to cut the bottom end to final length.

Use an angled offcut piece from the leg when setting the stop block in the mortising jig. Set it in place so the top of the leg is square. By doing so, the mortise will be in the same location on both faces of the leg.

Installing Drop-leaf Table Hinges

Drop-leaf hinge installation isn't intuitive. What seems normal – just placing the hinge barrel where the leaf and top meet, like a door to a stile – is totally wrong. Another wrong assumption is that the correct depth to set the hinges is simply to make them flush with the underside surface.

As with all hinges, the location of the pivot point is the ultimate concern. With the drop-leaf hinge, the pivot point, which is the center of the pin, must be centered on the radius of the matching profiles. In my case, the ½" radius of the rule joint requires the hinge pin to be ½" down from the top of the radius and ½" in from the side.

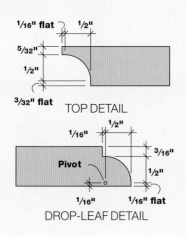

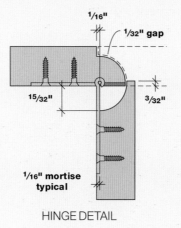

Rout the mating profile for the leaves using a cove bit. The bit height should leave a $^5/_{32}$" flat to match the mating profile's bead.

When both rule joint profiles are correct they nest together with the top surfaces flush and a $^1/_{32}$" gap between the profiles.

To form the tenons, refer to the poster for cutting the wider face cheeks. Because of the angled cut on the apron ends, the edge cheeks and shoulders are best cut by hand.

When the tenons are done, notch each long apron for its drop-leaf support arm. Following the drawings on page 45, use a hand saw or band saw to make the cutouts. The cut along the length of the notch is square to the face. When making the support pieces, the long bottom edge is square but the top edge is at 4° to match the apron edge. Attach the supports after assembly by screwing them in place, leaving them loose enough to swivel.

Base and Top Assembly

With the work on the legs and aprons complete, dry-fit the table base. After making any adjustments, glue it up. I made clamping cauls with one face at 4° to position the clamps square across the joint. I glued and clamped the base in two operations to avoid the typical panic associated with gluing it up all at once.

Next, glue the stock you need for the top and drop-leaves. Take a moment to organize the wood for the best grain pattern and color match. After the glue dries, trim the pieces to their final sizes.

The Rules of Rule Joints

The traditional drop-leaf table uses a rule joint at the transition between the fixed top and the leaf. It provides an attractive appearance when open or closed. Making the matching inside/outside radius profiles on the leaves and

Rout the leaf-hinge mortise using a template and guide bushing. Note the unequal lengths of hinge leaves. The short leaf goes on the tabletop side. Also, use the pencil line on the table surface to align the template. The pencil line on the template edges serve as the center point of the hinge pin.

top is not difficult, but properly locating the drop-leaf hinge on the mating parts requires a bit of knowledge and careful set-up (see "Installing Drop-leaf Table Hinges" on p. 31).

The edge profiles on the table parts can be made using a hand-held router or a router table. I opted for the router table because it allows for more control.

Some router-bit manufacturers offer matched bit sets to make the mating parts. These sets usually consist of a $^1/_2$"-radius bit and a $^1/_2$"-cove bit, each with a bearing guide. If you have one or both bits, the set isn't necessary.

Cut the profile on the table edge first. It has a $^1/_2$"-radius with a $^3/_{16}$" bead on top. Cut the profile in two passes so you don't tax your router. Make the same cut on a scrap piece, too. Next, install the cove bit and mill the mating leaf profile to the dimensions given in the drawing.

Now turn your attention to the drop-leaf hinges. Before you begin cutting the mortise for the hinges, remember this:

A shallow trough must be made to accommodate the hinge barrel. Use a fluting bit and an edge guide.

Drop-leaf Table

| NO. | ITEM | DIMENSIONS (INCHES) | | | MATERIAL |
		T	W	L	
4	Legs	1½	1½	28¼*	Cherry
2	Aprons	1	5	26¾**	Cherry
2	Aprons	1	5	9⅞**	Cherry
1	Top	¾	14¼	36	Cherry
2	Leaves	¾	7½	36	Cherry
2	Leaf supports	1	1½	12½	Cherry

* Dimension is slightly bigger than finished size; **Apron lengths from longest point at shoulder and includes ¾" tenons.

Your hinge may be different so base your measurements on the hinges you use.

Place the tabletop and leaves together and upside down on your workbench and gently clamp the three pieces together. Now measure in 6" from the edge along the rule joint to determine the general location of each hinge.

From the joint edges, make a line $\frac{1}{2}$" back on the tabletop side. This is the pin location on one axis. Repeat this procedure for all four hinge locations.

Now set up a router with a $\frac{1}{2}$" straight bit and guide bushing (mine had a $\frac{5}{8}$" outside diameter). Make a template using $\frac{1}{2}$" plywood with a cutout sized to the hinge and the bushing diameter. In my case, this is the hinge width or length plus $\frac{1}{8}$". After making the cutout, scribe a line on each side edge of the template opening in the exact location of the hinge-pin center. This is not centered because the hinge leaves are different lengths. The longer leaf is on the leaf side.

Now set the router's depth of cut to include the template thickness plus the required depth for the center point of the hinge pin. It should be about $\frac{3}{32}$."

Using the scrap test pieces for the rule-joint profile setup, test the template by routing the hinge-leaf mortise. Arrange the template so the lines scribed on the template align with the $\frac{1}{2}$" pencil line you marked earlier.

Before installing the hinge in the test pieces, remove some material to accommodate the hinge barrel. Install a $\frac{1}{4}$" fluting bit in your router along with an edge guide. Remove the clamp and the table leaves. Adjust the edge guide so the bit aligns with the hinge barrel location. Adjust the depth of cut to accommodate the hinge barrel. Now make the relief cut for the hinge barrel.

Install the hinge in your test pieces and check out the movement. There should be no binding, it should be fully closed when on the same plane and it should have a small gap when at 90°. When satisfied, rout the mortises in the three top pieces.

Now install the hinges. Leave one screw out and test the action. If good, insert that final screw.

To attach the tabletop to the base, make cleats that attach the apron sides and top. The top edge of the cleats must have the 4° angle to match the top apron edge.

To finish the table, I first sanded through progressive grits from #120 to #220 grit.

For a clear finish, I used one of my favorite "recipes" when I don't want a heavy film finish. My concoction calls for equal amounts of paint thinner, boiled linseed oil and oil-based varnish.

This liquid is thin enough to rag on and wipe off, and after a couple coats it offers reasonable surface protection compared to an oil finish alone. The finish is especially effective on cherry because the linseed oil accelerates the natural darkening and aging of the wood.

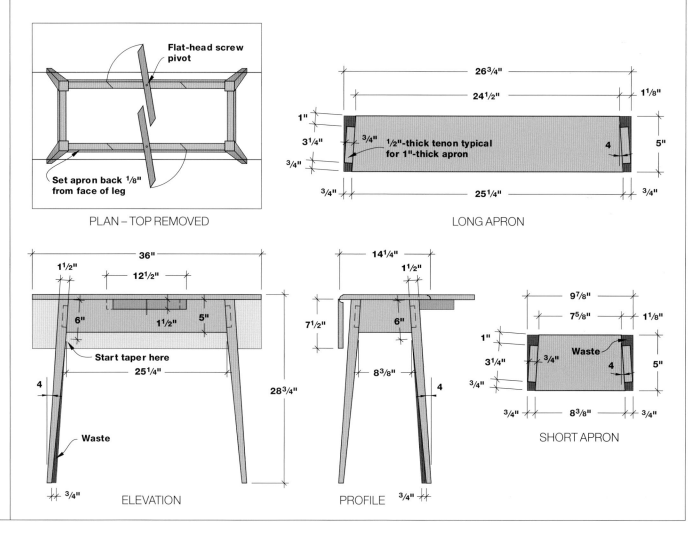

Tripod Table

BY KERRY PIERCE

Several years ago while teaching a chairmaking class at the Marc Adams School of Woodworking, I thanked Mario Rodriguez (who was teaching a hand-tool class at the school that same week) for writing a magazine article I had seen some years before in which simple tenons had been substituted for sliding dovetails to join the legs of a period tripod table to its pedestal. The article, I explained, had been a revelation, allowing me to simplify the construction of these tables without losing any real strength. Mario very kindly pointed out that he had not written the article, nor did he know who had.

Ouch.

Despite my confusion over its authorship, the article had been a revelation, one that changed the way I built these tables and one that caused me to take a long-overdue look at the issue of joint-making excess.

Complex mechanical joints (the very best examples can be found in period Chinese furniture) offer a high degree of strength even without the use of adhesives. This strength is achieved through the use of interlocking parts which – particularly when cut by hand – require skill, patience and time to create. They're often joints that are visually elegant and provide eloquent testimony to the furniture maker's skills.

What I had never really considered until reading the article I had mistakenly attributed to Rodriguez is that often these constructions represent joint-making excess. This is because the mechanical strength of a joint is limited by the resistance to breakage of the wood species from which the joint is cut. This very obvious truth is sometimes overlooked by those of us who fall in love with the joint-making process. In our zeal to create elegant joinery, we – perhaps willfully – forget that a joint cut in a fragile species will fail when the wood fails regardless of the mechanical complexity of the joint.

I work primarily in figured maple and cherry because these are the woods my customers prefer. They're not, however, among the strongest American hardwoods. This is a fact I put to the test many years ago using a collection of chairs I had made but had not offered for sale because of unsightly blemishes in the material. Several were built from cherry, several from figured maple, several from straight-grained hard maple, one from walnut and one from ash. To test the strength of each species, I smashed each chair against the concrete-block wall of my shop. I threw each into the air and allowed it to crash onto the driveway. I tried to drive the heel of my work boot down through the front ladder of each chair. What I learned is this: Hard maple and ash are virtually indestructible; cherry, figured maple and walnut (which fared slightly better than cherry) are not. In fact, I was astonished to see how easily I was able to destroy chairs made from the two wood species with which I most often worked.

The message was clear: Cherry and figured maple are not the woods of choice in applications requiring strength. And further, they are not ideal species to use for furniture requiring complex mechanical joinery – like the sliding dovetail – because the cherry and figured maple are likely to fail long before the elegant joinery.

The Shaker original, on which this example is based, appears in John Kassay's magnificent volume of photos and drawings, "The Book of Shaker Furniture" (University of Massachusetts Press). As is the case with nearly all 18th and 19th century tripod tables, the legs of that original are affixed to the base through the use of sliding dovetails, this despite the fact that the original, like my reproduction, was made of cherry.

You could argue that a furniture maker would be foolish to forego a joint that holds the legs to the pedestal on the still-functional Shaker original, 150 years after its construction. However, I'd be willing to bet my wife's shiny new car that my table – held together with lowly tenons – will still be functional in the

Mortise Layout

The leg-tenon mortises are laid out with the aide of my lathe's indexing head.

An indexing head is a disk centered on a lathe's axis of rotation. A number of equally spaced holes are bored near the circumference of that disk.

On my lathe, there are 36 equally spaced holes, which divide the indexing head (and any object centered on my lathe) into 36 10° increments. Increments can be counted through the use of the spring-loaded pin shown here. By retracting the pin, rotating the disk and re-engaging the pin, I can count a 10° section of an object's circumference.

I wanted to divide the circumference of this tripod-table pedestal into three equal sections. To do that, I counted 12 stops on the indexing head, then, with my marking gauge, I drew a line along that section of the pedestal base. I repeated the process a second time, then a third time. This divided the circumference of the pedestal into three perfectly equal sections.

home of my great, great, great grandchild 150 years after its construction.

Preparing Materials

I have lots of thick cherry in my shop because I often buy 12/4 material, which I then resaw for chair post blanks, but I recognize that not every furniture maker is so lucky. If necessary, the pedestal stock for this table could be glued up from two pieces of carefully matched 5/4 material.

The top on my example was glued up from two pieces of edge-jointed ¾" material cut from the same board. This practice – gluing up tops from two pieces cut from the same board – is one I employ whenever I'm making small tabletops because it results in much better color and figure matching than I can achieve by edge-jointing two pieces cut from two different boards. It takes a sharp eye to see where the joint is on this top.

Because one side of that board was marred by pitch streaks, I flattened the opposite face on my jointer. Then, as soon as I had a clear surface, I ran the material through my thickness planer, removing stock from the blemished side

until it had been reduced to a ⁹⁄₁₆" thickness.

Turning the Pedestal

With your roughing gouge and your lathe, reduce the pedestal blank to a cylinder. Then mark the various divisions along its length. (The measurements shown in the drawing on page 37 indicate the diameters at the marked locations.)

The 1"-diameter tenon at the top of the pedestal is created in two steps. First, use a fingernail gouge – ½" or ¾" – to reduce the diameter so that its smallest diameter is just more than 1". Make frequent checks of that smallest diameter with a set of calipers. Then, with a sharp butt chisel laid bevel side down, square up the outside diameter of the tenon.

The butt chisel alone can be used to create the straight-sided 1⅞"-diameter cylinder against which the legs will be fit.

Use a parting tool to set the diameter of the post where it meets the bottom of the cup. The cup can be shaped with the skew used as a plane or laid flat and used as a scraper. Then use a fingernail gouge to shape the long taper below the cup.

Marking Mortises

After you've sanded the pedestal, mark three equally spaced lines around the outside diameter of the base of the pedestal. These three lines will mark the centers of the three mortises you'll cut for the leg tenons.

There are several techniques you can use for dividing outside diameters into equal parts. If your lathe has an indexing head, like mine, the indexing head can be used to count off 10° increments of that outside diameter (see "Mortise Layout" on page 35). A set of 12 10° increments is equal to 120°, or one-third of the outside circumference of a circle.

Once the outside circumference has been divided into three equal parts, use a marking gauge – like the one shown below – to create three equally spaced lines on the surface of the pedestal base running parallel to the center of the pedestal.

This marking gauge can be made from two pieces of scrap: a vertical piece that holds the marking pencil (notice the set screw that locks the pencil in place in the photo below) and a horizontal piece that slides along the lathe bed. My

The lines being drawn with my marking gauge divide the circumference of the pedestal base into three equal sections. Each of these lines will become the center of a leg-tenon mortise.

Fix the pedestal on your bench with a pair of U-blocks and a clamp.

Tripod Table

NO.	ITEM	DIMENSIONS (INCHES)			MATERIAL	COMMENTS
		T	W	L		
1	Tabletop	⁹⁄₁₆	16¼ dia.		Cherry	
1	Support disc	¾	6⅞ dia.		Cherry	Attached with four No. 8 x 1" wood screws
1	Pedestal	2 dia.		19⅜	Cherry	
3	Legs	⅝	4¹⁄₁₆	11³⁄₁₆	Cherry	Note grain direction on leg profile
1	Sheet-metal disc	1¾ dia.			Sheet metal	Attached with three No. 6 x ¾" wood screws

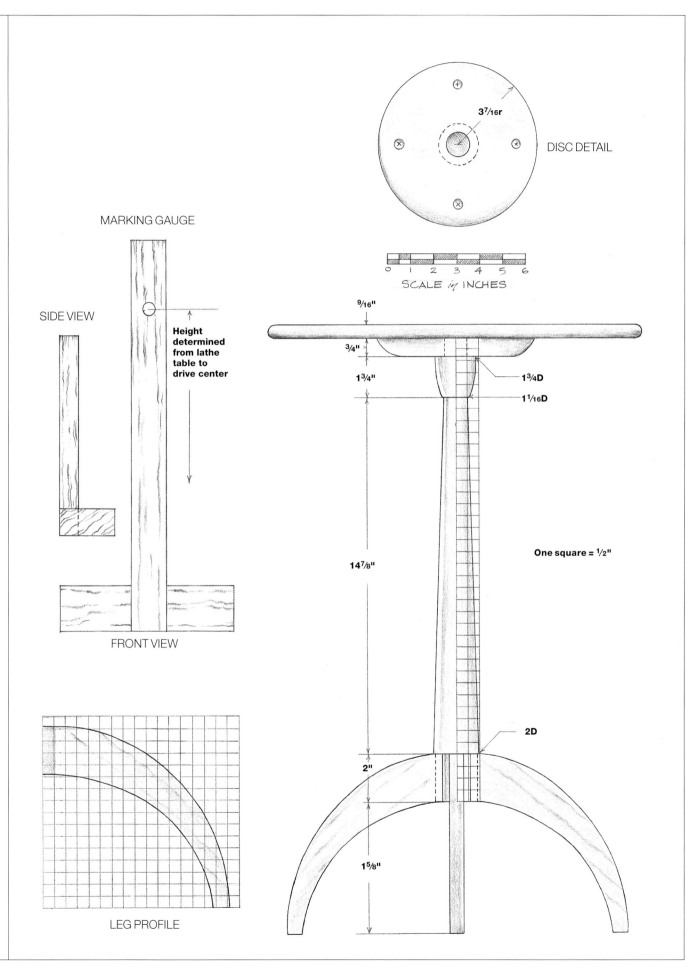

MARKING GAUGE

SIDE VIEW

FRONT VIEW

Height determined from lathe table to drive center

DISC DETAIL

$3^7/_{16}r$

SCALE *in* INCHES

0 1 2 3 4 5 6

$9/_{16}$"

$3/_4$"

$1^3/_4$"

$1^3/_4$D

$1^1/_{16}$D

$14^7/_8$"

One square = $^1/_2$"

2D

2"

$1^5/_8$"

LEG PROFILE

Intermediate line

With a backsaw, rough in the sides of each mortise.

Begin chopping out the waste with a mortise chisel.

lathe bed is a deck of 2 x 6s, so all I need is a flat block of wood for my horizontal piece. If your lathe bed is a tube or a piece of angle iron, you may need to construct a slightly different horizontal piece.

Next, mark a line ³⁄₁₆" on either side of each mortise's center line. These lines delineate the ³⁄₈" widths of the mortises you'll cut in the pedestal base.

Before removing the pedestal from the lathe, mark three more locations on the outside diameter of the pedestal base. These marks should be placed midway between each of the mortise center lines you created previously.

After removing the pedestal from your lathe, fix the pedestal on your bench with a pair of U-blocks and a clamp.

Draw lines on the end grain of the pedestal base connecting the intermediate marks with the center line of the mortise on the opposite side of the base. Complete the marking process by making lines ³⁄₁₆" on either side of the mortise center line on the pedestal's end grain. The mortises are now completely marked.

(If you take a moment to study the photos, this marking process will quickly become clear.)

Saw and Chop the Mortises

With a fine-toothed backsaw, rough in the sides of each mortise. Be careful to keep the saw kerf from extending beyond the limits of the mortise. Then begin chopping out the waste with a mortise chisel. Follow this with a paring chisel and work up to the lines. Then use your mortise chisel to create the flat at the bottom of the pedestal mortise.

Creating the Tenons

Cut out each leg on your band saw. Then clean up the saw marks with a rasp and sandpaper.

Use a knife against a straight-edge (I used an old flexible scraper) clamped to the work to mark the shoulders of each tenon. Then with a fine-toothed backsaw, cut each shoulder to depth. With the leg clamped in a vise – end-grain-up – rough in the tenon cheeks with that same backsaw.

Reclamp the leg onto your benchtop and pare the cheeks down to the line.

Fitting the Tenons

In order for the tenon shoulders – which are cut 90° from the surface of the leg – to mate up tightly with the round pedestal, the top edges of the mortises must be beveled slightly with a paring chisel. Proceed cautiously, testing the leg tenon in the mortise many times as you make your cuts.

Making the Top

You can make a compass for drawing large circles with a length of scrap used as a beam, a nail and a pencil. Close to one end of the scrap, drive a 4d nail so that the point extends through the thickness of the scrap. Bore a pencil-shaft-sized hole through the beam. The center of this hole should be a distance from the nail equal to the radius of the circle you're about to mark. Insert the pencil into the drilled hole, locking it in place with a set screw driven in one edge of the scrap.

To use the compass, set the nail in a shallow pilot hole that's drilled into the bottom of your stock. Then rotate the beam around the hole.

Now band saw the circle and clean up the edge with a rasp and sandpaper. Then use your router to cut a small radius on the top and bottom of the tabletop. Finish up with a rasp and sandpaper.

Mark the shoulders of each tenon and then, with a backsaw, cut each shoulder to depth. Then rough in the tenon cheeks.

Making the Disk

The tenon at the top of the pedestal fits into a disk that is screwed to the bottom of the tabletop. By orienting the grain in this disk so that it runs perpendicular to the grain in the top, the disk acts to stabilize the thin top, reducing the likelihood of cupping.

The curve on the bottom edge of that disk is too large to form with a router; however, you can easily create that profile on your lathe with a fingernail gouge. Begin by fastening the disk to a faceplate with four screws. Then turn the faceplate on your lathe's drive center.

It's important that you work the fingernail gouge downhill, that you begin each pass on the edge face of the disk closest to you and work away from the disk's center point, toward the face of the disk closest to the lathe's drive center. If you work the other way, you'll be working uphill, against the grain. This inevitably results in significant tear-out. Working downhill won't eliminate tear-out, but it will make the tear-out that occurs much less significant.

Fasten the disk to the bottom of the tabletop with four wood screws. Choose a screw length that will allow the screws to penetrate almost completely through the top when the screw head is recessed in the disk. Notice the pitch streaks on the bottom side of my tabletop. This is a common defect in cherry, but it can be placed, as I did here, on hidden surfaces.

The 'Spider'

The Shakers screwed a small disk of metal, called a spider, to the bottoms of the legs on the original to help hold the legs and pedestal together. On the Shaker original, the metal disk had three legs, extending out 1" or 2" along the bottoms of each leg. I opted for a simpler form – shown here – which still gives me enough reach along each leg to secure it.

Bevel the top edges of the mortise with a paring chisel to mate accurately with the leg's tenon shoulders. Check the fit multiple times. You don't want to cut too far.

Orient the grain in the disk so that it runs perpendicular to the grain in the tabletop. This will allow the disk to resist the top's natural inclination to cup. When fastening the disk to the bottom of the tabletop, choose a screw length that will allow the screws to penetrate almost completely through the top when the screw head is recessed in the disk.

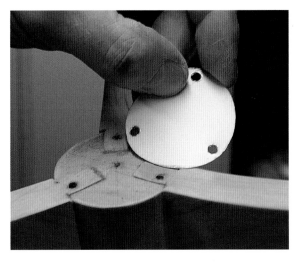

Here is the small disk of metal, called a spider, that's screwed to the bottom of the legs to help hold them together. Use clearance holes in the legs to avoid splitting the tenons.

White Water Table

BY CHRISTOPHER SCHWARZ

The first time I encountered this table in the White Water Shaker collection, it was locked in a storeroom with more than a dozen other pieces. To my eye, there was something unusual about it.

Was it the size? It's 25" high – a bit shorter than typical. Was it the single drawer surrounded by a solid apron? That's atypical for Shakers. Or was it something else?

I put my fingers around the front knob and slid the drawer out. And that's when the mysteries really began. The craftsmanship on the table's base is impeccable. Tight joints. Neat pins. Clean tapers. And the maker chose excellent wood – the aprons are all quartersawn walnut.

But the drawer was a different story. The drawer had one giant dovetail at each corner, and the half-blind tails at the drawer's front left a scant $1/16$" of drawer front. Further, the groove that held the drawer bottom was visible on the ends of the drawer front. That's usually a no-no.

Then I turned my attention to the tabletop. Unlike the table's base, the top was flatsawn walnut and was thinner along its edges with an enormously wide rabbet on the underside. The top was glued and nailed to the base.

Several weeks later, I measured the table and all its details. I sat before it and stared for a long time, hoping that I would find the answers to the questions racing through my head.

Was the drawer original? Was it made by a different maker? Was the top a replacement? And what was this table used for? It's a little big for a side table. And it's too small and low for a typical worktable. But I liked it, and I resolved to build one to donate to the organization restoring the White Water village – Friends of White Water Shaker Village.

The Restoration

I decided to build this table so the wood selection and craftsmanship matched on all the components. That meant a quartersawn walnut top attached with wooden buttons and a more finely dovetailed drawer. This approach troubled me – I don't like to guess about these things. But as the table came together on my workbench, I convinced myself that I had

I decided to cut my drawer front from the front apron. So I ripped a $5/8$"-wide strip off the front apron. After cutting the drawer front from the apron, I glued this strip back on.

made the right decision.

On the first day of working on the project, I glued up the slab for the top from three quartersawn walnut boards and set it aside. Then I turned my attention to the aprons, especially the front one.

After inspecting the original, I suspect the drawer opening was cut from the front apron. I decided I wanted the drawer front's grain to match the apron. So I cut the drawer front from the apron.

Here's how I did it: I started with an apron piece that was a bit wider than needed. I ripped a $5/8$" strip from the top of the front apron (this would later become the apron's top rail). Then I cut the drawer front free from the apron using a backsaw and then a plunge-cutting Japanese saw. Then I glued the $5/8$" strip back on and I had an apron with a 3" x 10" drawer hole in it.

Short & Simple Legs

The legs are $1^{11}/16$" square and taper to 1" at the floor on the two inside faces. The taper begins 1" below the apron. When selecting the stock for the legs, look for growth rings that run diagonally from corner to corner. This will ensure the legs look consistent on all four faces.

Mark out the $1/4$"-wide x $1^{1}/4$"-deep x 4"-long mortises on all four legs. Note that you want the aprons to be set back $1/32$" from the front face of the legs, so be sure to include that detail in your layout. Excavate the mortises.

Then you can taper the legs. I cut the tapers using a band saw and cleaned

An *azebiki nokogiri* is a Japanese saw with curved cutting blades (one for rips; the other for crosscuts). Used against a guide, you can start your cut in the middle of the apron and plunge through. This releases the drawer front from the apron.

To clean up the bottom of the drawer opening, clamp a guide to the apron and use a chisel with its flat face against the guide. Skew the tool to shear the wood and you'll find the work quite easy.

up the cuts with a jointer plane (which is safer than most table saw jigs for this operation).

(Almost) Traditional Tenons

Then turn your attention to the matching $1^{1}/8$"-long tenons. I sawed mine by hand. It's a challenge in wide stock such as this, but if you take your time your tenons can fit right from the saw.

I cut the face shoulders of my tenons using a Japanese flush-cutting saw and a block of wood as a guide. I simply clamped the guide on my knife line,

To cut the tenons' face shoulders you can use a scrap of wood to guide a flush-cutting saw. Just make sure the saw has no set and you've clamped the guide right on your knifed-in shoulder line.

pressed the saw against the guide and sawed a perfect shoulder.

I couldn't bear to nail and glue the top to the table's base. So I cut mortises in the four aprons that would hold buttons to allow for seasonal movement.

Then I cleaned up the legs and aprons, and prepared them for finishing.

Gluing & Pegging

I usually glue up tables in two stages. First I glue the front legs to the front apron and the back legs to the rear apron. Then I peg those tenons and legs together. Next I glue the side aprons to the front and rear assemblies, and I peg those joints.

Pegging joints can be stressful. Here's how I do it. First I make sure that my pegs and drill bit will play together nicely by making a sample joint. Sometimes pegs can be undersized, which will leave an ugly gap behind.

Then I apply painter's tape over all my joints and lay out where I want my pegs to go on the tape. To drill the hole for the peg, I use a $1/4$" brad-point bit and run the drill in reverse for a few rotations to score the perimeter of the hole. This little trick reduces tearing at the rim.

Then I drive the $1/4$" peg in with some glue and cut it flush with a flush-cut saw. The tape protects the wood from the glue and from the occasional wayward saw stroke.

The Raised-panel Tabletop

The tabletop is a bit like a raised panel. The edges are thinned down to $1/2$" while the center field is left $3/4$" thick. This wide and shallow rabbet (3" x $1/4$") can be made

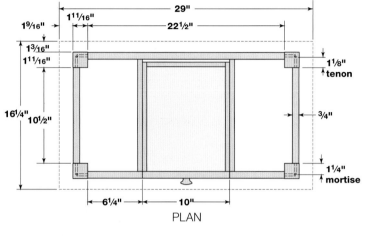

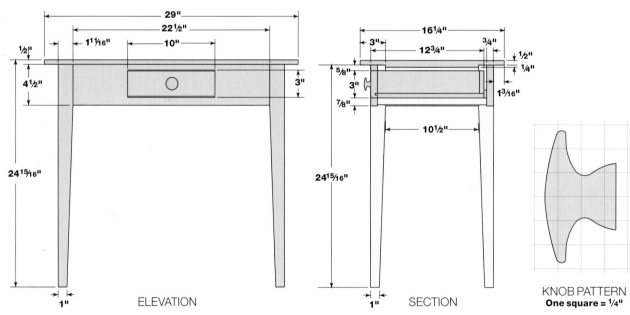

White Water Table

NO.	ITEM	DIMENSIONS (INCHES)			MATERIAL	COMMENTS
		T	W	L		
4	Legs	$1^{11}/_{16}$	$1^{11}/_{16}$	$24^{15}/_{16}$	Walnut	
2	Long aprons	$3/4$	$4^{1}/_{2}$	$24^{3}/_{4}$	Walnut	$1^{1}/_{8}$" tenon both ends
2	Short aprons	$3/4$	$4^{1}/_{2}$	$12^{3}/_{4}$	Walnut	$1^{1}/_{8}$" tenon both ends
1	Top	$3/4$	$16^{1}/_{4}$	29	Walnut	
1	Drawer front	$3/4$	3	10	Walnut	Cut from front apron
2	Drawer runners	$1^{5}/_{8}$	1	$12^{5}/_{16}$	Poplar	
6	Buttons	$1/2$	1	$1^{1}/_{2}$	Poplar	
1	Knob	$3/4$	$1^{3}/_{8}$ dia.		Walnut	

Before assembling the table's base, you should cut mortises for the buttons that will secure the tabletop to the base. I did these using a mortising machine. The mortises are ¼" wide, 2" long and ½" deep. Poke one mortise in each end apron and two mortises in the front and back aprons.

A strip of painter's tape can protect your finished work from glue squeeze-out and from the teeth of the saw. After you cut the peg flush, remove the tape.

on the table saw or router table, but it's also quick work with hand tools. Here's how.

First cut a kerf around the center field of the panel and use a cutting gauge to define the finished ½" thickness on all four edges. Take a rabbeting plane, tip it about 45° and run it in the kerf. Work the long edges of the tabletop first. After a few strokes, begin tilting the rabbeting plane with each stroke so it's eventually almost upright. This will create a wide "V." Work down until the "V" is ¼" deep.

Then waste away most of the rest of the wood with a fore plane or a scrub plane. Clean up the results with a block plane. After you work the long edges of the tabletop down, work the short edges in the same manner.

Attach the tabletop using shopmade wooden buttons – mine were ½" x 1" x 1½". The buttons have a ¼" x ¾" lip that reaches into the mortises in the aprons. When you screw the buttons to the tabletop, the top stays in place, yet it can move with the seasons. (Note: For the buttons in the long aprons, don't bottom them out in the mortises.)

Drawers & Their Runners

The table's two drawer runners are nailed to the front and rear aprons – from the outside of the table. To make the drawer runners, take a long length of 1" x 1⅝" wood and cut a ½" x ⅞" rabbet in its long edge. Crosscut the two runners you need and fit them inside the table's base.

When you have them positioned in the right place, secure them with two cut nails (don't forget to drill pilot holes for your cut nails).

For the drawer, you can make it like the original, you can build it like I did (with three half-blind tails in the drawer's front) or build it so it suits you. I took a traditional path with my drawer. The two tails at the two back corners of the drawer are through-dovetails. The bottom is let into a ¼" x ¼" groove in the drawer sides and drawer front. The drawer bottom (like the tabletop) is also like a raised panel and slides in under the drawer's back, which is ½" narrower than the drawer sides.

The drawer is finished up with a ³⁄₁₆" bead on the top and bottom edge of the front and a walnut knob. After the drawer slides smoothly, glue in a couple stops to the rear apron to make the drawer fit flush at front.

Finish & Final Thoughts

After breaking all the edges of the table with sandpaper, I added a simple and traditional finish: an oil and varnish blend. The oil gave the walnut warmth; the varnish gave it some protection. Five coats did the trick.

You can buy this finish off the shelf (Watco is one brand). Or you can make it by mixing equal parts alkyd varnish, boiled linseed oil and low-odor mineral spirits (paint thinner). Wipe on thin coats and sand away the dust nibs between coats with #320-grit sandpaper.

As a faithful reproduction, this table is a failure. I changed it too much, from the unusual original drawer to the unconventional way the top was attached on the original. But my changes were sympathetic to the time period. So though I can say this table wasn't the same as the one built in the early 19th century in southern Ohio, I can say that my version wouldn't look out of place there, either.

Remove the fence from your rabbet plane and tip the corner of the tool into the kerf as shown. After a few strokes you will reach your finished depth. Stop.

A block plane will remove most of the tool-marks from creating this large rabbet. This block plane is a rabbeting block, which allows the tool to get right into the corner.

A combination square can help line up your drawer runners and the opening for the drawer. Once everything lines up, drill your pilot holes and nail the runners in place.

The only decorative detail on the table is a small bead at the top and bottom of the drawer front. You can make this with a moulding plane or scratch stock.

Shaker-style Coffee Table

BY MEGAN FITZPATRICK

offee tables didn't exist as a furniture form until the 1920s (when they were known as cocktail tables). So while there is no true Shaker coffee table, I needed a table to put in front of my couch that would work well with the other Shaker-influenced furniture in my living room. And to my mind, that's one of the best things about being a woodworker – the ability to design and make exactly what you want. So that's what I did.

This table has the same turned feet and post-and-rail base construction that I used for my stepback (from the February 2009 issue, #174), I used the same hardware as on the "Bibliophile's Bookcase" (from the December 2009 issue, #180) and all three pieces are built from cherry. They're clearly part of the same family, but different enough that they don't look like a store-bought suite.

Best Foot Back
I began by squaring six pieces of 8/4 stock for the legs (my turning skills are at best sophomoric, so I wanted two extra legs in case something went terribly wrong).

I labored over one foot until I was satisfied with its appearance, then set that one directly behind the lathe so I could look at it as I turned the others. Though I used calipers to get the top bead and swelling close to the same size on each foot, they're not identical. That doesn't bother me. They're close enough that, when spread apart to the four corners of the table, you don't notice the differences except with close scrutiny.

After all the feet were turned, I decided on the final leg arrangement, (which was in part dictated by the glaring white sapwood on the corner of one leg that had to face to the inside), then marked out the mortise locations. I cut the $1\frac{1}{2}$"-deep mortises with a $\frac{1}{4}$" hollow-chisel mortiser.

Rails, Stiles & End Panels
With the legs done, I moved on to the rails, stiles and end panels. After cutting the four rails, two middle stiles and two end panels to size, it was time to tenon. I wasn't feeling adventuresome enough to cut all the tenons by hand, so I loaded up the dado stack in the table saw to make the tenons on the rails and end panels.

Il tried a bunch of different leg arrangements until I had all the best faces facing out – the white wood on the front right leg in the picture is on the far side of the table from my couch; only the cats will notice it.

To cut a good tenon by hand, it's best to tilt the workpiece at 45° or so in your vise so you can saw to two lines. Then tilt it toward you to saw down to the baseline on the other side. With those two cuts made, there's a V-shape of waste to saw out of the middle, with the workpiece straight up in the vise. Make the shoulder cut using a crosscut saw and a bench hook.

It's quite a trick to apply glue and get all the tenons in place before a sticky mess ensues. I've seen it done – but I have yet to achieve it.

With the base done, the project is starting to look like a table.

Because the middle stile on each side doesn't have to be as structurally sound, I decided to practice my handsaw skills by cutting the tenons on those two pieces by hand – and they actually fit better right off the saw. I had to clean up the table saw tenons with a router plane, but had very little work to do on the hand-cut ones – next time, it's handsaws for all joinery cuts.

Because the tenons on the end panels traverse $7\frac{1}{2}$", I decided on split tenons (I'd cut the mortises accordingly). I

sawed straight down, coped out the majority of the waste, then cleaned up the resulting shoulder with a chisel.

Base Glue-up
With all the pieces for the base done, it was time to get out the glue. I started with the front and back assemblies, and because there are mortises in the top and bottom and on both ends, I had glue dripping everywhere. So much for my sanding-avoidance techniques – I had to wipe off the drips with a damp rag,

With a panel this long and no roller stand, it's helpful to have another person support the end of the board through the cut. But if another person isn't around to help, a handscrew attached to the crosscut sled will do (though you have to use more downward pressure to keep the piece flat to the saw table to compensate for some sag).

which raised the grain on my carefully planed surfaces.

After those two assemblies dried, I glued in the two end panels, checked everything for square, then set the completed base aside to dry.

Top(ic) of Debate

My next step involved some debate amongst the editors. Is it better to attach the top before making and fitting the drawers? Or is it better to make and fit the drawers with the top unattached, so you can easily reach inside the carcase to make adjustments?

I decided to make and attach the top first, perhaps in part because a top made the thing look closer to finished, but also because I had some trepidation about fitting the through-drawers. I was concerned the base might shift a little as I tightened the buttons to secure the top, and that would affect the drawer fit (three out of four editors agreed).

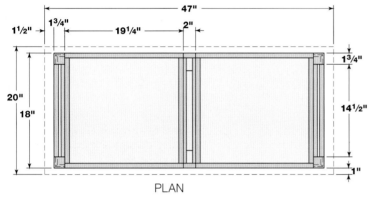

PLAN

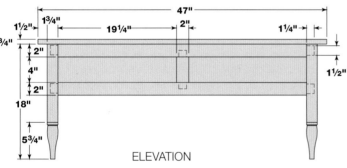

ELEVATION

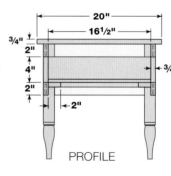

PROFILE

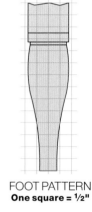

FOOT PATTERN
One square = 1/2"

Shaker-style Coffee Table

NO.	ITEM	DIMENSIONS (INCHES) T	W	L	MATERIAL	COMMENTS
4	Legs	1¾	1¾	18	Cherry	5¾" turned foot
4	Rails	¾	2	43	Cherry	TBE* (1¼")
2	Center stiles	¾	2	6½	Cherry	TBE (1¼")
2	End aprons	¾	8	17	Cherry	Split tenon ends
1	Top	¾	20	47	Cherry	
2	Drawers	4	19¼	18	Cherry/Pine	Make to fit
Web frame						
2	Rails	¾	2	40½	White pine	
2	End stiles	¾	2	12½	White pine	
1	Middle stile	¾	6	12½	White pine	
2	Drawer guides, ends	¾	1¼	14½	White pine	
2	Drawer guides, interior	¾	¾	16½	White pine	
* Tenon both ends						

So it was on to the top. I wanted a two-board glue-up to make the 20" panel, and the piece of wood I'd bought with that in mind was 11" wide. But, there was sapwood running at an angle on both edges, so I couldn't simply cut two pieces to length and join them in the middle. Instead, after cutting each piece of the panel a couple inches overlong, with the face that would become the top facing up on the band saw table, I cut off the sapwood where it met the heartwood at what would become the glueline. (The sapwood was wider on the bottom, and I wasn't concerned with a white stripe on the bottom center; nothing except spiders will see it.)

I then straightened those cuts at the jointer, and glued up the panel. What resulted was a parallelogram, which I squared up at the table saw after the glue was dry.

To attach the top, I cut white oak buttons (from scrap that was underneath my bench), drilled and countersunk screw holes in the buttons, then screwed them to the top, with the tongues fitted in $1/4$" mortises that I cut on the inside edges of the table with a biscuit joiner. There are two buttons on each side and one on either end (and I have a few extras stored in one of the drawers that I can add later if necessary – say, if in the July heat and humidity it starts to curl up at the corners).

Web Frame

Typically, the web frame on which the drawers rest would be notched around the legs. But I'm cheap (and perhaps a bit lazy) and wanted to use the $3/4$" pine scraps that were under my bench.

I had no pieces wide enough to work as stiles notched around the legs, and no pieces long enough to use as notched rails. Nor could I use mortise-and-tenon construction without milling some longer pieces. So instead, I used pocket screws to make a web frame that stretches from end to end on the inside corners. It's simply glued in place to the front and back rails. That made it easy to locate the drawer guides on each end. I simply butted a $3/4$" x $1 1/4$" x $14 1/2$" piece in at each end against the frame, then taped and wedged them in place while the glue dried. The $3/4$" x $3/4$" $16 1/2$" interior guides

The drawer guides on either end were simply butted against and glued to the web frame. Tape and wedges held them in place while the glue dried.

run from center stile to center stile, and were installed with glue after the drawers were done, so I could easily achieve a good fit.

Drawers

With but two drawers to make, the final steps in the build should have been a cakewalk. Of course, they weren't.

I'd picked out some nicely figured cherry for the drawer fronts; it was a little twisted but it was close to $7/8$" thick, so I thought that if I cut the four fronts just a little overlong, I'd be able to take out the twist as I milled each front. Nope. By the time the pieces were flat, they were just a hair under $1/2$" thick – too thin for half-blind dovetails.

But gosh was the figure nice; I was determined to use those pieces as my fronts. So instead of cutting half-blinds for the eight drawer corners, I made through-dovetailed pine drawers that were $1/2$" too short for the openings, milled the cherry fronts down to $1/4$" thick and cut them to size, then glued them on to each pine front. Had I been a little smarter, I'd have used cherry for the front substrate and you'd not be able to tell they weren't through-dovetails. But the drawers were glued up by the time I

Supplies

Rejuvenation

rejuvenation.com or 888-401-1900

8 • square bin pull, oil-rubbed bronze #C1481, $12 ea.

Price correct at time of publication.

The drawers are through-dovetailed with $1/4$"-thick pieces of cherry glued to each front. Clamping the glue-up to your benchtop helps to spread the pressure evenly across the face.

You have to look closely at the completed drawers to tell they aren't constructed with half-blind dovetails.

realized that, and they fit well – it seemed like asking for more trouble to remake them.

One of my drawers was a wee bit short of perfectly square, so I had to add a narrow shim on one guide to even up the reveals. Once everything looked good and fit tightly, I planed a couple thousandths off the bottom side of each drawer and waxed the guides for a smooth ride.

After sanding the base up to #220-grit (the top is planed), I sprayed on two coats of amber shellac topped with two coats of dull-rubbed-effect pre-catalyzed lacquer, then went over it with a brown paper bag to remove any dust nibs and dull the finish a bit more.

While the design picks up on the other pieces in the room, the height was determined by the height of my couch cushions. I wanted to stretch out my legs and not have the edge of the table bite into my calves. But after I got the table in place, my ratty old couch looked even worse in comparison … so I ordered a new one. But I neglected to check the cushion height. I'm waiting for it to arrive, and keeping my fingers crossed.

2

Cabinets &
Chests

Blanket Chest

BY GLEN D. HUEY

was flipping through a copy of The Magazine Antiques one afternoon when I noticed an attractive blanket chest in an advertisement for an antiques dealer in New York. The ad said the Shaker chest was from the John Roberts house in Canaan, N.Y., and had been built in 1850. All I knew was I wanted to build one. With a bit of research on traditional Shaker joinery, it was off to the shop.

The chest is built exactly as Shakers did in the 19th century – with the notable exceptions of biscuits to attach the feet, aliphatic resin glue and a few power tools that would have shocked and excited the brethren. You'll probably need to glue up a few boards to create panels wide enough for the sides, front and top, unless you have access to some lumber in legendary 19th-century widths. Prepare the panels for the sides, front, upper back and top. You might also have to glue up panels for the larger drawer pieces.

Start with the two sides. Determine the best face and mark it for the outside, then mark the location of the three dadoes for the bottom and the two drawer divider webs as shown in the diagram. The dadoes are $\frac{3}{4}$" wide and $\frac{1}{4}$" deep and run the entire width of the sides. With the dadoes cut, next turn to the $\frac{3}{4}$" x $\frac{5}{16}$" deep rabbet on the back edge of each side. This rabbet should stop 5" up from the bottom of each side to leave a solid gluing

surface for the rear feet.

Notch the sides on the front edge $\frac{3}{8}$" deep to allow the front to overlap the sides. This notch will match the front width. Finally, cut a half-circle on each side to form the feet of the base. Use a $4\frac{1}{2}$" radius to mark the half-circle then cut it out with a jigsaw.

With the sides complete, turn to the front piece and cut a $\frac{3}{8}$" x $\frac{3}{4}$" rabbet on each end and the bottom. The rabbets allow the front to fit into the notches on the front edge of each side, and they also allow the bottom to fit snugly into the front. The last step before assembling the case is to prepare the drawer web frames. The drawer runners have a $\frac{3}{4}$"-long tenon cut on either end that fits into matching mortises cut in the front and rear dividers. Glue the front mortise-and-tenon joint but leave the back one loose to allow the frame to expand and contract.

Attach the front and rear feet to the bottom divider frame and case sides with biscuits. The Shakers might have used only glue at this joint, but because we have the technology, cut biscuit slots for all the feet.

The case is now ready to assemble, but I'd recommend first taking a couple of minutes to finish sand the interior of the blanket chest area. It's tough to get into those corners once the chest is together. Little glue should be used to assemble

the chest. A dot of glue at the center of the bottom dado and a dot at the ends of the web frame dadoes is sufficient. Nail the web frames in place with a single nail through the sides and into the end of the dividers. Nail the front and back pieces in place without glue because the joints are long-grain to short-grain joints.

Complete the case assembly by gluing the front and rear feet in place. When the glue is dry, cut the radius on the front feet to match the curve on the sides and sand your handiwork. Finally, nail the shiplapped back pieces in place using nickels as spacers.

Next prepare the chest for the top. The chest top needs a stout hinge that requires more than the $\frac{3}{4}$" back to support it. To accomplish this, glue and nail build-up blocks to the chest back. Once fixed in place, use your router and a straight bit to cut a mortise in the back and block for the hinge leaf.

Now prepare the moulding that's attached to the front edge and sides of the top. The moulding is more than decorative, it also forms a dust seal across the lid. First bevel the moulding on the bottom edge to soften the corner, miter the pieces, and then nail it flush to the top edge.

Position the top on the chest with the back edges flush. Mark the hinge location on the top, then attach the hinges.

Now it's time to work on the drawers.

The front feet are different than the back feet and are cut to allow the grain to run diagonally from the corner of the base area. In addition, the front feet are radius cut on the inside. Attach the feet first, then cut the radius to shape to ease glue up.

With the case glued up and the upper back in place, the loose lower back pieces are ready to be nailed in place. The half-lap design provides a closed back, but allows the wood to expand and contract with the wood movement.

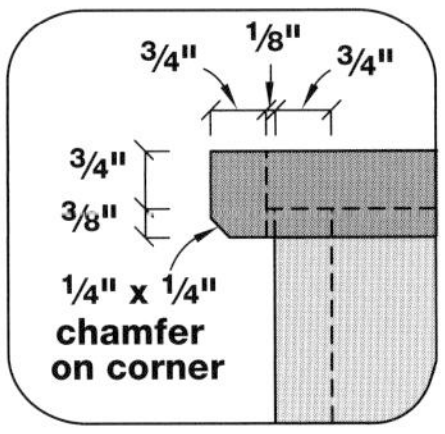

MOULDING DETAIL

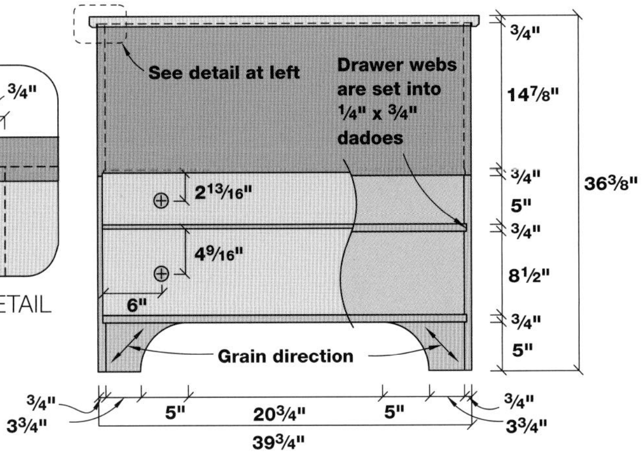

ELEVATION

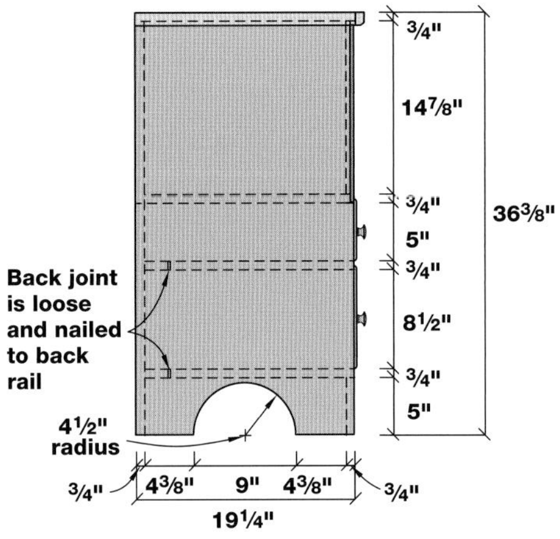

PROFILE

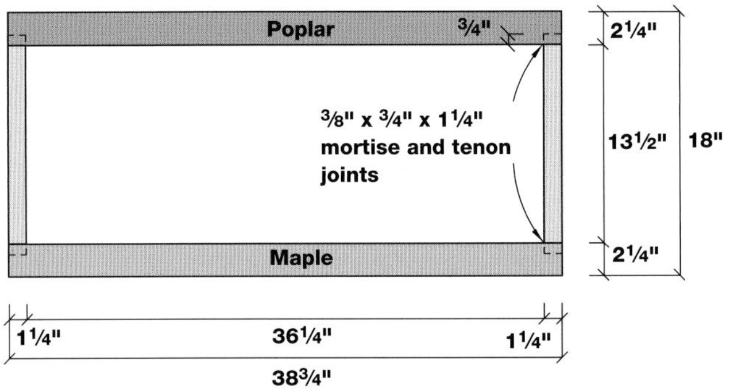

PLAN OF DRAWER WEB FRAME

Supplies

Horton Brass
800-754-9127

1 Pair • 8" strap hinges, #HF-9

Ball and Ball
800-257-3711

1 • Box lock, #TJI-062

Blanket Chest

NO.	ITEM	DIMENSIONS (INCHES) T	W	L	MATERIAL
2	Sides	3/4	19 1/4	35 5/8	Maple
1	Front	3/4	16	39 3/4	Maple
1	Back	3/4	16	39 1/8	Maple
1	Bottom	3/4	18 1/8	38 3/4	Poplar
1	Top	3/4	19 3/8	40	Maple
4	Drawer dividers	3/4	2 1/4	38 3/4	Maple/Poplar
4	Drawer runners*	3/4	1 1/4	15 3/8	Poplar
2	Rear feet	3/4	5	5	Poplar
2	Front feet	3/4	6 1/2	4 1/2	Maple
2	Build-up blocks	3/4	2 1/2	4	Maple
1	Small drwr front †	13/16	5 5/16	38 7/8	Maple
1	Large drwr front †	13/16	8 13/16	38 7/8	Maple
1	Small drwr back	9/16	4 7/8	38 1/4	Poplar
1	Large drwr back	9/16	8 3/8	38 1/4	Poplar
2	Small drwr sides	9/16	4 7/8	17	Poplar
2	Large drwr sides	9/16	8 3/8	17	Poplar
2	Drawer bottoms	5/8	17 1/4	37 1/2	Poplar
	Back boards ‡	5/8	15	39 1/8	Poplar
	6 lineal feet of 5/8" x 11/16" bevel edged top moulding				
4	1 1/2" diameter wooden knobs				

* 3/4" tenon on both ends; † 5/16" lip side and top, 1/8" bottom; ‡ Size given is size of complete, half-lapped back

The drawers are assembled using rabbeted half-blind dovetails at the front and through-dovetails at the rear. First rabbet the drawer fronts to form a $5/16$" lip on the top and sides, and an $1/8$" lip on the bottom edge. The dovetail joint attaches to the rear of the lip formed by the rabbets. To keep the work traditional, the drawer bottoms are made from $5/8$"-thick solid wood, and the three sides of the bottom are beveled to reduce the thickness in order to slide into the $1/4$" x $1/4$" grooves in the sides and drawer fronts. Next tack the bottom into the drawer back to square up the drawer.

Some final hardware and you're ready to finish the piece. Check the instructions (if any) on mounting the chest lock and install the locking hardware. Drill and attach the knobs to the drawers.

To give the piece an appropriate 19th century finish, I used Moser's Early American Cherry aniline dye and applied a couple of coats of lacquer to protect it.

My wife isn't always happy with the number of magazine subscriptions I have. But when I can turn up an idea like this chest from a magazine ad, I'm allowed to keep those subscriptions current.

The drawers are assembled in traditional Shaker fashion using half-blind dovetails on the front–but that doesn't mean you can't cheat on what tools you use. After marking and cutting the pins on the fronts, the band saw makes quick work of what would have been a lot of hand-cutting to create the tails.

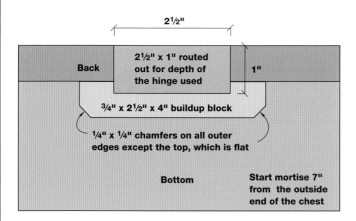

2½"

Back

2½" x 1" routed out for depth of the hinge used

1"

¾" x 2½" x 4" buildup block

¼" x ¼" chamfers on all outer edges except the top, which is flat

Bottom

Start mortise 7" from the outside end of the chest

PLAN DETAIL OF HINGE BUILDUP

With the hinge blocks glued in place against the cabinet back, mark the hinge shape on the top of the block and the back. Next rout out the hinge mortise to the full depth of both hinge leaves.

Hanging Cabinet

BY CHRISTOPHER SCHWARZ

If you own any books about the Shakers or their furniture, you probably have seen a small storage cabinet like this one hanging in the background behind the more celebrated pieces.

I first spotted a close relative of this cabinet in William F. Winter's "Shaker Furniture" (Dover). After a long and glowing description of the chairs shown in the same photograph, Winter notes only: "This small, pine, wall cupboard (from the North family, New Lebanon) is a typical convenience of the sisters' shops."

When I visited the Shaker Village of Pleasant Hill (shakervillageky.org) in Harrodsburg, Ky., I saw a similar cabinet hanging on a peg in one of the second-floor rooms. While eating sweet-potato casserole in the Trustees' Office Inn that evening, everyone else at the table was raving about the built-in cabinets; I was smitten with the little hanging cabinet (and the casserole).

Then, years later, I noticed that Thomas Moser published a more refined version in his seminal "How to Build Shaker Furniture" (Sterling).

The way I see it, this small cabinet has what few woodworking projects can truly lay claim to. It is both simple to build and exceptionally well-proportioned. For that, it deserves center stage.

4 Important Lessons

When building this hanging cabinet there are four important things to pay attention to:

• Rabbet joinery: This cabinet – in one way or another – is built using mostly rabbets. Become familiar with this joint before you attempt this project.

• Wood selection: This cabinet will not look right if you choose the wrong boards for the front. The rails and stiles must have the straightest grain possible. Curvy, diagonal or irregular grain will distract from the simple lines of the piece. Save the most dramatic grain patterns, such as a cathedral grain, for the door's panel.

One common mistake many beginners make is that they try to make a project with as few boards as possible. While no one likes to waste wood, the bigger sin is to build a project that could have looked a lot better in the end. So buy some extra wood and save the scraps for the interior pieces that won't show on a future project.

When picking boards for the two side parts, choose pieces that have straight grain at the edges. This grain pattern will match the straight grain on the case stiles, making the sides look pleasing and – if you're lucky – almost seamless.

• Fitting a door: Beginners hate fitting doors. Experts know there is a trick to making them right with little fuss. Follow the directions carefully and you'll see how straightforward it can be.

• Wood movement: The back is made from a solid-wood panel, so it will expand and contract about $\frac{1}{8}$" with changes in humidity. This means you have to attach the back in a special way to prevent it from splitting or wrenching your cabinet apart as it answers nature's call.

Making a Strong Case

Once you select your boards and joint and plane them down to the correct thickness, you should mill all the parts for the carcase. Joint one long edge of each board, rip them to width and then crosscut them to finished length. Leave the door parts and frame stiles long for now – you will cut them to fit the assembled carcase.

The first joints to cut with this project are the three rabbets in each side piece. Set

I recommend using a dado stack for cutting rabbets because it requires only one setup. The featherboard makes the operation safer and more accurate by keeping your work pressed firmly against the saw's table.

up your table saw to cut a $\frac{3}{4}$"-wide x $\frac{1}{4}$"-deep rabbet. Make a test cut in some scrap that's the same thickness as your sides. Check your work with a square and some care. If this joint does not have a dead-on 90° corner, your carcase won't have one either. If it is square, check the dimension of the rabbet using a dial caliper. This might sound like overkill, but it's not. Here's why: If this joint is just a little off, then all the joints that follow it will have to compensate for this small error – espe-

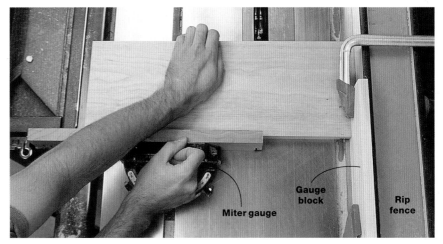

The gauge block, which is clamped to the rip fence, sets the location of the dado on the side pieces. But because the gauge block sits in front of the saw blade, there's no danger of trapping your side piece between the rip fence and the blade while making this cut – a major source of kickback. If you have a stock miter gauge, this would be an excellent time to add a piece of adhesive sandpaper (I prefer #100-grit) to its smooth metal face to improve grip during this operation.

Gauge block

Miter gauge

Rip fence

Angled nails wedge the joint

Stile

Mind the gap

Nails are not an act of the devil. Someday the glue will fail, and it's the nails that will hold everything together. Make sure you angle your nails (18-gauge brads are good) as shown so that the fasteners wedge the side piece against its mates.

This is a highly visible joint, so make extra sure you watch out for gaps between the stiles and the sides.

cially when you start building the door and fitting it to the case. Small errors like this tend to add up during the course of a project.

When you're satisfied with the setup of your dado stack and rip fence, lock the height of the arbor. This is important for a couple of reasons. With some less-expensive table saws, you can actually force the arbor to creep downward dur-

ing a cut with a dado stack. I've seen it happen – your dado will look like a ramp for skateboarders instead of a properly made joint. Also, you will be keeping this exact height for the next two joinery operations, so locking in your setting is a good idea. With your saw set, cut this rabbet on the ends of the two side pieces. This joint holds the top and bottom of the case in place.

Next, cut the rabbet in the sides that will hold the back panel. To create this rabbet, you need only adjust your rip fence to make a $1/2$"-wide x $1/4$"-deep rab-

bet and cut that rabbet on the long back edge of each side piece.

After that, cut the dados in the side pieces that will hold the two $1/2$"-thick shelves in place. To make your life easier, make sure you do not change the height of the dado stack you just used to cut the rabbets. Remove the dado stack from the arbor and install the correct number of wings, chippers and shims to produce a perfect $1/2$"-wide dado.

The dados for the shelves are $1/4$" deep. By leaving the height of the blades alone, you ensure that the shelves, top

Hanging Cabinet

NO.	PART	DIMENSIONS (INCHES)			MATERIAL	COMMENTS
		T	W	L		
Carcase						
2	Sides	$3/4$	7	19	Cherry	$3/4$"-wide x $1/4$"-deep rabbets on ends
2	Inside top & bottom	$3/4$	$6 1/2$	17	Cherry	
2	Shelves	$1/2$	$6 1/2$	17	Cherry	In $1/2$"-wide x $1/4$"-deep dados
2	Stiles	$3/4$	$2 1/2$	19	Cherry	Glued to carcase
1	Notched outside top	$1/2$	$8 3/4$*	19	Cherry	
1	Outside bottom	$1/2$	$8 1/4$	19	Cherry	
1	Back	$1/2$	18*	$24 1/2$	Cherry	
Door						
2	Door stiles	$3/4$	$1 1/2$*	20*	Cherry	$1/4$"-wide x $1/2$"-deep groove on one edge
2	Door rails	$3/4$	$1 1/2$*	$11 1/4$	Cherry	$1/4$"-wide x $1/2$"-deep groove on one edge, $1/2$" TBE
1	Door panel	$1/2$	11	17	Cherry	$1/2$"-wide x $1/4$"-deep rabbet on four back edges

* Dimensions listed are oversized. See the text for details. TBE = tenon both ends

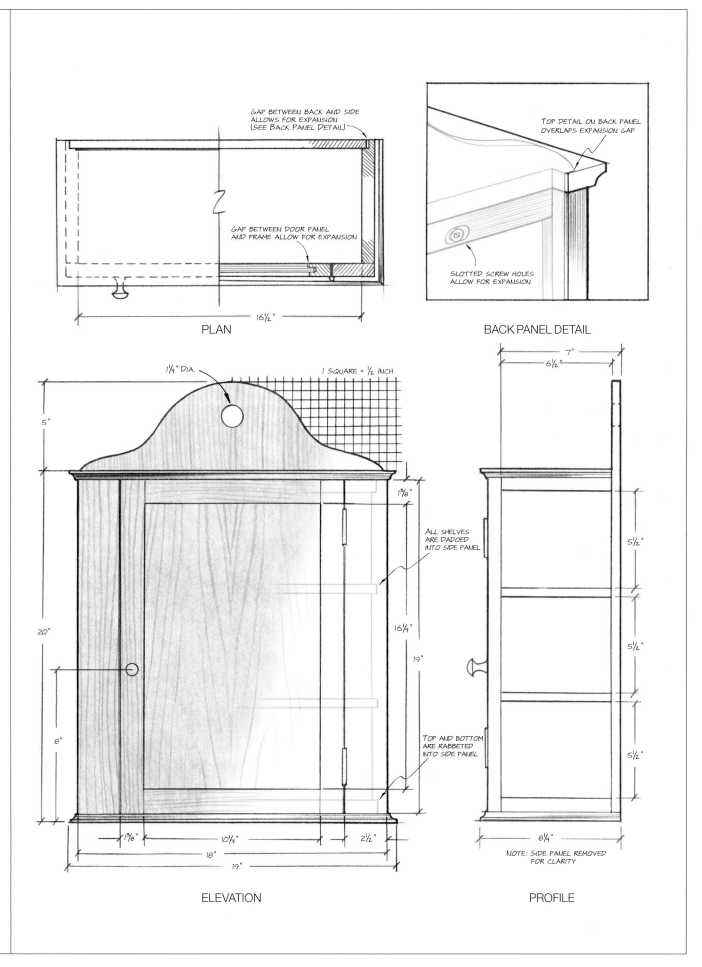

GAP BETWEEN BACK AND SIDE
ALLOWS FOR EXPANSION
(SEE BACK PANEL DETAIL)

GAP BETWEEN DOOR PANEL
AND FRAME ALLOW FOR EXPANSION

16½"

PLAN

TOP DETAIL ON BACK PANEL
OVERLAPS EXPANSION GAP

SLOTTED SCREW HOLES
ALLOW FOR EXPANSION

BACK PANEL DETAIL

1¼" DIA.

1 SQUARE = ½ INCH

5"

20"

8"

1⅜"

16¼"

19"

ALL SHELVES
ARE DADOED
INTO SIDE PANEL

TOP AND BOTTOM
ARE RABBETED
INTO SIDE PANEL

1⅜"   10¼"   2½"

18"

19"

ELEVATION

7"

6½"

5½"

5½"

5½"

8¼"

NOTE: SIDE PANEL REMOVED
FOR CLARITY

PROFILE

Cutting an accurate stopped notch like this is a pain. By ripping the oversized top down and regluing smaller blocks on the ends of the top, you create the perfect notch for the back piece.

and bottom will keep your case square. If you change the height of the blades even a tiny bit before cutting the dados, one of two bad things will happen. If your cut is too deep, your shelves won't seat all the way down into the bottoms of the dados without some extraordinary clamping pressure. (If you manage to close this joint, your carcase will end up with an hourglass shape and the rabbets at the top and bottom will be gappy and weak.) If your dado cut is too shallow, the shelves will cause the sides to bulge out in the center and the rabbets at the top and bottom will be gappy, unattractive and weak.

To make the dados in the sides, use your table saw's miter gauge (set to 90°) and a gauge block clamped to your rip fence, as shown in the photo below. Mark on your side pieces the locations of both dados. Sure, it will take an extra minute, but it prevents mistakes. Also mark the top and bottom of each of the sides so you don't get the right and left sides confused – a common mistake that even professionals make.

With the dados cut, you are almost ready to assemble the basic carcase. It's always a good idea to prepare your interior surfaces for finishing before assembly. Finish-sand the inside faces of your pieces (start with #100-grit paper and work up to #220), or plane and scrape the surfaces to your liking.

Test the fit of the joints and clamp the case together without any glue. Do not skip this step. A rehearsal is worthwhile for several reasons: You'll figure out exactly how many clamps you need so you don't have to go rushing across the room for more as the glue sets up. You'll also figure out the best procedure for clamping the case without your parts flopping around. And you'll make sure your rabbets and dados fit soundly.

As you make this milk run, make sure you keep the front edges of the top, bottom and shelves perfectly flush with the front edge of the side pieces. The top, bottom and shelves, if you haven't noticed, are $1/2$" narrower than the sides.

Before you take the clamps off, pay

particular attention to the squareness of the case. Measure the case from corner to corner and compare the two dimensions. If they're the same, everything's square. If they're not, put a clamp across the two corners that produced the longer measurement and apply the tiniest bit of clamping pressure. Compare the corner-to-corner measurements again. Repeat until everything is perfect. I like to check the squareness now because the cabinet usually behaves the same once you add the glue.

Now add glue in your rabbets and dados. If you are new to woodworking, I recommend a slow-setting glue for casework. There are several varieties, the most common being Titebond Extend. The glue's extra "open time," which is when the glue is wet and your parts can move around, will allow you to tweak the position of your parts. When applying the glue, a thin but consistent film will bond your joints without making a big mess. When you apply the clamps, a little glue squeeze-out is good – it means you haven't starved your joints of glue.

After 45 minutes, take the case out of the clamps and nail the sides to the top and bottom pieces, using the above photo as a guide.

World's Simplest Face Frame
Traditionally, face frames are built using both vertical pieces (stiles) and horizontal pieces (rails). Not so with this project, which has only stiles. This makes things a lot easier.

Cut your stiles to finished width and length, and finish-sand or plane them. If you're handy with a block plane, it's wise to cut your stiles about $1/32$" long and trim them flush to the case at the top and bottom after affixing them to the carcase. If you're not so confident, just take extra care in cutting your stiles to length.

Attach the stiles to the carcase using glue and clamps. Nails aren't necessary here. Make an effort to ensure the long edge of each stile is perfectly flush with its mating side piece; otherwise the opening for your door will not be square.

To complete the opening for the cabinet's door, you need to attach the additional $1/2$"-thick top and bottom pieces that have the decorative cove cut milled on them, which is easy to do.

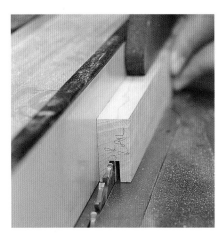

Centering grooves on your work is child's play if you cut them in two passes. Here you can see that I milled one half of the groove and have turned the piece around to mill the other half.

Make the tenons by cutting a rabbet on both sides of the rails. Use your miter gauge and fence to make this cut. It's a safe operation because you can't trap your work between the blade and fence.

As you study the cutting list below, you'll notice that the outside top and bottom are different widths – the top is ¹⁄₂" wider than the bottom. That's not a mistake. It's actually a clever way to create a notch in the back edge of the outside top piece (cutting stopped notches is no fun). Let me tell you what you're going to do to that top piece: First you're going to rout the cove detail on three edges of both the top and bottom.

The best way to do this operation is on a router table that's set up with a ⁵⁄₈" cove bit, though you can do it hand-held in a pinch. Either way, make sure you rout the detail on the ends first, then come back and rout the long edge. This will clean up a good deal of splintering that occurs when you exit the cuts on the ends.

Next take only the top piece to the table saw and rip the back edge off the board so it's 7³⁄₄" wide. Take the fall-off strip and rip it so it's ¹⁄₂" wide. Crosscut 1" off each end of that falloff piece and reglue each end to the back edge of the top piece, making sure the cove detail matches. Voilà! You have an instant stopped notch in your top.

Attaching the top and bottom pieces to the carcase is easy if your case is square and your joints are flush. Before you attach the top and bottom, check their fit against the carcase itself. You want a tight joint at the front and the sides. If you don't get a seamless fit with only hand pressure, you'll need to tweak the carcase until you do. Relying on your clamps to close an imperfect joint is asking for trouble.

Sometimes this process takes a bit of detective work to figure out what's wrong. For example, the top of my carcase had an inexplicable but slight bulge in the center, so the top piece would rock back and forth on it. A sharp block plane made short work of the problem. As you remove material, try to stay away from the edges of the carcase. That's where you can create problems that will show in the finished piece.

When satisfied with the fit of the top and bottom pieces, apply a liberal amount of glue to the carcase and position the top and bottom in place. When you've got them where you want them, nail them in place through the inside of the cabinet. Use only a couple of nails in

each; their job is to hold the top in place as you clamp it. Apply clamps around the cabinet to secure the top and bottom to the carcase and check for gaps.

The Stub-tenon Door

Because this is a light-duty door, we can build what's called a "stub-tenon" door.

Essentially, it's a traditional mortise-and-tenon door that uses short (some would say "stubby") tenons that are only ¹⁄₂" long. A bigger traditional door would use tenons at least 1" long.

The advantage to these short tenons is they allow you to build the door without having to cut mortises in the stiles. The

A Better Hinge

Installing hinges for an inset door can be a brutal lesson in precision. Inset doors, as their name implies, sit inside the cabinet or the cabinet's face frame. The space between the door and the cabinet – called the "reveal" – has to be perfectly equal all the way around the door or it won't look right. Overlay doors, on the other hand, are much more forgiving to install because a rabbeted lip on the door covers up the gap between the cabinet and the door. If you're a little off – or sometimes even a lot – no one will notice. But overlay doors don't generally have the look of a fine and refined piece of furniture. They say "kitchen cabinet" instead of "prized possession."

So if you want to install inset doors, you're going to have to wrestle with mortising a butt hinge into both your cabinet and door, right? Wrong. During the last five years we have become huge fans of a hinge made by Amerock that is remarkable for three reasons: One, it lets you install the hinge without cutting a mortise. Two, once you install the hinge you can tweak its position until the door is perfect and then lock in your final setting. And three, these hinges look great on traditional cabinets.

The secret to these remarkable hinges is that they have oval-shaped holes for screws that allow you to shift the door slightly up and down in its opening and even cock it deliberately out of square to match a door opening that's not perfect. Once you get the door just right, you secure the hinge permanently with either a final screw or a brad – depending if the hinge is designed for a face-frame cabinet (which uses what Amerock calls a "full back-to-back wrap-around hinge") or a frameless cabinet (which uses a "partial wrap-around hinge").

In the hinge pictured at left, you can see the holes for the brads in the leaf that attaches to the case. Curiously, you have to supply your own brads to lock this leaf in place; my only gripe with this hinge is that they aren't included.

On the leaf that attaches to the door you can see the two screw holes that lock in that setting. (One of the holes has a screw in it; the other does not.)

The Amerock hinges are available in a variety of finishes, including wrought

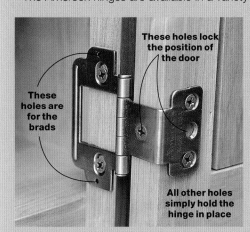

These holes lock the position of the door

These holes are for the brads

All other holes simply hold the hinge in place

If you struggle with installing hinges for inset doors, this can make it easier.

iron, brushed nickel, dark antique brass, antique brass and polished brass. Plus they are available in a variety of styles that match many styles of furniture with a finial tip, a ball tip or just a plain button. These hinges aren't cheap – about $6 per pair no matter where you go. But that price includes high-quality screws for installing them. Once you try these hinges, we don't think you'll go back to traditional mortise hinges unless you have to.

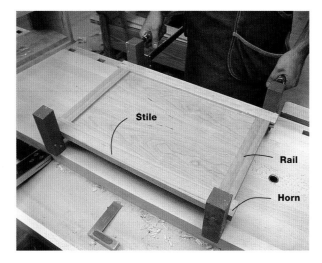

You can see here how the stiles stick out past the rails of the door. These are the so-called "horns," which you then trim off to make the door the perfect size.

$1/4$"-wide x $1/2$"-deep groove you cut for the door's panel also serves as the mortise for the tenons on the rails.

While stub-tenon doors are a good trick, the real trick to making perfect doors is to learn about "horns." What are horns? Again, take a look at the cutting list and you'll notice that the stiles are 1" longer than they need to be to fit in the door's opening. And both the rails and stiles are $1/8$" wider than called for in the drawing.

This extra length and width create what look like horns on the assembled door. These horns allow you to make a door that is slightly oversized when compared to the hole in the cabinet. Once the door is assembled, rip and crosscut it square to fit perfectly in the door opening. There is no easier way to fit a door.

So let's build the door. Cut your stiles, rails and panel to the sizes listed in the cutting list. Now mill the $1/4$"-wide x $1/2$"-deep groove in one long edge of the rails and stiles. The best way to do this is with a rip blade set to make a $1/2$"-deep cut. A rip blade is best because the top of its teeth are flat, so the bottom of your groove also will be flat. Crosscut teeth will leave "V"-shaped channels in the bottom of the groove. Position your saw's rip fence so there's a $1/4$"-wide gap between the teeth and the rip fence.

Cut the groove first with one face of your work against the fence, then turn it around and make the cut with the other face against the fence. This method ensures that the groove is perfectly centered on your rails and stiles. If there happens to be a thin scrap hanging in the middle (as shown in the photo on p. 58, you can adjust the fence and make a third pass to eliminate it.

Next get your rails and prepare to cut the tenons on the ends. These tenons are made by cutting a rabbet on both faces of the board. Two rabbets make a tenon, as shown in the photo on p. 58.

Set up your dado stack with an accessory fence just like you did when you cut the rabbets on the side pieces. Bury the dado stack in the accessory fence so that you're making a cut that is exactly $1/2$" wide x $1/4$" deep.

Use your miter gauge to guide your rails across the spinning dado stack. Make a couple of test cuts on scrap that is the same thickness as your door stock. Test the fit of your scrap tenon in the

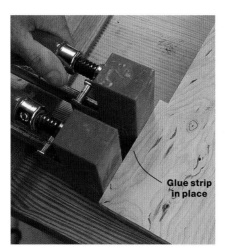

To make this notching operation go smoothly, make sure you rip the narrow strips from the back using a sharp rip blade. This will ensure that you'll get a clean cut and the blocks will be easier to reglue and get a seamless joint.

grooves you cut in the rails. Fine-tune your fence setup and cut the tenons on the ends of both rails.

Now fetch your $1/2$"-thick panel. To fit this panel in the grooves in the rails and stiles you must first cut a rabbet that is $1/2$" wide x $1/4$" deep on the panel's four back edges. Coincidentally (OK, it's not really a coincidence), this is the same setup you just used to make your tenons.

Now finish-sand your door parts and dry-fit the door. You'll notice how the stiles extend past the rails. These are the horns I told you about earlier. The tenons must close tightly with only minimal clamping pressure. If you are straining to close the joint you are almost certainly twisting your door so it's not flat. Take the joint apart and investigate the problem. Usually there's gunk that's preventing a good fit, or the tenon is too long for the depth of the groove.

Once you have a seamless door frame clamped up, take the whole thing apart and glue the tenons in the grooves. (Never glue a solid-wood panel in place in a door. It has to expand and contract with changes in humidity.)

After about 45 minutes, remove the clamps from the door. Measure your door opening and temporarily screw the hinges to the carcase. Now true one stile of your assembled door by running it over the jointer. Rip the door to its finished width on your table saw, trimming evenly from the left and right stile. Then crosscut it to the correct length. Test the fit in the door's opening and fine-tune things until the door has a

This elongated hole allows the back to expand and contract and still stay tightly secured under the screw. I make these holes by wiggling my drill bit. The other option is to drill a round hole and elongate it with a small rat-tail file.

Shelf Support Basics

Storage doesn't do you much good if you can't divide it to suit your needs. That's what shelving is all about and there are a number of ways to put your shelves in just the right position. We've gathered the best of the pack here with quick explanations of their best applications.

Though there are a number of good choices listed, the most common support with the best price and function is the spoon pin, with or without the sleeve. We also appreci-ate the invisible application found with either the low-profile pin or the hidden shelf wire. When using any of the supports that require carefully located holes in your cabinet sides, we recommend cutting a piece of $\frac{1}{4}$" hardboard or plywood to about 3" wide and nearly the height of your opening. Drill a single line of shelf holes in this piece and use it as a template for all the holes.
– David Thiel

Standard with Clip

One of the most common, inexpensive, versatile and ugliest shelf supports ever manufactured. While you can easily adjust shelf locations in 1" increments, the metal track is always visible and requires a groove machined in the sides. This support looks best in office furniture – not a project you spent hours building. Available in ugly nickel or zinc plate, ugly white and uglier brown.

Reinforced Support

An economical option, this plastic support slips into a hole (or multiple holes to allow for adjustment) that you drill in the cabinet sides. Like the metal track above, these are also common in office furniture and are not attractive. They also hold the shelf away from the side by as much as $\frac{1}{4}$".

Locking Support

Top lock

This support also fits into holes drilled in the cabinet sides. As an added feature, it locks the shelf in place from above, avoiding accidental tipping. Economical, but still rather unsightly, it also holds the shelf away from the cabinet sides. Use this for commercial furniture or for shop cabinets where you don't want a shelf to ever come crashing down – not for that Queen Anne highboy.

Right-angle Support

Slightly less unsightly, this support is almost invisible (with the shelf in place). The optional rubber pad keeps the shelf from sliding off, but it still leaves an unattractive gap between the cabinet side and each shelf. This is a good choice for furniture in a child's room or in a rumpus room.

Adjustable Support

Studs

Pins

This support compensates for sloppy drilling. By trapping the shelf between the studs, the pin can rotate in the hole to find a balance between the four holes. A nice feature, but the ugly gap is still there, and now you've got a stud showing above the shelf. Save this support as a last option if (or when) you've messed things up.

Straight Pin

This is a true pin. Although low visibility, it has some problems. If the hole is slightly oversized, the pin can work loose, dumping the shelf. If the holes are not drilled perfectly, the shelf will wobble. On the other hand, if small notches are cut on the underside of the shelf, the pin can nestle in the notch, holding the shelf firmly.

Spoon Pin

Optional sleeve

A refined version of the straight pin, this pin can be used with or without the sleeve. It's then slipped into a hole or holes drilled in the cabinet side. The pin allows the shelf to fit all the way against the cabinet side without any visible gap, but still has a shoulder to hold the shelf in place.

Screw-in Spoon Pin

Taking the pin and sleeve concept a bit further, this pin screws into its sleeve. It's a nice idea, but ultimately a little like gilding the lily, and best reserved for high-end glass casework. These pins are pretty darn expensive because you have to buy a threaded sleeve for every shelf-pin hole.

Low-profile Pin

The most invisible and still very economical, this support requires a little extra machining. The plastic pins are still slipped into holes drilled in the cabinet sides, but the shelves themselves have stopped saw kerfs along the ends that accept the blade of the pin. The shelf fits around the pins (in place) and the support disappears.

Hidden Shelf Wire

Another invisible variation is a hidden shelf wire. Rather than using two independent pins that slip into grooves in the shelves, this system uses a wire support. Essentially requiring the same amount of machining and drilling, this actually provides a more stable support and puts less stress on the shelf. The wire spreads the support over the depth of the shelf rather than focusing it on two bearing points.

perfectly consistent gap all around. You can use a table saw to do this, but I prefer a hand plane because I mess things up in a much slower fashion than with a power tool. Once your door fits, you can tweak its position in its opening if you use the hinges we recommend in the Supplies box below. Add the knob of your choice and a catch (the magnetic ones are the easiest to install).

More Notches in Your Back

As I designed this project, I tried different ways to make it so the back was not one piece of $17\frac{1}{2}$"-wide solid wood. The solutions were more complex than I liked or they didn't look right, so I decided to stick with the original wide back.

To make this work, I first had to calculate how much the back would expand and contract in a typical Midwestern environment (which has some pretty radical humidity fluctuations, I can tell you). Using the formulas in R. Bruce Hoadley's "Understanding Wood" (Taunton Press), I figured out how much movement to expect. According to Hoadley's formulas, the panel will expand about $\frac{1}{8}$" when the humidity fluctuates between 8 percent and 14 percent. This is a reasonable range to expect in our climate.

So now you need to measure the space between the two rabbets on the backside of your assembled carcase. It should measure 17". So the lower part of the back piece should measure $16\frac{7}{8}$" wide. That's simple enough. The real difficulty comes when dealing with the curvy top part of the back. It's $17\frac{1}{2}$" wide. That extra width

overhangs the top of the cabinet. Once again this means you have to create a stopped notch on the two long edges of the back.

The simplest procedure is to use the same trick you used for creating the notch on the top piece: Gluing small pieces on the back to make a notch. And that's a fine way to do it as long as you pay close attention to matching the grain. This is a very visible part of the cabinet.

Make your back piece a bit wider to start with: 18" is about right. Rip two strips off each long edge so the back ends up $16\frac{7}{8}$" wide. Keep track of which edge each strip came from because that will make it easier to match the grain when regluing the blocks in place. Now take those narrow strips and crosscut 5" off the top of each. Reglue these blocks to the back.

After the glue dries, mark the curvy shape on the back and cut to that line. A band saw, scroll saw or coping saw will do. Just make sure it's a fine-tooth blade. Clean up the rough saw-cut edges with sandpaper, files or a spokeshave. Then drill the $1\frac{1}{4}$"-diameter hanging hole in the location shown in the drawing. Finish-sand your back.

Attaching the back is easy if you pay attention to the issue of wood movement. The back is attached by screwing through it into the top and bottom pieces. You want to secure the back in the center of the cabinet so it expands equally on either side. Here's how to do that: Drill six screw holes in the back, three along the top and three along the bottom. The middle hole should be a standard round clearance hole. But the holes to the left and right should be elongated left-to-right. It's these elongated holes that allow the back to expand and contract with changes in humidity.

I've seen people make a template to rout perfect elongated ovals. Then they make the countersink using a template and a chamfer bit. This is not necessary. All you really need to worry about is allowing the shaft of the screw to pivot as the back moves. The screw's head can remain basically in the same place.

Here's how I make elongated holes: Drill a standard clearance hole for your screw that allows the screw's shaft and threads to pass through without biting

into the wood. Next, angle your drill 45° one way and drill out a bit of one side of your clearance hole. Then angle the drill 45° the other way and drill out the other side of your hole. Finally, come back with your countersinking bit and countersink your clearance hole. Once done, then you can screw the back to the case using some #8 x 1"-long screws.

Finishing Cherry

Before you apply a finish to this project, take a few minutes to break the sharp edges with #120-grit sandpaper. This will make your project more enjoyable to touch and less likely to get damaged. Now remove the back and door.

Because cherry darkens nicely with age, I prefer not to add much coloring. In any case, staining cherry can be difficult because it blotches.

But new cherry with a clear finish looks a bit anemic until it gets a couple of years of coloring, so I like to help the process along. Begin by wiping on a coat of boiled linseed oil that's thinned down to a water-like consistency with paint thinner. Wait about 30 minutes and wipe off the excess. Then take your project outside and let it bask in the warm sun for an afternoon or two. This will jump-start the coloring process.

After a couple of days of letting the oil cure, you can add a protective top coat. The simplest finish for this is a wiping varnish – essentially a thinned-down off-the-shelf varnish.

If you want to hang this project like the Shakers did, you'll need to build and hang a board with Shaker-style pegs. The length of the board is up to you and the scale of your room. We've included a supplier of cherry Shaker pegs at left.

The last trick is to find a place in your home that really shows off the proportions and workmanship of this fine piece. You don't want this project to ever languish in the background.

Supplies

Rockler
800-279-4441 or rockler.com

2 • Amerock ball-tip, full wrap-around hinges in antique brass, #31300, $8.99/pair

1 • Cherry Shaker $\frac{7}{8}$" knob, $\frac{3}{8}$" tenon, #78469, $9.49 pair.

1 • Narrow magnetic catch, #26559, $2.49 each

• Cherry classic Shaker pegs, #23382, package of eight/$8.99 (Also available in oak and maple.)

Prices correct at time of publication.

Smart Ways to Hang Cabinets

The hanging process should actually begin with the design phase of the project. With the cabinet shown here, we've followed the Shaker tradition and mounted a peg board to the wall, with the cabinet hung from a peg.

Other methods (more common today) are to mount the cabinet to the wall through the back of the cabinet (either with just the back or with a hanging strip) or to use a French cleat, which is invisible and convenient.

Screwing Through the Back

Depending on the size of your cabinet, you may have used a ¼"-thick back or thicker (½" or ¾"). With a thicker back, mounting the hanging cabinet to the wall is simply a matter of finding a stud and marking that stud location on the inside of the cabinet. Then you drill a clearance hole for the screw (usually ³⁄₁₆" diameter), hold the cabinet in place and level on the wall, and screw the cabinet to the stud with a #10 x 3"-long screw. If the cabinet is wider than 16", you'll be able to put a second screw through the back and into a second stud. This should be enough to support most cabinets.

If your cabinet is less than 16" wide, you'll need a drywall "molly" to reinforce the second screw. Mollys are sold in the picture-hanging section of your local hardware store and allow you to put a screw almost anywhere in a wall. There are half a dozen kinds of mollys that are suited for different weights.

If you're hanging a large cabinet and want to use a ¼"-thick back (to make it less expensive and lighter in weight), a hanging strip will make mounting the cabinet easier. This strip (shown top right) can be built into the design of the cabinet or simply applied to the back. It goes inside the cabinet and below the top. Actually building the strip into the sides adds some strength, but it also adds an extra step or two to the project.

Screwing through this strip instead of just the thin back will give you more strength and reduces the chance of tearing through the thin back material with the screw.

Using a French Cleat

French cleats offer invisibility and incredible strength, but they do steal some storage space from the inside of the cabinet. These cleats can be purchased (made from aluminum or steel) for the truly lazy, or made from simple ¾"- or ½"-thick scrap. The cleat is in two pieces, each with a 45° bevel on one long edge. One goes on the back of the cabinet; the other attaches to the wall. When you nest the 45° bevels together, the cabinet hangs firmly on the wall. You should be able to do pull-ups on your cabinet if it is properly installed this way – no kidding.

To use a French cleat, you have to design a gap behind the back of the cabinet to house it. Essentially the cabinet is built with the back recessed into the cabinet, so the top, sides and bottom still touch the wall.

Beyond the strength gained by using a cleat (as long as you catch a stud or use mollys), cleats are easy to level. The wall section of the cleat is attached with one screw and that section is leveled and fixed in place. Then the cabinet is simply slipped in place over the wall cleat.

– David Thiel

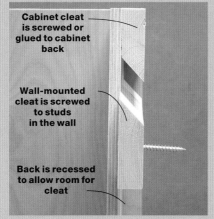

Cabinet cleat is screwed or glued to cabinet back

Wall-mounted cleat is screwed to studs in the wall

Back is recessed to allow room for cleat

The shop-made French cleat in action. This French cleat is made for a board ripped at a 45° angle, but the cleat also could be made with interlocking rabbets. Either way, you get some amazing strength and convenience.

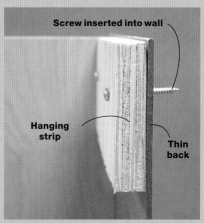

Screw inserted into wall

Hanging strip

Thin back

With a larger cabinet, a thin back makes more sense but will not be sufficient to secure the cabinet to the wall. By adding a hanging strip, the weight of the cabinet is more evenly transferred to the cabinet box.

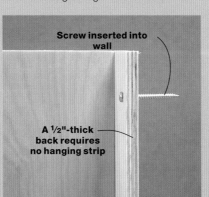

Screw inserted into wall

A ½"-thick back requires no hanging strip

With smaller cabinets, a thicker back (usually ½" or more) can be used without any major weight concern. This thicker back also allows you to simply screw through the back of the cabinet directly into the wall and stud.

Back is recessed to allow room for cleat

This store-bought version of a French cleat takes up less room behind the cabinet and is priced at about $13 for 10 sets. Place one hanger every foot to hold heavy cabinets.

Simple Hanging Cabinet

BY TROY SEXTON

've built hundreds of single-door cabinets like this one. Some people use them as spice cabinets. Others use them in the bathroom as a medicine cabinet.

As I was building this particular cabinet, it occurred to me that it would be an excellent project for beginners. It has all the traditional components of larger-scale cabinetry, yet it doesn't need a lot of material or tooling. Once you've built this cabinet, you can build something bigger using the same principles. Intermediate woodworkers might also pick up a trick or two because I build my cabinets just a bit differently.

Choose Your Wood

I used tiger maple for this project, but if this is your first cabinet, you might want to use poplar and then paint the finished item. Poplar is easy to work with and less expensive than maple, especially if the maple has some figure.

As in larger cabinets, most of the major components are made from $3/4$"-thick stock: the case sides, top, bottom, plus the rails and stiles for the door and the face frame. This cabinet has a solid wood shiplapped back that's made from $1/2$"-thick pieces; the door panel is $5/8$" thick.

Face Frame: the Place to Start

It seems logical to begin by constructing the case. Don't. The size of your case and door are all determined by your face frame. Build it first and then you'll use your face frame to lay out your case and door. All face frames are made up of rails and stiles, much like a door. The stiles are the vertical pieces. The rails are the horizontal pieces that go between the stiles.

When you rip your stiles to width on your table saw, make the rip $1/16$" wider than stated on the Schedule of Materials. You need this extra to overhang the sides of your case so you can trim it flush with a flush-cutting bit in a router. Once your pieces are cut to size, join the rails and stiles using mortise-and-tenon joints.

Begin by cutting the tenons on the rail ends. I know the books say to cut the mortise first, but I've found it's easier to lay out your mortises after your tenons are cut. Try it, and I think you'll agree.

The tenons should be $3/8$" thick (one-half as thick as your stock), centered on the rail and 1" long. I cut $1/2$" shoulders on the tenons. If they're any smaller, the mortise might blow out. Now use your tenons to lay out your mortises on the stiles. Hold the tenon flat against the edge where the mortise will go and use the tenon like a ruler to mark your mortise.

Now cut your mortises. Make them all $1^{1}/16$" deep, which will prevent your 1"- long tenons from bottoming out. You don't want your tenons to wobble in your mortises, yet you don't want to have to beat the tenon in place.

Dry-fit your face frame, then put glue on the mortise walls and clamp it up. While you're waiting for it to dry, turn your attention to the bead moulding that goes on the inside edge of the face frames.

Years ago, I used to cut the beading into the rails and stiles. Then I would have to miter the bead and cut away the beading where the rails and stiles were joined. It sounds like a pain, and it was. Now I simply make my bead moulding separate from my face frame and miter, nail and glue it in place. It looks just as good.

To make the bead moulding, put a $1/4$" beading bit in your router and mount it in a router table. Then take a $3/4$"-thick board that's about 4" wide and cut the bead on one edge. Take that board to your table saw, set your rip fence to make a $3/8$"-wide cut and rip the bead from the wide board. Repeat this process three more times.

Now take your strips and run them through your planer to reduce them in thickness to $5/16$". Miter the corners; then glue and nail them in place. Sand both sides of your face frame with 100 grit sandpaper and move on to building the door.

The Door

Why make the door next? Well, for one thing, it is easier to hang your door in your face frame before you nail the face frame to your case.

I build my doors so they are the same size as my opening, then I shave off a little so there's a $1/16$" gap all around. This way if the door or face frame is out of square, I can taper the door edges to fit,

hiding my error.

The door is built much like the face frame, using the same size mortises and tenons. The biggest difference is that you will need to cut a groove in your rails and stiles for the door panel, so your tenons must be haunched. A "haunch" is a little extra width in the tenon's shoulder that fills in the groove on the end of the stile.

Begin by cutting a $3/8$"-deep x $3/8$"-wide groove down the center of one long edge of your rails and stiles. Cut your tenons on your rails. Then cut your mortises on your stiles. Dry fit the pieces together and measure how big the center panel should be.

You want the panel to float to allow seasonal expansion and contraction, so cut the panel to allow $1/8$" expansion on either side. Now raise the door panel using your table saw or a cutter in your router table. Practice on scrap pieces of $5/8$" stock so you achieve the right lip, angle and fit.

When the panel is complete, sand the raised section, then glue up the door. Be careful not to get any glue in the groove that holds the panel. When the glue is dry, hang the door in your face frame.

Finally, the Case

The case is simple. The top and bottom pieces fit into $1/4$"-deep dadoes and rabbets on the sides. The back rests in a rabbet on the sides and is nailed to the back edge of the top and bottom pieces.

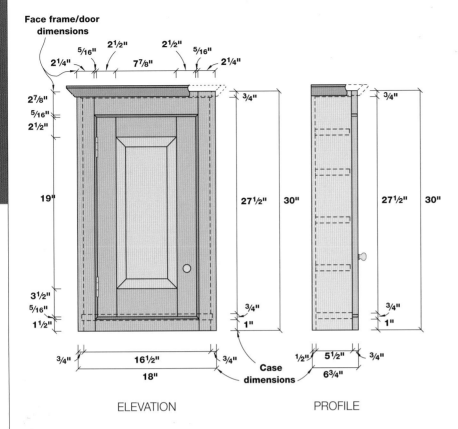

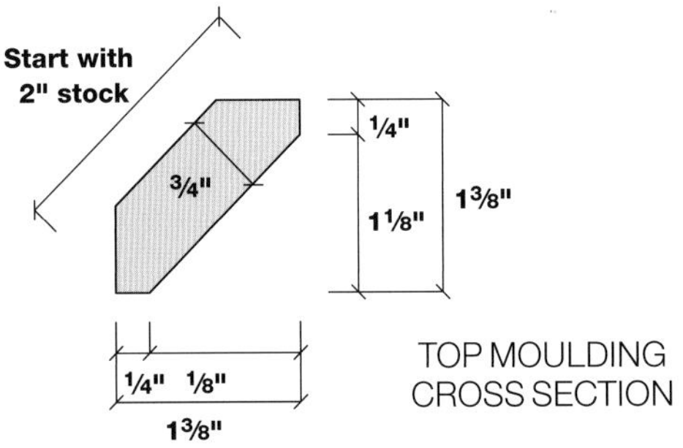

Face frame/door dimensions

2¼" · 5/16" · 2½" · 2½" · 5/16" · 2¼"

7⅞"

2⅞"
5/16"
2½"

19"

3½"
5/16"
1½"

¾"   16½"   ¾"
18"

ELEVATION

¾"
27½"   30"

¾"
1"

½"   5½"   ¾"
6¾"

Case dimensions

27½"   30"

¾"
1"

PROFILE

Start with 2" stock

¾"   ¼"   1⅛"   1⅜"

¼"   ⅛"
1⅜"

TOP MOULDING
CROSS SECTION

Adding this beaded moulding to the inside of the face frame creates a nice shadow line around the door. Miter, glue and nail it in place. Don't forget to putty your nail holes.

You'll use your face frame to lay out your joints on the sides. You want the bottom piece to end up 3/16" higher than the top edge of the bottom rail on your face frame. This allows your bottom to act as a stop for the door. Mark the location of that ¼"-deep dado and cut. The top piece rests in a ¼"-deep x ¾"-wide rabbet on the sides. Cut that using your table saw. Then cut the ½"-deep x ¼"-wide rabbet on the back edge of the sides.

Drill holes for shelf pins and space them 1" apart on the sides. Sand the inside of the case. You'll notice that the top and bottom are ½" narrower than the sides. This is to give you a good place to nail the back pieces to the case. Assemble the case using glue and nails, making sure the top, bottom and sides are all flush at the front.

Attach the face frame to the case using glue and nails. Trim the face frame

Simple Hanging Cabinet

NO.	ITEM	DIMENSIONS (INCHES)		
		T	W	L
2	Face frame stiles	¾	2¼	30
1	Top face frame rail	¾	2⅞	15½
1	Bot face frame rail	¾	1½	5½
2	Door stiles	¾	2½	25
1	Top door rail	¾	2½	9⅞
1	Bot door rail	¾	3½	9⅞
1	Door panel	⅝	8⅜	19½
2	Case sides	¾	6	30
2	Top & Bot	¾	5½	17
4	Shelves	¾	5⁷/₁₆	16⁷/₁₆
	Back boards	½	17	30
	Top moulding	¾	2	36

Fit your door in the face frame before you attach the face frame to the case. Everything lays flat on your bench as you work. You'll find this procedure is a faster and easier way to get perfect results.

Here you can see how the bottom of the case acts as a door stop. This is one of the reasons I build my face frames first: I can make sure my bottom will be in perfect position.

Fit the face frame on the case. The stiles should hang ¹⁄₁₆" over the edge of the case so you can rout (or plane) them flush later.

flush to the case using a bearing-guided flush-cutting bit in your router. Finish sand the cabinet to 180 grit.

Take your scrap pieces and use them to make a shiplapped back. Cut a ¹⁄₄" x ¹⁄₂" rabbet on the edges and then cut a bead on one edge using a ¹⁄₄" beading bit in your router table. You want to give the back pieces room to expand and contract, about ¹⁄₈" between each board should be fine.

Cut the moulding for the top so it resembles the drawing detail at left. Finish sand everything, then nail the moulding to the top.

I like to peg the tenons in my doors to add a little strength. Drill a ¹⁄₄" diameter hole most of the way through the stile

and tenon. Then whittle a square piece of stock so it's round on one end, put glue in the hole and pound it in place. Cut the peg nearly flush. You want it to be a little proud of the stile – it's a traditional touch.

Break all the edges of the case with 120-grit sandpaper, and putty all your nail holes. Paint, dye or stain the all the components (I used a water-based aniline dye). Then add two coats of clear finish and nail the back pieces in place. Hang the cabinet by screwing through the back boards into a stud in your wall.

Supplies

Rockler
800-279-4441

• #31495 hinges for door, $8.99/pair

Horton Brasses Inc.
800-754-9127

• 1" dia. #K-12 w/MSF (machine screw fitting), $7.25

Tailor's Cabinet

BY GLEN D. HUEY

This tailor's cabinet was brought to my attention by a customer who wanted one just like it. She had seen the piece in John Kassay's "The Book of Shaker Furniture." The original was made in Watervliet, N.Y., during the first half of the 19th century using plain and figured maple, and pine for the panels and interior pieces. The book also describes the drop-leaf on the original as being of walnut, indicating it may have been added later. My customer wasn't looking for a walnut leaf or pine sides, and I assured her I could make those changes.

This is a great storage piece for any number of rooms in the house, and while the leaf adds character, it doesn't add all that much space. While the leaf may never be used, I like the way it looks; so it's well worth the effort.

The basic construction of the cabinet is frame and loose panel for the sides and back. The front is a mortise-and-tenoned frame filled with drawers. Construction starts with the legs. Cut them to size according to the Schedule of Materials, then mark the foot of each leg for the simple tapered turning. The taper starts $4\frac{7}{8}$" from the bottom. At the top of the taper the leg is turned from a $1\frac{5}{8}$" square post to a $1\frac{1}{2}$" round, then tapered to 1" at the base.

With all four legs tapered, determine the arrangement of the legs to show off the best figure and mark them to keep them straight. The sides and back of the cabinet are made of panels and rails with tenons that fit into grooves that are cut on the inside faces of the legs. The grooves are $\frac{3}{8}$" wide x $1\frac{1}{8}$" deep and are run $\frac{1}{4}$" in from the outside edge of the leg. I used a router table to run the grooves, lowering the leg onto the bit to start the cut and lifting at the end of the cut. Use indexing marks on the router table fence to indicate when to start and stop the groove. Make the same groove in the side and back rails and stiles to hold the panels in place. The groove will be off-center on the rails, so determine which face is most attractive and run the grooves with the best side on the $\frac{1}{4}$" off-set while the router table is set up.

The next step is to cut the mortises in the legs, then form the tenons on the front rails. You'll see in the photo above that the front rails have double tenons for extra strength. Mark the mortise locations on the front legs, then use a mortiser or router to cut the mortises. While using the mortiser, mark the locations for the 10 drawer runners on the inside of the face rails and cut those mortises as well. Then set your table saw to cut the double tenons on the ends of the front rails.

The front stile dividing the upper four drawers is attached to the second rail with a half-lap or bridle joint, cut exactly in the center of the rail and the stile. I made these cuts on the table saw, nibbling away with repeated passes.

Assemble the front frame by starting with the stile, attaching it to the top and third rails using pegs through the rails.

Next cut the tenons on the ends of the side and back rails and back stiles. I again used the table saw to make these cuts. The tenons are centered on the pieces and offset from the center to match the grooves.

Cut rabbets on all four sides of the side and back panels. As these are $\frac{1}{2}$"-thick pieces, a $\frac{1}{8}$" rabbet forms the tenon easily so that the inside faces of the panels and the rails will be flush on the inside. By setting your table saw's rip fence to $\frac{3}{8}$" (with the blade set at $\frac{1}{2}$" high) the rabbets can be easily cut on the saw by running the panels on end.

To add a nice detail to the piece, put a beading bit in your router and run a $\frac{1}{4}$" detail on both edges of the side center rail and on the inside edges of the top and bottom rails. Cut the notches for the drop leaf support in the top back rail according to the diagram, then assemble the back and rear legs. Use glue on the rail and stile tenons, but don't glue the panels so the wood can move.

Drawer Supports

While the glue is drying, turn to the drawer supports. There are four side supports and two center supports for the upper drawers, and four side supports for the lower drawers.

Cut the supports to the sizes given in the Schedule of Materials. The supports are all a little different, but let's start with the front end. Make $\frac{3}{8}$" x $1\frac{3}{4}$" x $\frac{3}{8}$"-long

With the tenons and mortises formed, and the legs turned, the puzzle begins to take shape by gluing up the front frame. Notice the double-tenon used in the legs for extra strength.

It never hurts to check the fit when so many pieces come together in one place. Check the spacing of the panels and rails into the legs and adjust as necessary.

With everything sitting in place, it's time to add the back and clamp everything down. Notice the two drawer support rails attached to the back.

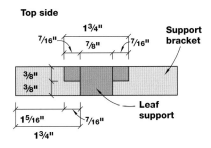

Top side

1³⁄₄"
⁷⁄₁₆" ⁷⁄₈" ⁷⁄₁₆"

Support bracket

³⁄₈"
³⁄₈"

Leaf support

1⁵⁄₁₆" ⁷⁄₁₆"
1³⁄₄"

LEAF SUPPORTS & BRACKETS

To guide the drawers smoothly, I attach simple poplar strips with a brad nailer to the drawer supports. A little wax on the supports and the drawer runs smooth as silk.

The three-piece leaf supports are kind of clever if I do say so myself. By trapping the support itself between the front and back of the case, the support has a built-in stop in both the open and closed position.

tenons on the front of all the side supports. Make ³⁄₈" x 2" x ³⁄₈"-long tenons on the front of the two center supports. Only the six top supports have tenons on the back end. Make the side support tenons ³⁄₈" x 1³⁄₄" x 1" long, and the two center supports ³⁄₈" x 2" x 1" long. The four lower drawer supports are notched ³⁄₄" x 1" around the the rear leg, and then tapered on the inside edge. These are then nailed in place, with reproduction nails, to the rear leg after assembly.

To attach the upper drawer supports at the rear of the cabinet, mortise and then nail two support battens in place on the back legs.

You're now ready to assemble. Test fit the side panels and rails in the back legs,

and check the fit of the front frame to the sides. If everything fits well, lay the face frame on your work surface and glue the side rails to the front legs (again leaving the panels glue-free) then glue the drawer supports into their mortises in the front

Shaker Tailor's Cabinet

NO.	ITEM	DIMENSIONS (INCHES)			MATERIAL	COMMENTS
		T	W	L		
4	Legs	1⁵⁄₈	1⁵⁄₈	30¹⁄₂	Primary (P)	
4	Side rails, top/bott.	³⁄₄	2¹⁄₂	20³⁄₄	P	1" TBE
2	Side rails, middle	³⁄₄	2³⁄₄	20³⁄₄	P	1" TBE
2	Back rails, top/bott.	³⁄₄	2¹⁄₂	33⁷⁄₈	P	1" TBE
1	Back rail, middle	³⁄₄	2³⁄₄	33⁷⁄₈	P	1" TBE
2	Back stiles	³⁄₄	2³⁄₄	10¹³⁄₁₆	P	1" TBE
5	Front rails	⁷⁄₈	1⁵⁄₈	33⁷⁄₈	P	1" TBE
1	Front stile	⁷⁄₈	1⁵⁄₈	10³⁄₈	P	Half-lap
4	End panels	¹⁄₂	9³⁄₈	19³⁄₈	P	³⁄₈" TAS
4	Back panels	¹⁄₂	9³⁄₈	15³⁄₁₆	P	³⁄₈" TAS
4	Drwr runners	³⁄₄	2¹⁄₈	18⁷⁄₈	Secondary (S)	³⁄₈" TOE
2	Drwr supports	³⁄₄	1⁵⁄₈	33¹⁄₈	S	
4	Drwr runners	³⁄₄	2¹⁄₈	18⁷⁄₈	S	³⁄₈"/1" T
2	Drwr runners	³⁄₄	3	18⁷⁄₈	S	³⁄₈"/1" T
8	Drwr sides	¹⁄₂	4¹⁄₂	19	S	
4	Drwr backs	¹⁄₂	3³⁄₄	15³⁄₈	S	
4	Drwr fronts	⁷⁄₈	5	16¹⁄₈	P	³⁄₈" lip 3X
4	Drwr bottoms	⁵⁄₈	16	19¹⁄₄	S	CTF
4	Drwr sides	¹⁄₂	5¹⁄₂	19	S	
2	Drwr backs	¹⁄₂	4³⁄₄	31³⁄₄	S	
2	Drwr fronts	⁷⁄₈	6	32³⁄₈	P	³⁄₈" lip 3X
2	Drwr bottoms	⁵⁄₈	32	19¹⁄₄	S	CTF
1	Top	³⁄₄	24	45¹⁄₈	P	
1	Leaf	³⁄₄	6³⁄₄	45¹⁄₈	P	
4	Support brackets	³⁄₄	1³⁄₄	19³⁄₁₆	S	
2	Leaf supports	³⁄₄	1³⁄₄	21	S	
10	Drawer guides	³⁄₄	⁷⁄₈	16	S	

* TBE = tenons both ends; TAS = tenons all sides; TOE = tenon one end; x/xT = size of tenon on each end; 3X = on three sides; CTF = cut to fit frame. Lower the back into place, leaving the tenons on the drawer supports glue-free. Check for square and clamp the cabinet until the glue is dry.

The drawer supports provide support for the bottom of the drawers, but to get them to move well they also need some guides to control side-to-side movement. These $\frac{3}{4}$" x $\frac{7}{8}$"-wide strips are simply tacked in place to the drawer supports to guide the drawer sides.

While you're still working on the inside of the cabinet, cut the leaf supports and the four brackets to support them to size. Each pair of brackets is rabbeted $\frac{3}{8}$" x $\frac{7}{16}$" on one side, and the leaf supports are rabbeted on both sides to form a stubby "T" cross-section. Then notch

the support as shown in the photo and chamfer or round the end to avoid sharp corners. Later you will screw the brackets to the underside of the top with the arm protruding through the notches you cut in the back rail.

Drawers & Details

The drawers are of standard construction (by 19th century standards, that is) with hand-cut dovetails and a solid wood bottom. Cut a $\frac{3}{8}$" x $\frac{1}{2}$" rabbet on three sides of the drawer fronts, then use the same beading detail as on the side rails to dress up all four edges of each drawer.

It's now time to get to the rule joint that attaches the drop-leaf to the top. First glue up the large top, leaving it

Supplies

Rockler
800-279-4441

• 3 brass-plated table hinges, 1$\frac{1}{2}$" wide and 3$\frac{3}{16}$" long. item # 29249, $11.99 a pair.

• Metal tabletop fasteners, item# 34215, $2.99/pack of eight

Prices correct at time of publication.

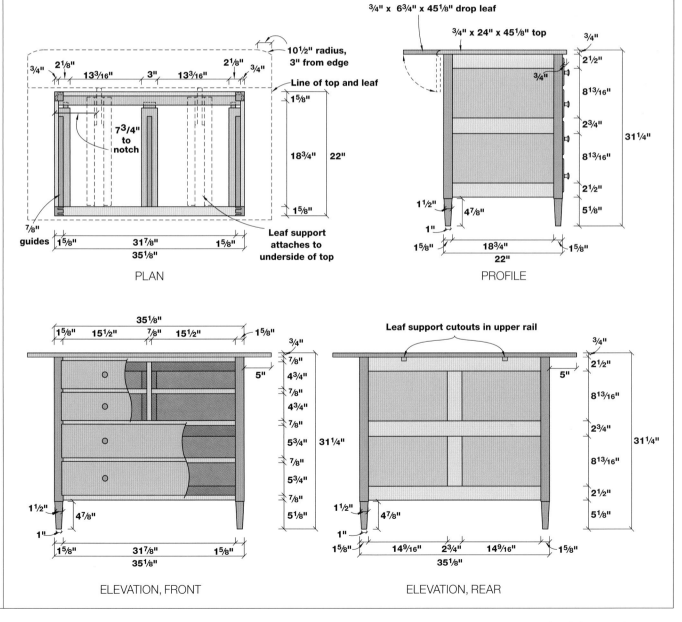

PLAN

PROFILE

ELEVATION, FRONT

ELEVATION, REAR

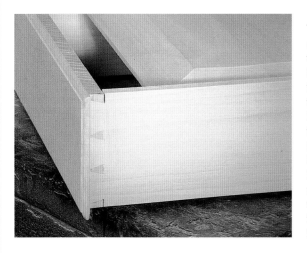

The drawers are constructed using dovetails (half-blind on the front and through at the back) and a beveled bottom slipped into grooves in the front and sides (right). A trick from our clever ancestors was to cut a slot in the back edge of the solid wood bottom and nail the bottom in place at the slot (below), with the bottom glued to the front. This allows the bottom to move with changes in humidity.

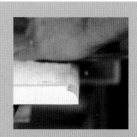

oversized for length until after the top and leaf have been attached by the hinges so the lengths will match perfectly. Use the information at left to cut the rule joint. I use standard hinges for my drop-leaf. If you purchase special drop-leaf hinges, then you won't have to rout a recess for the barrel as shown.

The top is attached to the cabinet by using rectangular wooden "buttons" that have a short tongue. The tongue slips into grooves cut in the side rails with a router and a slot cutter. If you don't feel like making your own buttons, you can purchase metal clips through most hardware catalogs. Cut the slots wide enough to allow the top room for wood movement. Attach the leaf supports to the top at this time.

After a good sanding, the cabinet is ready to finish. If you've read any of my earlier pieces in Popular Woodworking you may have noticed I have a favorite finish for curly maple furniture. I used that finish again on this piece. (Moser's Golden Amber Maple, a water-based aniline dye, available from Woodworker's Supply, 800-645-9292 as item #W14901 for $10.99) After the dye is dry, lightly sand the entire piece to remove any raised grain, then top coat the piece with lacquer or your favorite choice of protective finish.

Making a Rule Joint

The rule joint for the top and leaf attachment requires a certain amount of accuracy, but it pays off in the end. With a little care, a test piece isn't even necessary. I used $\frac{1}{2}$"cove and roundover bits sold separately. You can find sets in other catalogs.

The first step is to run the roundover bit on the top piece, leaving about an $\frac{1}{8}$" shoulder at the top.

Next, use the cove bit to run the profile on the leaf, making the cut less deep than should be necessary. Then place the two pieces together to check the fit, and adjust the depth of the cove cut deeper until the top surfaces are flush.

Next, turn the top and leaf over and mark the locations for the hinges so that the center of the barrel is $\frac{1}{2}$" from the lip of the top. With the location marked, use a $\frac{5}{16}$" straight bit to make a relief cut in the underside of the top piece that's deep enough for the barrel of the hinge to slip into. Allow for the thickness of the hinge leaf when determining the depth of the recess.

With the barrel recessed into the top, mark the hinge location on the top and leaf, and rout a recess for the hinge leaves into both pieces. The same bit used to rout in the barrel should work for this operation as well.

When you rout for the hinge leaf recess, make the cuts short of the pencil line, then use a chisel to clean up the recess. Start the clean-up by defining the perimeter of the recess using a chisel. Pare the material at the pencil marks. Then use the chisel held flat to remove the waste. Now simply attach the hinges, mark the length of the top and cut the top and leaf to length.

Wall Cupboard

BY CHRISTOPHER SCHWARZ

If you don't like nails, then perhaps you should turn the page. This small wall cupboard from the New Lebanon Shaker community bristles with them.

The carcase and stiles are nailed together with cut brads. The back is attached with clout nails. And the door is held flat with battens that are secured by clenched nails. I think the nails add to the piece, and, because there are so many different kinds, this project is an excellent introduction to 19th-century cut nails.

Quick Joinery – Quick Results

I've built quite a few of these cabinets in the last couple years because they are an excellent way to teach someone tradition-al joinery and they can be made quickly (my father received one last year that I banged out in a day).

Begin with the carcase. The carcase sides are the only pieces that have real joinery. Cut $3/8$"-wide by $3/16$"-deep rab-bets in the bottom edges of the sides. These receive the interior bottom piece. Cut $3/8$"-wide by $3/16$"-deep dados for the shelf.

Glue and nail the sides, bottom and shelf together. I used $2d$ cut headless brads that I set $1/32$" below the surface.

True up all the edges of the assembled carcase then fit the two stiles on the front. They hold the carcase square. Glue and nail these in place with $2d$ cut head-less brads and set those.

The thin top and bottom pieces are each attached in an unusual way. First round over the front edge and ends of each piece. The thin bottom is merely glued on to the carcase. Note that the bottom extends $1/4$" beyond the back of the carcase, which creates a rabbet for the

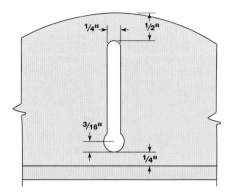

SLOT DETAIL

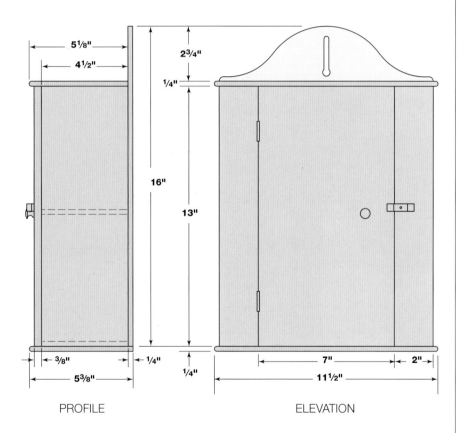

PROFILE   ELEVATION

Wall Cupboard

NO.	ITEM	DIMENSIONS (INCHES)		
		T	W	L
2	Carcase sides	$3/8$	$4^1/2$	13
2	Stiles	$3/8$	2	13
2	Shelf & bottom	$3/8$	$4^1/2$	$10^5/8$
1	Top	$1/4$	$5^1/8$	$11^1/2$
1	Exterior bottom	$1/4$	$5^3/8$	$11^1/2$
1	Back	$1/4$	11	16
1	Door	$3/8$	7	13
2	Battens	$3/8$	$1^1/2$	$6^7/8$

back. The top is glued and nailed to the stiles and carcase sides (don't worry – it's the back of the cupboard that handles all the weight).

Now deal with the back. Cut the ogee shapes on the top of the back piece. Then cut the slot that allows you to hang this cupboard on a peg or nail. Here's how. Drill a ¼" hole at the top of the slot. Drill a ⅜" hole at the bottom. Connect the two slots using a coping saw. Attach the back to the carcase using 2d clout nails (no glue).

Keep Your Door Flat

The door is a flat panel of wood. If you don't apply some cross-grain battens to the back, it will warp in short order.

So fit the door in its opening and cut the mortises for your hinges. With the door moving freely, remove it from the cupboard and drill pilot holes through the door and battens for nails.

You will clench these nails, which means you'll bend them over on the inside of the door. I used 2d cut headless brads. Drive them through the front of the door and through each batten.

When all the nails are driven in, turn the assembled door over onto a metal surface and hammer the tips of the nails. This will bend them over into the wood, securing them. Then cut the hinge gains, hang the door and make a turn to hold the door closed. The original also had a little knob, which is best turned on a lathe.

While the finished cabinet will have too much metal to pass through airport security, I guarantee the nails will help your piece last as long as the original.

Drill a ¼" hole for the top of the slot and a ⅜" hole at the bottom. Connect the holes with a coping saw.

Drive the tips of your headless brads back into the battens while the door rests on a metal surface.

The thin exterior bottom piece is glued on. Clamp the assembly to your benchtop to help distribute the clamping forces.

Storage Cabinet

BY TROY SEXTON

The Shakers always had a knack for packing a lot of storage into a small space and making it look good. The three-sided built-in in the Center family residence at Pleasant Hill, Ky., is a prime example. You've probably seen a photo of it. It's the impressive cherry unit that's in an attic with a skylight that illuminates all 45 drawers.

It is in that spirit that I designed this two-door cabinet for a client in Ohio. The family needed to store an enormous number of board games and toys in a small space. The doors had to hide everything.

How to Pack Lots of Stuff Into Small Spaces

Organizing clutter is an interesting problem that you also might face as you design storage in your home or case pieces. Here's what I did: Behind the left door I put a series of five $3/4$"-thick adjustable solid-wood shelves. These would handle the heavier games and books. Behind the right door is a series of $1/4$"-thick tempered Masonite shelves. These 10 shelves slide in and out of $1/4$" x $1/4$" dados.

The Masonite won't hold a lot of weight, but it's just right for storing lightweight objects. Think home office, and you'll know what I mean. Masonite (sometimes called "hardboard") shelves are perfect for storing letterhead, envelopes, CDs and any other paper goods in an office. The other challenge in this piece was getting the shelves, doors and face frame positioned so they didn't interfere with one another. As you'll see in the drawings, it took a few pieces of "blocking" to get everything to work in this cabinet.

Face Frame First

This seems backwards, I know, but begin construction by building the face frame. The size of the case and doors are determined by your face frame, so it's clearly the place to begin.

When ripping out the material for the face frame stiles, cut them each about $1/16$" wider than the dimension called for in the cutting list. This will make your face frame hang over the edge of the case sides. Once the face frame is attached, you can trim it flush for a perfect fit.

I use mortise-and-tenon joinery to build both the face frames and doors. The tenons are $3/8$" thick and 1" long, and I usually cut a $3/8$" to $1/2$" shoulder on the edges. Be sure to cut your mortises $11/16$" deep so your tenons don't bottom out. When everything fits, put glue in the mortises, clamp the frame and allow the glue to cure.

Doors are Second

Next, build the doors. It's much easier to fit the doors into your face frame before it's attached to the case. Build the doors much like you did your face frame by using mortise-and-tenon joints. The only difference is that you need to cut a $3/8$" x $3/8$" groove in the rails and stiles to hold the door panels.

I cut my grooves along the entire length of the stiles; as a result, I cut my tenons with a "haunch" to fill in that extra space on the ends of the stiles. The panels are flat on the front, and beveled on the backside so they fit in the grooves in the rails and stiles. I cut that bevel by setting my table saw blade to 7° and slicing off a little of the backside of each door until the panels fit snug and without rattling.

Sand the panels up to your final grit

(120 will be fine for a painted piece) and assemble the doors. Sand the assembled doors and face frame and then peg the tenons if you like. I used square pegs that I pounded into round holes.

Finally, the Case

The case goes together quickly thanks to my nail gun. Begin construction by cutting a $3/4$"-wide by $1/4$"-deep dado in the side pieces for the bottom of the cabinet. I like to use a dado stack in my table saw for this operation. Now cut a $1/2$" x $1/2$" rabbet on the back edges of the sides to hold the plywood back in place. Sand the inside of the case and get ready for the first bit of assembly.

Put the case together on its back. First put glue in the dados in the sides and fit the bottom in there. Nail the bottom in place from the outside of the case. I use a finish nailer for this task.

Now put the nailing strip in place at the top of the case. The diagrams show you where this needs to be, but essentially it's flush with both the rabbets in the sides and top of the case. Nail it home. Glue and nail the face frame to the case using brads. Trim the face frame flush to the case.

All the Insides

There's nothing complicated about the insides once you have a plan. Begin by cutting the $1/4$" x $1/4$" dados in the dividers. These are spaced 2" apart, and there are 21 of them. I used a dado stack in my table saw and simply moved the fence $1 3/4$" after each pass.

Now it's time to add the dividers to the case. Turn the case on its head. Cut a notch in each divider so it will fit around the nailing strip. Get the divider right where it needs to be and nail it in place through the bottom and the nailing strip. Now nail the two blocking pieces shown on the diagram in place. The blocking does a couple things. First, it allows the Masonite shelves to be slid in and out without having to swing the doors wide open. Second, the thinner piece of blocking fills in the gap between

I'm not perfect, and neither are you. If your face frame is exactly the width of your case, it's going to be difficult to fasten it square. Make life easier by ripping your stiles ¹⁄₁₆" oversize in width. After you nail and glue the face frame to the case, use a flush-trimming bit in your router to trim the face frame flush with the side of the cabinet's case.

Supplies

Woodworker's Supply
800-645-9292

Amerock non-mortising hinges, #891-749, $4.49 each

Horton Brasses
800-754-9127

Maple knobs, #WK-3, 1¾" diameter, $2.50 each

You can see the haunch on the tenons on the rail closest to the camera. When it comes to fitting your panels, remember to work tight in summer and loose in winter. Panels of this size will shrink and contract noticeably.

the divider and face frame and leaves room for the hinges.

Now drill the holes in the left side of the case and the center divider for the adjustable solid-wood shelves. I'm partial to 5 mm holes spaced 1⅜" on center.

Mark the base cutouts on the sides, front and plywood back of the case using the diagrams as a guide. Use a jigsaw to make these cuts and clean up your work with sandpaper.

Cut your top to size. I used a piece of bird's-eye maple. You have a couple options for attaching the top. You could use pocket holes, figure-8 fasteners or

You could use a router and a straight bit to make this cut as long as you had a reliable way of guiding the router (such as an edge guide). I find a table saw is much faster for this operation.

Storage Cabinet

NO.	ITEM	T	W	L	MATERIAL
			DIMENSIONS (INCHES)		
Face Frame					
2	Stiles	¾	2½	51¼	Poplar
1	Top rail*	¾	2	45	Poplar
1	Bottom rail*	¾	5½	45	Poplar
Doors					
4	Stiles	¾	2½	43¾	Poplar
6	Rails*	¾	2½	18½	Poplar
4	Panels	⅝	17	18⅝	Poplar
Carcase					
1	Top	¾	19	50	Maple
2	Sides	¾	17¼	51¼	Poplar
1	Bottom	¾	16¾	47	Poplar
2	Dividers	¾	16¼	45½	Poplar
1	Nailing strip	¾	1½	46½	Poplar
1	Blocking 1	¾	2¼	45½	Poplar
1	Blocking 2	½	1¾	45½	Poplar
5	Adj. shelves	¾	16¼	22⅝	Poplar
10	Masonite shelves	¼	16¼	20¼	Masonite
1	Back	½	47	51¼	Ply

* = 1" tenon on both ends

wooden cleats. No matter which way you go, prepare the case for the top but don't attach it. I like to glue the top to the front edge of the case after finishing.

Finishing

On the knobs, top and all the inside pieces (except the Masonite), I wiped on a light honey-colored stain. Then I painted the case a dark red and added a topcoat of lacquer to protect the paint. Hang the doors, nail in the back and add the knobs.

I have no idea how the Shakers would feel about seeing one of their cabinets filled with "Parcheesi," "Connect Four" and "Uncle Wiggly" games. But I'm sure at least they would approve of the efficient use of space.

Once you nail the dividers in place through the bottom piece, turn the case over on its feet and nail through the nailing strip into the dividers.

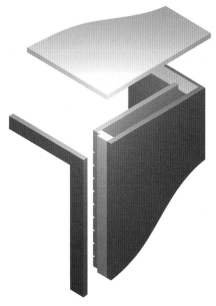

TOP RIGHT CORNER – EXPLODED

In addition to cutting this detail on the sides and front, I also cut it on the bottom of the plywood back, which gives it a finished look when the cabinet is viewed from down low or from a distance.

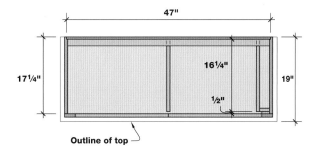

PLAN – TOP REMOVED

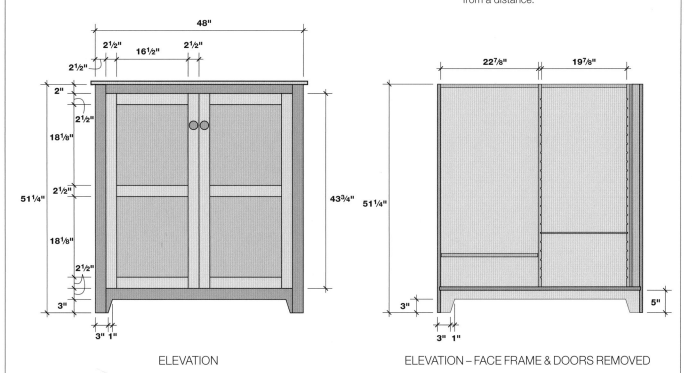

ELEVATION

ELEVATION – FACE FRAME & DOORS REMOVED

Press Cupboard

BY GLEN D. HUEY

When I first discovered this cupboard in John Kassay's "The Book of Shaker Furniture" (University of Massachusetts Press), it jumped from the pages and begged me to build it. The original version that I built featured a blind-door cupboard, but a friend at a furniture show suggested I build it with glass doors. I followed her advice, and what a difference it made.

This piece originated in the Pleasant Hill, Ky., Shaker community in the late 1800s. It's called a press cupboard because its flat, sturdy construction helped to press the linens stacked neatly inside. With the addition of the glass doors, this piece becomes a showplace for any treasured collection.

Lower Section First

To begin, mill the parts for the lower case according to the cutting list. Then turn the legs using the diagram provided. If you're not a turner, I recommend you taper the legs on the two inside edges instead. The taper should begin 1" below the lower front rail and sides, and the legs should taper to $1\frac{5}{16}$" square at the floor.

Now mark the layout of the mortises on the legs. Because the sides and back are wide pieces of solid wood, you should use a double tenon to accommodate seasonal wood movement. Next cut the $\frac{1}{4}$"-thick mortises on the legs.

Don't forget to cut the mortises in the top and lower rails and back piece to receive the two rail supports and the two drawer runners.

If you're using a hollow-chisel mortiser, use the step method of cutting mortises – skip every other cut and return to clean out the sections between after reaching the end of each mortise. This will prevent excessive wear on your chisel.

Now cut your tenons on the table saw. I use a shop-made tenon jig, but a commercial jig will do fine. Test the fit of the pieces of the lower case. If everything works, proceed to finish sand your parts, and glue and assemble the lower section. First glue the front and back subassemblies, then finish by assembling the side pieces. Remember to install the rail support pieces at this stage.

Next, notch the drawer runners so they fit around the legs. Glue them into the mortises you cut in the lower front rail and nail them to the rear of the back leg. Nail the drawer guides to the runners, flush to the leg blocks.

Next build the drawer. The drawer front is flush with the face of the cupboard. You can see the layout of the hand-cut dovetails at right. I used half-blind dovetails at the front and through-dovetails at the back. The solid-wood bottom is a raised panel that fits into grooves in the sides and drawer front.

Once you've built the drawer, slide it into the lower section and align the drawer front with the case front. Then measure and cut the stops for the drawer. Attach the stops with a screw and glue each to the back leg (see the photo on the top of page 84).

Next remove the drawer, then lay out and drill holes in the legs and through the case's tenons for the square pegs. Set the pegs and cut them flush with the case.

Now glue up the boards you'll need for the top of the lower section. To attach it, I used shop-made wooden clips. I used a biscuit joiner to cut the recess in the sides, back and top front rail to accept the clips.

Upper Section Next

To begin the cupboard's upper section, cut your sides and shelves to size. Lay out and cut the $\frac{1}{4}$" x $\frac{3}{4}$"-deep dados for the shelves – use the diagram to lay out your dados. Note that these are stopped dados that don't extend through the front of the sides. Also, cut the $\frac{7}{16}$" x $\frac{3}{4}$" rabbet for the backboards. Notch the front corners of the shelves so they fit in the stopped dado cuts.

Next, using a $\frac{1}{2}$" core box bit

Before I glued the drawer parts together, I ran the bottom edge of my drawer front over the jointer with the fence set at a 5° angle and the machine set to make a $\frac{1}{16}$"-deep cut. This creates a slight bevel that allows the drawer to close without the bottom edge catching on the lower front rail.

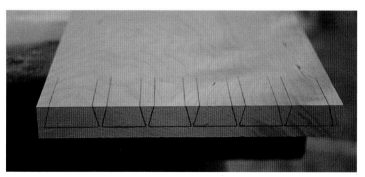

Here you can see the layout of the hand-cut dovetails used to build the drawer.

chucked in a router and another shelf as a straightedge, cut a plate groove into the back of the lower three shelves that's approximately $1\frac{1}{4}$" from the back edge. Make sure to begin and end the cut just shy of the shelf ends.

Finish sand the shelves and the insides of the sides, then glue the unit together. Check for squareness by measuring the case diagonally from corner to corner. When the glue is dry, add the square pegs through the sides and into the shelves as you did to the lower section.

Simple Mullioned Doors

For the doors, lay out and cut the mortises on the stiles. Because these are glass-pane doors, cut a $\frac{3}{8}$" x $\frac{1}{2}$" rabbet on the interiors of all eight door pieces.

Now cut the rails to finished size and get ready to cut the tenons on both ends. This tenon fits around the rabbet in the stiles. Here's how to make it: Set your table saw's blade height to $\frac{1}{4}$" and define the tenons' shoulders on the face sides of the rails.

Next, move the fence $\frac{3}{8}$" closer to the blade and define the shoulders on the back of the rails as well as the shoulder on the edge. Then finish the tenons by completing the necessary cheek cuts. Test fit all of the pieces and then assemble the door frames.

Now rout the mortises for the door

hinges and install the hinges. Hang the doors. Now cut down the door stiles so they overlap $\frac{5}{16}$" in the center. Remember to keep the stiles the same width.

One of these doors will open with a latching knob, and the other one will open using a release inside the cupboard. Remove the door that will have the latching knob and cut a $\frac{3}{8}$" x $\frac{3}{8}$" rabbet on the back side of its interior stile. Reinstall this door and allow the rabbet to overlap onto the opposite door's stile.

Mark the overlap on the opposite door and cut a matching rabbet to produce the half-lap joint shown above.

Next, with the doors installed, mark

Shaker Press Cupboard

NO.	ITEM	T	W	L	MATERIAL	COMMENTS
			DIMENSIONS (INCHES)			
Lower Section Case Pieces						
4	Legs	$1\frac{7}{8}$	$1\frac{7}{8}$	$34\frac{1}{4}$	Maple	
2	Sides	$\frac{3}{4}$	11	$17\frac{1}{4}$	Maple	$1\frac{1}{4}$" TBE*
1	Back	$\frac{3}{4}$	11	$42\frac{1}{4}$	Poplar	$1\frac{1}{4}$" TBE
1	Top front rail	$\frac{3}{4}$	$1\frac{1}{4}$	$42\frac{1}{4}$	Maple	$1\frac{1}{4}$" TBE
1	Lower front rail	$\frac{3}{4}$	$1\frac{1}{4}$	$42\frac{1}{4}$	Maple	$1\frac{1}{4}$" TBE
2	Rail supports	$\frac{3}{4}$	2	$18\frac{1}{8}$	Poplar	$\frac{1}{2}$" TBE
2	Drawer runners	$\frac{3}{4}$	$2\frac{1}{8}$	$17\frac{3}{8}$	Poplar	$\frac{1}{2}$" TOE**
2	Drawer guides	$\frac{1}{2}$	$1\frac{3}{16}$	$14\frac{5}{8}$	Poplar	
1	Top	$\frac{3}{4}$	20	$47\frac{1}{2}$	Maple	
1	Drawer front	$\frac{7}{8}$	$8\frac{3}{8}$	$39\frac{5}{8}$	Maple	
2	Drawer sides	$\frac{1}{2}$	$8\frac{1}{4}$	$15\frac{1}{2}$	Poplar	
1	Drawer back	$\frac{1}{2}$	$8\frac{1}{4}$	$39\frac{5}{8}$	Poplar	
1	Drawer bottom	$\frac{5}{8}$	$15\frac{1}{2}$	39	Poplar	
2	Wooden knobs			2	Maple	
Upper Section Case Pieces						
2	Sides	$\frac{3}{4}$	12	45	Maple	
1	Top front case rail	$\frac{3}{4}$	$5\frac{1}{2}$	39	Maple	
1	Bottom front case rail	$\frac{3}{4}$	$1\frac{3}{4}$	39	Maple	
4	Top, bottom & shelves	$\frac{3}{4}$	$11\frac{1}{4}$	$37\frac{3}{4}$	Maple	
3	Door stiles	$\frac{3}{4}$	3	$37\frac{1}{2}$	Maple	
1	Door stiles	$\frac{3}{4}$	$3\frac{1}{4}$	$37\frac{1}{2}$	Maple	
2	Upper door rails	$\frac{3}{4}$	$3\frac{3}{4}$	16	Maple	$1\frac{1}{4}$" TBE
2	Lower door rails	$\frac{3}{4}$	$4\frac{1}{2}$	16	Maple	$1\frac{1}{4}$" TBE
4	Exterior door grills	$\frac{1}{4}$	$\frac{3}{4}$	30	Maple	
4	Interior door pieces	$\frac{1}{4}$	$\frac{1}{2}$	30	Maple	
2	Bottom moulding	$\frac{5}{8}$	$1\frac{1}{2}$	16	Maple	
1	Bottom moulding	$\frac{5}{8}$	$1\frac{1}{2}$	42	Maple	
2	Crown moulding	$\frac{3}{4}$	4	16	Maple	
1	Crown moulding	$\frac{3}{4}$	4	42	Maple	
1	Back boards	$\frac{5}{8}$	$38\frac{3}{8}$	$42\frac{1}{2}$	Maple	made in many pieces
1	Fixed door catch	$\frac{3}{4}$	1	$3\frac{1}{4}$	Poplar	
2	Wooden knobs			$1\frac{1}{4}$	Maple	

*TBE = tenon both ends; **TOE = tenon one end

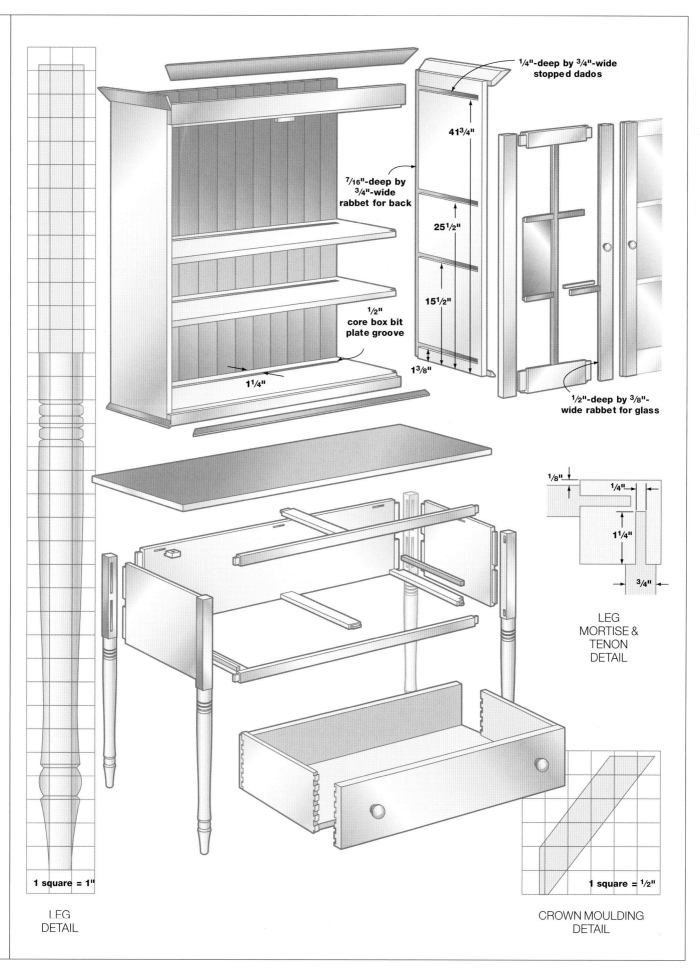

¼"-deep by ¾"-wide
stopped dados

41¾"

⁷⁄₁₆"-deep by
¾"-wide
rabbet for back

25½"

15½"

½"
core box bit
plate groove

1⅜"

1¼"

½"-deep by ⅜"-
wide rabbet for glass

⅛"

¼"

1¼"

¾"

LEG
MORTISE &
TENON
DETAIL

1 square = 1"

LEG
DETAIL

1 square = ½"

CROWN MOULDING
DETAIL

After you've built the drawer, slide it into the lower section and align the drawer front with the case front. Measure and cut stops for the drawer, then attach them with a screw and glue to the back leg as shown here.

Gang all the door stiles for the job and do the layout work in one step. This will increase your accuracy.

the location of the top and bottom of each shelf on the door stiles. This will properly place the glass dividers on the door so they conceal the shelves when the doors are shut. Also mark for a ¾"-wide vertical divider on the edge of the two rails of each door.

Now cut the long strips of ¼" x ½" material for the interior dividers and the ¼" x ¾" strips for the exterior glass dividers. With the door face down, fit and glue the interior horizontal pieces, allowing them to rest on the lip created by the rabbet cut on the inside of the door.

Flip the door so it's face up, and fit the long vertical exterior piece into the center of the opening. Glue this to the two previously installed pieces. These three pieces form the basis of the opening for the glass.

Cut, fit and install the remaining pieces necessary to complete the door. Then repeat the procedure on the other door.

Finishing Touches
When the glue in the upper unit is dry, mill the top and bottom front case rails a bit longer than required, sand the insides

and glue them to the sides of the upper unit. After the glue dries, drill and install square pegs through these rails. (By allowing the glue to dry, you reduce the risk of the wood splitting at the joint.) Cut the extra length flush to the case.

Now make the crown moulding according to the illustration. Set the blade of your table saw to 40° and make the first cut with the board face against the fence. The fence is set on the left side of the blade. Then, set the fence to the

right side of the blade, and lay the face flat on the table saw in order to cut the complementary angle on the opposite edge of the board, achieving 90°.

Keep your table saw settings the same and cut the angle on the bottom moulding for the upper section. Sand both mouldings, progressing to #180-grit sandpaper.

Sand the outside of the case to #180 grit, then fit the crown moulding to the case and attach it with reproduction fin-

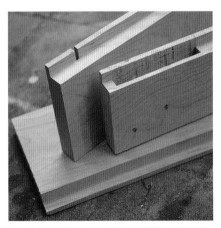

Here's what the door stiles look like after cutting the rabbet for the glass.

This is how the tenoned ends look after you complete all the cuts.

Create a half-lap joint by marking the location on the latched door and creating a matching rabbet on the other door.

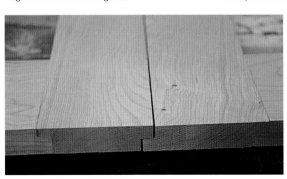

Supplies

Door hinges, 2 pairs, 2½" in length

Slot-head wood screws, No. 8 x 1¼"

1½" shingle nails for backboards

1½" fine finish nails for mouldings

The exterior glass dividers form the basis of the door's glass grid. The interior horizontal pieces rest on the lip created by the rabbet cut on the door pieces. The exterior vertical piece is fitted into the center of the opening and glued to the two horizontal pieces.

ish nails for an authentic look. Dowel the top edge of the crown moulding from the side into the front piece and sand it smooth.

Align the bottom moulding with the inside of the front and sides of the case. Make the 45° cuts at the front corners, square cut the back corners and attach with No. 8 x 1¼" slot-head wood screws into the sides. Glue and screw the moulding to the front. Then dowel the front corners as you did on the crown moulding.

Cut the half-lap joints on the long edges of the back boards. Then finish sand the pieces.

On the door without a knob, install the catch. Using a biscuit joiner, cut a ¼" slot in the bottom of the second shelf to accept the catch shown below. After finishing, align the catch with the slot and install with a No. 8 x 1¼" slot-head wood screw. Then make a latch (also called a turn) for the other door. It will latch against its neighbor's stile.

I used a reddish aniline dye to finish this piece. After the dye-job is complete, attach the top to the lower case using wooden clips and apply your protective top coat. I selected lacquer as the cupboard's finish.

Nail the backboards into place using reproduction nails, then install the glass in the doors. On this cupboard, I used Bendheim's light restoration glass (for more information, visit the company's web site at www.bendheim.com).

This case is unusual in that you install the top and bottom case rails after assembling the case. They are applied to the front edge of the sides. Cut them long, glue them in place and trim them to fit.

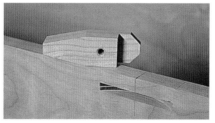

This is the catch for the door without a knob. It turns into a ¼" slot in the bottom of the second shelf that you cut using a biscuit joiner.

This is what the latching knob looks like.

Use water putty for installing glass panes into the doors. Water putty gives a yellowed look that simulates age. I use Durham's Rock Hard Water Putty.

Pleasant Hill Cupboard

BY KERRY PIERCE

I began my study of the Shaker furniture at Pleasant Hill, Ky., with a quick survey of the contents of the enormous Centre Family Dwelling, sticking my head in the door of each room, making a mental note of everything that caught my eye: a table here, a chair there, a little blanket chest, a tripled clothes hanger.

Each item on my mental list had something about it that set it apart from other objects in the Dwelling. In some cases, it was a splash of color, in others a bit of intriguing joinery, in others a form that deviated from Shaker norms. In this manner, I chugged along for maybe half an hour: Looking, storing and getting excited about the prospect of looking more closely later on.

Then, in a room on the second floor, I saw this cupboard hanging from a peg rail above a wash stand. I stuck my head in, caught my breath, released it and then slowly entered the room. The cupboard was familiar (Christian Becksvoort's book "The Shaker Legacy" [Taunton]), but I had forgotten about it. I know I wasn't expecting to see it there.

I stepped over the low railing erected to keep the public at a distance. (I had permission from the curator.) I stuck my nose close to the piece to study the pegs that penetrated the joinery of the frame-and-panel door, then backed off. This was something special, something profoundly Shaker, something that – unlike many pieces in the Pleasant Hill collection – could never be attributed to country origins.

The editors at *Popular Woodworking* had sent me and the magazine's photographer, Al Parrish, to the Shaker Village to write and illustrate a couple of articles about Western Shaker construction methods and design.

Nobody told me to do any measured drawings, but when I took the job, I was pretty sure I'd end up drawing at least a few pieces, and as soon as I saw this cupboard, "pretty sure" changed to dead certain.

Material from a Home Center

I usually buy lumber from hardwood dealers – businesses that typically require a 100 board feet (bf) minimum order. So I can't buy, for instance, 75 bf of curly maple or 50 bf of cherry.

In most cases, I don't mind these minimums. I always need cherry, walnut and curly maple. But sometimes, I don't really want 100 bf of a particular species, and anyone buying small lots of hardwood at stores catering to woodworking hobbyists will find he needs the support of a full-time cardiologist when they check out at the cash register.

Recently, I've been experimenting with another source for poplar: my local home-center store. All the big home-center stores charge more per board foot than hardwood dealers. But there are some good reasons to consider these type of suppliers for poplar (and pine).

For one thing, the material has been surfaced, and let's face it: One of the more odious chores is flattening and

thicknessing material. But here's a more important reason: I can buy only perfect boards. If there's a knot, a split, a bit of wane, I don't buy it. If it's not perfectly flat – and I mean billiard-table flat – I put it back.

Try that with a hardwood dealer. He might let you set aside a few boards with egregious defects, but if you reject eight boards out of 10, he might decide he doesn't want your business after all.

In fact, I have developed the habit of buying all my secondary wood this way. Every time I go to the store, I sort through all the poplar and clear white pine, and I buy every perfect board. This little cupboard is built of poplar I'd culled from the home-center's stock over the previous month.

Assembling the Case

I chose to use 8*d* coated nails to assemble the cupboard because the nail heads visible on the original are about the size of 8*d* nail heads, and I knew 8*d* nails, which are 2½" long, would result in a solid construction. Eight penny nails are big for this application, and I think you could have good results with a 7*d* nail as well, but I wouldn't recommend anything smaller than that.

Initially, the whole nail thing made me uncomfortable. I've spent too many years cutting wood-to-wood joinery to embrace this (sacrilegious?) method of work. But early in the construction process, I had to remove a piece I'd nailed in the wrong location, and let's just say I'm

Although it's possible to drive nails into "green" hardwood without pre-drilling, thoroughly dry hardwood requires pre-drilled holes – that is if you want to avoid split stock. The through hole should be nearly the same diameter as the shank of the nail. The hole that penetrates the second piece of stock should be a bit smaller in order to give the material a good grip on the nail.

Tap the shelf into its dados using a protective block of scrap.

Use a plane to level the edges of the cupboard's case before you attach the face frame.

Although the bead on the Shaker original was likely made with a scratch stock (because there is evidence of this tool everywhere at Pleasant Hill), I chose an ⅛" side-bead plane.

convinced this little cupboard will never come apart.

These nails require the drilling of two holes. The first is a through hole in the board you're nailing through. This hole should be just large enough for the shank of an 8d penny nail to pass without being driven by your hammer.

The second hole should be the full length of your 8d nail and just a bit smaller than the shank of the nail. It has to be small enough so that you have to drive the nail in with your hammer but

not so small that seating the nail results in split material. As always, experiment on scrap before you work on the good stuff.

If you look at the photo on the previous page, you'll see me drilling the smaller hole in a partially assembled joint. The drill for the larger, through hole, sits on the bench behind me.

After nailing the carcase together, fit the shelf and tap it into its dados.

The original cupboard has only one shelf, although there are dados for two

equally spaced shelves. I thought that an interior divided into only two compartments, instead of three, made more sense on this modest-sized cupboard, so I eliminated the second shelf the original cupboard had at birth. This gave me a fairly small compartment above and a larger compartment below.

After the shelf has been nailed into place, level the cabinet front and back with a plane

The cupboard has ⅛" beads along each of the front corners and around the door frame. The beads on the corners are cut on both the front and side of the vertical parts of the cupboard front. This produces a bead that's visible from either perspective.

If you haven't used a moulding plane, an ⅛" side-bead plane (shows at left) is a great place to start. You can find these relatively common planes at flea markets, antique malls and, of course, on eBay. But you must be sure to purchase a plane with a reasonably straight sole. Some have bowed beyond repair in the century and a half since their creation. "Reasonably" straight, however, doesn't mean "perfectly" straight. This little ⅛" side-bead plane I'm using here has a bit of a bow but it still works fine.

Unlike most moulding planes, which

Pleasant Hill Cupboard

NO.	ITEM	DIMENSIONS (INCHES)			MATERIAL	COMMENTS
		T	W	L		
1	Top	⅜	7½	31⅞	Poplar	
1	Bottom	13/16	7½	32	Poplar	Stock can be slightly oversize
2	Sides	13/16	5⅞	17¹³/₁₆	Poplar	
1	Face frame top rail	13/16	2⁷/₁₆	20	Poplar	
1	Face frame rail	13/16	1⅞	20	Poplar	
2	Face frame stiles	13/16	5⁷/₁₆	17¹³/₁₆	Poplar	
2	Sub top/bottom	⅞	5⅞	29¼	Poplar	
2	Sides	13/16	5⅞	17¹³/₁₆	Poplar	
1	Shelf	¾	5⅞	30	Poplar	In ¾"x ⅜" d. dados
2	Door rails	13/16	2⅞	16⅛	Poplar	2" tenons on each end
2	Door stiles	13/16	3¹⁵/₁₆	13½	Poplar	
1	Door panel	5/16	8⅝	13	Poplar	1/16" gap all around
2	Hangers	5/16	2⅞	27	Poplar	
	Backboards	5/16	30⅞	17¹³/₁₆	Poplar	Random widths to fill 30⅞"
1	Knob *	1	1	1¹¹/₁₆	Walnut	
1	Catch	¼	⁷/₁₆	¾	Walnut	

* I made the knob ⅛" longer than the original knob. This was a mistake, one I didn't notice until I prepared the materials list. The extra length is in the long cove. The length I give in the materials list is the length of the Shaker original to match the drawing. ** The hinges on my reproduction also are historically inaccurate. The hinges on the original are 1¾" long (as they appear on my drawing). Here, too, I made a mistake. I marked and mortised for a pair of 2"-long hinges, thinking – for some reason – I was working with 1¾"-long hinges.

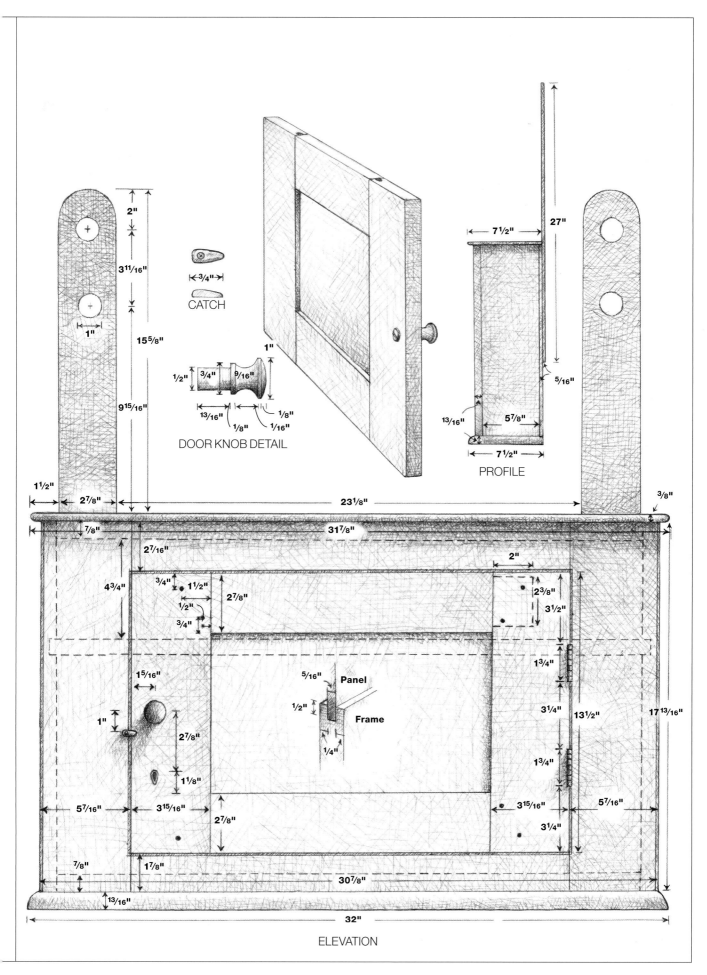

CATCH

DOOR KNOB DETAIL

PROFILE

Panel

Frame

ELEVATION

The junction of the horizontal and vertical beads must be completed with a little paring chisel work.

Carefully drive the nails that attach the face frame. (If you miss and ding up your stock, don't despair. Just spoon a bit of water onto the ding. As the fibers swell to accept the water, the surface of the wood will return to its original configuration.)

are designed to be held at an angle (the spring angle), side-bead planes are designed to be held upright, their sides perpendicular to the surfaces being worked. Set the iron so that it's barely visible when you sight along the sole of the plane, tap the wedge firm, then crowd the plane's fence against the edge of the work and push the plane forward. If you have the right amount of iron exposed, a tiny shaving will squirt out the side of the plane. (Test the plane's setting on scrap before working on the cupboard stock. A rank iron – one set too deep – can tear out the bead.) After a half dozen passes, you will have defined a neat little bead and quirk.

If you prefer routers, there are ⅛" bead cutters available that will simulate the work of this plane.

Cutting the bead around the door on the face frame stiles of the cupboard front requires a little trickery because you simply can't do it with a properly set up side-bead plane. This is because the bead doesn't run all the way to the ends of the boards on the face-frame stiles (although the bead does run from end to end on the face-frame rails so these beads can be cut in the way I'm demonstrating here.)

Caveat: The Shaker maker might have done this with a scratch stock. A scratch stock is nothing more than two pieces of scrap wood between which is sandwiched a small bit of metal filed to the necessary profile. The wood part of the scratch stock provides a way to hold the metal at the necessary angle without damaging the craftsman's fingers (it also stabilizes the metal), while the metal

Bench planes can be made to do a fair amount of edge shaping. Here, I'm using a bench plane to create the radius between a line drawn on the edge and a line drawn on the top of the cupboard bottom.

cuts the bead with a scraping action. It's simple but effective when properly sharpened.

You can, however, cut the stopped bead on the face-frame stiles of the cabinet front with a side-bead plane if you cheat a little. Tap the iron down so that it hangs an extra ⅛" or so from the sole of the plane. That will allow the iron to engage the work when the sole of the plane is not riding down on the bead you're cutting. You are in effect, using the side-bead plane as a beading tool. This too is something you should experiment with on scrap before trying it out on the good stuff.

Nail the components of the face frame into place.

After the frame has been attached, you'll then finish the bead around the door with a paring chisel as shown above, followed by sandpaper.

These narrow, deep mortises can be tricky to chop with hand tools.

The cupboard top and bottom both have radiused edges. The top has a 180° radius, the bottom only a 90° radius. These radii can be formed with moulding planes (or roundover bits in a router), but I've always made this shape with a bench plane as I'm doing above. You'll be amazed at how quickly you can do this work – much more quickly than you could set up a router to perform the same operation, and of course working with a plane means no dust and no noise. The shop remains quiet enough so you can plan the next few steps in the construction process.

If you choose my method, you'll first need some pencil lines to plane between. One of these lines should identify the midpoint of the board's edge. The other line should be placed on an adjacent surface a distance from the edge that is equal to half the thickness of the board.

To create the radius, simply remove shavings in the area between these lines until, working by eye, you've established the rounded edge.

You should create the radii on the ends of the board before tackling the long-grain radius to avoid tear-out at the corners.

Nail the shiplapped backboards onto the back of the carcase. Then nail the top and bottom in place.

Making the Door

The cabinet took me maybe three hours to assemble. The door took a day and a half to build and fit. In part, this is because the door is the only element with any traditional joinery, but primarily, it was because doors require a lot of careful fitting.

The original door has $\frac{1}{4}$"-thick x 2"-wide x 4"-long through tenons on the rails. And so did the first door I made for this particular reproduction.

But the mortises must have been a little out of whack because when I assembled the door, it had an unacceptable amount of twist, a result probably of an incorrectly cut mortise. This is something that's easy to do when chopping long and very thin mortises by hand. So I made a second door, this time with mortises only 2" deep. These were much easier to cut accurately, and a tightly fit 2"-long tenon has more than enough glue surface for this door, particularly when the glue joints are reinforced with $\frac{1}{4}$" walnut pegs.

The photo at the top of the page shows the door components before the door was glued up. Notice the $\frac{1}{4}$"-wide, $\frac{1}{2}$"-deep through grooves milled into all of the inside edges of the door's rails and stiles. The flat center panel floats in these grooves.

The door is opened with a turned walnut knob. I turned two knobs from the spindle shown because I had decided to make a pair of these hanging cupboards.

The final touches on the door are the $\frac{1}{4}$"-diameter pegs that reinforce each tenon. Cut off a length of walnut (or some other durable, easily split hardwood) that is a bit longer than the thickness of the door components. Then, with a wide chisel, tapped with a hammer, split off squares about $\frac{5}{16}$" on a side. Pare

these squares into approximate rounds, holding the individual pegs as shown above.

The splits in the center of the photo are the splits from which the pegs are shaved. The pegs on the left have been shaved close to their final shapes.

Cut and shape the hangers as shown in the illustration. Nail them to the back – place the nails so you catch a shelf and the sub top of the carcase.

Finishing

The original cupboard was stained red, but I opted for paint in order to conceal the nail heads. I began with a coat of latex primer, which I sanded, then followed that with two coats of a "designer" red that approximated the color of the original piece.

Of course, the problem with paint is the dimensional change it causes. Each layer of paint adds measurably to the width and thickness of the part to which it's applied. A door stile that was 4" wide after sanding, might be $4\frac{1}{8}$" wide after applying three coats of paint. So even though I had fit the door with a comfortable $\frac{1}{16}$" gap all around, after painting, I had to remove the door and plane off additional width from all the rails and all the stiles and then repaint those planed edges in order to get the door to open and close properly.

My wife asked me how the Shakers

might have used the original cupboard. I had to tell her I didn't know.

Because it was poplar – rather than, say, cherry or curly maple – it probably was a utility cabinet of some kind, maybe something that hung in a washroom, something that might once have held soaps or cleaning brushes, but because it was so portable – just remove it from the pegs in one room and hang it from the pegs in another – it might have had several incarnations in its original life, as the Shakers moved it from room to room to suit the needs of a community dwindling steadily in size over the years.

My wife decided to hang hers in the kitchen. She's going to fill it with spices, and then use the top surface to display her collection of antique tin cans with brightly lithographed color labels.

Before you glue up the door, lay out the parts and make certain that they will all come together during glue-up.

Use a skew to shape the top of the knob and a fingernail gouge to cut the cove. The tenon can be cut with a paring chisel laid flat on the rest with the bevel down.

Riven pegs are not only historically accurate, they are also stronger than sawn pegs because they eliminate the possibility of grain run-out.

The original cupboard had been stained. I chose to use a primer and paint combination in order to best mimic the look of the aged original finish.

Pleasant Hill Mini Chest

BY KERRY PIERCE

Furniture reproductions are never exactly like the originals on which they're based. In some cases, that's because the skill and artistry of the reproducer don't measure up to the skill and artistry of the original craftsman. In other cases, it's because the reproducer consciously made the decision to vary from the original, substituting, for example, curly maple for cherry or machine-cut dovetails for hand-cut dovetails. In other cases, it's because the reproducer decided that the original could be improved on in some way.

The last is true of my version of this delightful little blanket chest from the Shaker Village of Pleasant Hill, which is located outside Harrodsburg, Ky.

The original was appealing in several ways: diminutive size, charming country-style details and solid joinery. But it also had some problems. Instead of the chest bottom's edges being let into grooves cut on the inside surfaces of the four sides of the case, the bottom of the original was simply nailed inside the case with the result that, when the solid-wood bottom underwent inevitable shrinkage across its width, gaps appeared on either side, visible when you look into the case from above. Also, the material was, I believe, simply too thick for this relatively dainty form. The material of the original was dressed to a chunky ⅞", a thickness that would have been more appropriate for this chest's bigger, full-sized brothers.

I opted for ⅝" material throughout, and I set the edges of the bottom into grooves, although in the drawing, I showed the original ⅞" material.

I have a theory about the original. I think it might have been an apprentice piece. The master in the shop would have

discouraged the youngster from testing his skills on a full-sized piece with a full-sized appetite for material, directing that youngster instead to this little miniature.

At least that's my theory.

So why would I reproduce a piece that I think might have been the work of an apprentice?

Well, I like it.

The Big Three-hearted Tree

Material selection and arrangement is always critical, but it is, I think, doubly so in the case of a simple piece like this on which there isn't any carving or veneering.

When I'm gluing up panels for such a simple piece, I begin by pulling boards with similar color and figure.

I then begin to lay out the cuttings on the surfaces of those boards, making an effort to ensure each panel will be glued up of pieces taken from the same board. This means, for example, that the five pieces from which the lid is glued up were all taken from the same board. Three 25"-long sections of that board came together for the lid's main panel. The breadboard ends were then ripped from the offcut left behind. This approach is critical, I believe, because even though all the boards I might pull for a particular piece will have similar color and figure, the very best matches are those taken from the same board.

We woodworkers are often tempted to cut our stock from the edges of our boards. That is, after all, the logical way to proceed. You joint one edge, set the table saw to the desired width, then rip off what you need. That's an efficient use of time and material, but it doesn't always result in the most visually pleas-

ing arrangement of material. My method is to draw rectangles anywhere on the boards that have the kind of color, figure and absence of defects I'm trying to attain. Then I band saw the first long edge of the piece, joint that edge, and cut the other side on the table saw.

I consciously look for opportunities to employ material exhibiting a mix of heart and sapwood, particularly in the cases of walnut and cherry where the contrasts are so dramatic. However, the use of sapwood places on me the obligation to use that material in some kind of aesthetically coherent manner. In the case of this blanket chest, I decided I would use sapwood only on the lid and only in a very controlled context. Specifically, I would create two swaths of light-colored material running the full length of the lid, stopped and held visually in place by breadboard ends cut from heartwood.

To create these two swaths of light-colored material, I aligned the material so that the joints between boards would occur only in the sapwood where, I knew from long experience, they would disappear, leaving the arresting appearance of a board cut from a three-hearted tree.

The moulded edges on the original chest are battered. They were not, I suspect, very cleanly cut in the first place, and they have been abused by a century-and-a-half of use at Pleasant Hill and elsewhere. The result is that it was difficult to tell exactly how they were originally intended to look. The drawing represents my best guess about the original maker's intentions, but the moulding I used for my reproduction is the profile cut by a stock router bit I picked up at Lowe's – a ⁵⁄₃₂" Roman ogee on a ¼" shank – a bit that cuts a profile that's reasonably close but not exactly like what I think the original maker intended.

Build a Box & a Half

This chest consists of two boxes: the case and the plinth. The front, back and sides of each box are assembled with dovetails.

After you've glued up the panels from which each of the primary box's elements will be cut, level and smooth the panels with your planer or a set of handplanes. Then joint one edge of each panel and rip it to width (leaving a little surplus width to remove when you remove the saw

If possible, cut lengths from the same board for each piece of a panel you are going to glue up. This strategy offers the best possible color and figure match.

marks). Then cut each panel to length.

Before you start cutting dovetails, plow the grooves on the inside surfaces of the chest's larger box in which the box's bottom will be housed. You don't need stopped grooves for this particular chest because the grooves will be hidden by the plinth so the through grooves that would otherwise show on the ends of the chest are concealed.

Then begin cutting dovetails. I cut my dovetails by hand because that's the only way I know how, but I understand they can be cut just as easily with a jig and a router. Apply glue to all mating surfaces

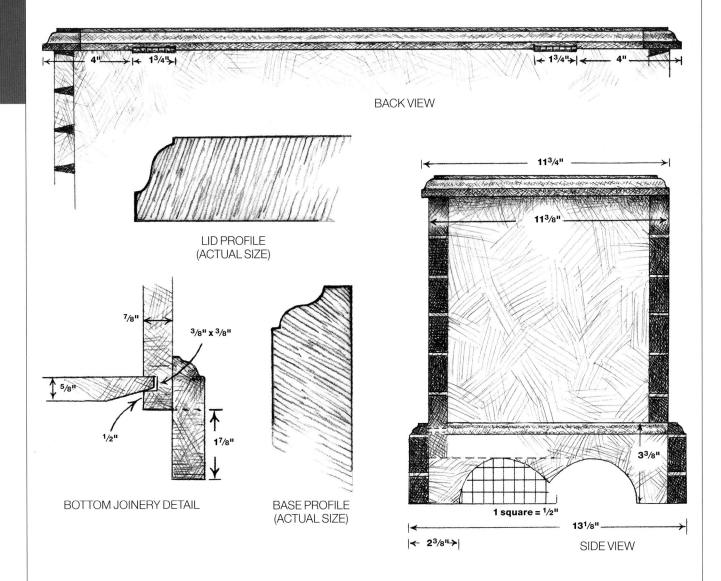

BACK VIEW

LID PROFILE
(ACTUAL SIZE)

BOTTOM JOINERY DETAIL

BASE PROFILE
(ACTUAL SIZE)

SIDE VIEW

1 square = 1/2"

Pleasant Hill Mini Chest

NO.	ITEM	DIMENSIONS (INCHES)			MATERIAL
		T	W	L	
2	Front and back	5/8	11	26 3/8	Cherry
2	Ends	5/8	11	11 3/8	Cherry
1	Bottom	5/8	10 5/8	25 7/8	Pine
1	Lid main panel	5/8	11 3/4	241/4	Cherry
2	Lid breadboard ends	5/8	1 5/8	11 3/4	Cherry
2	Lid cleats	5/8	2 1/2	9 3/4	Cherry
2	Plinth front & back	5/8	3 3/8	27 3/4	Cherry
2	Plinth ends	5/8	3 3/8	13 1/8	Cherry

Note: All measurements are finished sizes. Add extra lengths, particularly to dovetailed parts. Also, the illustration shows the original piece in 7/8" material; the cutlist shows the piece in 5/8", as built by the author.

of the dovetails and assemble the larger box around the chest bottom (which you have already raised so the edges of that bottom will fit in the grooves you've plowed for its edges). Check the case for square by measuring the diagonals. If there is an error, correct that error by racking the longer diagonal until the two measurements are the same (within maybe $\frac{1}{32}$"). Then wipe away all the glue squeeze-out on the inside and outside of the chest.

Once the glue has cured, fix the chest to your bench and, with a plane, pare down the surplus length from the pins and tails of your joinery. Prior to cutting a set of dovetails, I set my marking gauge so that there is at least $\frac{1}{32}$" of extra length on these elements so I can plane the surplus flush without retaining the end grain tear-out that is part of every saw crosscut. This work could also be done with a belt sander.

I believe this planing is the most difficult part of the joinery process because it takes a fair amount of force to power even a sharp, well-tuned handplane through the joint's end grain. That means the case must be securely fastened to your workbench.

When you apply significant clamping pressure to a glued-up panel, the pressure can cause the panel to cup. Cleats can be clamped to the panel as shown to eliminate that cupping.

Next, assemble the four parts of the plinth using dovetails here as well. I chose to cut the joinery before I shaped the moulding because I wasn't sure how I would mark the dovetails on an edge that had already been shaped.

Check the fit against the case dry to ensure there are no gaps. Then run the stock past the bit on your router table to create the moulded edge. Before you glue up the four parts of the plinth, dry assemble them one more time, and mark

the shape of the bracket feet at the corners. You can very quickly remove most of the waste on your band saw.

Then glue up the plinth and, while the glue is still wet, attach the plinth to the case using $1\frac{1}{4}$" x #8 drywall screws from inside the bottom. (I probably could have gone with 1" screws because the two pieces I'm joining here have a total thickness of only $1\frac{1}{4}$", but I wanted the holding power of the longer screws, so before I used them, I touched the tip of each to

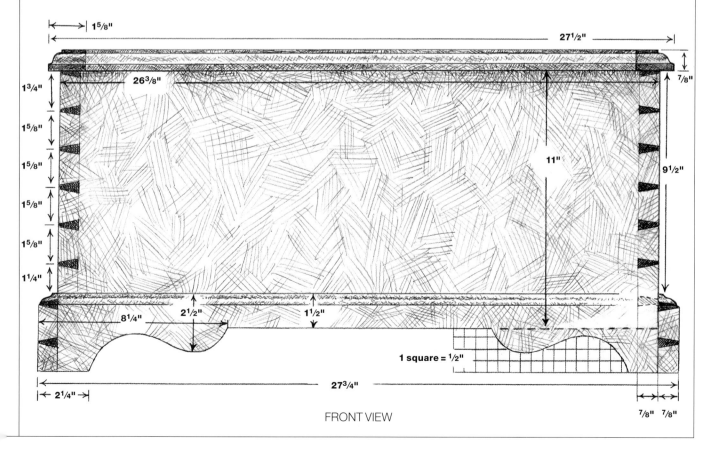

FRONT VIEW

After squaring lines across the end grain, I cut the tails free-hand, without first marking their angles. This gives me joinery that is certifiably handcut, with each tail just a little different than the one beside it.

Because I cut the pins and tails a little long, I use cleats to apply clamping pressure behind these elements when I'm bringing a case together.

my grinding wheel to reduce the length to a bit more than 1⅛".)

The moulded corners of the plinth will require a little fussy work with hand tools in that end section. I used a shoulder plane to extend the little fillet at the base of the moulded edge all the way to the corner. I then formed the rest of the moulded edge with a paring chisel and a carving gouge. And a little sandpaper.

I couldn't really tell how the original lid's breadboard ends were attached. What I can say is this: There's no evidence of a tongue-and-groove joint (the joinery I would have expected). That is, there is no tongue visible on the front edge of the lid. It's conceivable, however, that the tongue and groove were stopped, but that's a level of joinery sophistication I found nowhere else on this piece. In fact, for the most part, the joinery on

this chest is simple and straightforward – very Shaker. I chose to use a 20th-century standby, the lowly dowel. As you can see in the picture at right, I applied glue only to the three center dowels. My thinking is that might permit a bit more movement across the grain of the center panel. While you might normally drill elongated holes for the dowels, I've found that their location and slightly undersized fit allow plenty of room for wood movement.

All lids/tops cup. It's a natural law with results as predictable as gravity. It doesn't matter how you align the grain when you're gluing up the lid/top. It doesn't matter how carefully the material

is seasoned or whether you've finished both the top and bottom surfaces. All lids cup, and I have dedicated a good part of my woodworking life to finding ways to interfere with the expression of this natural law. In most casework, you can fasten the sides of the top to the sides of the case with good results, but you can't do that with a lid like the one on this chest. Many years ago I began installing cleats on the undersides of unsupported lids, and they do work, but they must be wide enough to resist cupping, and for best results you have to cheat with your cleats. Before I install them, I plane a ¹⁄₁₆" crown on the edge that will contact the underside of the lid. This gives me some leverage in

Supplies

Woodworker's Supply

800-645-9292 or woodworker.com

1 • brass escutcheon
   #940-732, $1.78

1 • cigar box lock
   #115-841, $33.99

Prices correct at time of publication.

Check the fit of the plinth elements around the case before you glue them together. Notice that I haven't yet cut the moulded edge on the top edge of the pieces to the plinth.

I used a Skil ⁵⁄₃₂" Roman ogee bit to cut the moulded edge. I used the same bit with the same set-up to cut the moulded edge around the assembled top.

Before you glue up the plinth, mark and cut away on your band saw the surplus stock at each corner.

my war on cupping. I may not use it all at once. If for example, there isn't much cupping on the day I install the cleats, I may install them with either end just a bit above the surface of the lid. Then later, if I need to, I can draw them down.

But I should point out that these cleats are not on the original lid, which is, I should also point out, cupped.

Haste Makes Slop

Take your time when installing the hardware because a little haste here can ruin an otherwise handsome project.

Begin with the hinges. In the finished piece, the back side of the lid is aligned with the back side of the case. Next attach the two lid stays. These nifty bits of hardware were not on the original, but I think it's a mistake to attach any lid without also attaching something to prevent the lid from accidentally flopping all the way back and maybe pulling out the hinge screws.

I bought the lock from Woodworker's Supply. I like this little lock because the post on the strike plate simplifies the installation process. Lock-and-strike-plate alignment can be frustrating. There is little room for error, and if you do make a slight mistake or if there is a slight mistake in lock manufacture, you may find yourself muttering in the shop.

Finishing

Unfortunately, finishing is all about sanding. Lots of sanding. Use a sanding block to keep the surface level and start with #100 grit, progress to #150, then #220, and finish-sand twice with #320.

Use clamps (and protective clamping blocks) to bring the plinth together and – this is important – screw it to the case before the glue in the dovetails cures. (If you look closely, you can see the bevels around the field of the raised panel on the chest bottom. These bevels were cut freehand with a jack plane.)

In a small shop like mine, without a dedicated finishing room, I think woodworkers are much better off with wipe-on finishes. I've used many different brands, and all performed well. In the case of this chest, I tried Minwax Wipe-On Poly for the first time, and two coats built up enough surface to lay a foundation for my paste wax. I sanded with #400 grit-wet/dry paper after the first coat of poly. I sanded with #600 grit wet/dry after the second coat. I then applied the wax.

I applied glue only to the center three dowels, thinking that might allow a bit more movement across the grain of the center panel.

Shaker Stepback

BY MEGAN FITZPATRICK

have a love-hate relationship with my television. I love (too much, perhaps) to watch shows, but I hate having the TV out in the open as the focal point of my living room. But I also dislike most commercial entertainment centers, as I've a penchant for antique and antique-style furniture.

So, I flipped through a pile of books on Shaker furniture and auction-house catalogs to cull design ideas for a step-back cupboard that could be repurposed as a modern entertainment center that would not only allow me to hide a 32" flat-panel TV behind doors, but also house the cable box, DVD player and various stereo components. (Of course, if you want to use it in your dining room, just omit all the holes in the backboards for air flow and cord management.)

A Plethora of Panels

While this project is quite large, it's suprisingly easy to build – though it's an exercise in organization to keep all the parts straight. The upper face frame, lower carcase and all four doors are simple mortise-and-tenon joints, with panels floating in grooves in the doors and carcase sides.

The first step is to mill and glue up all the panels. Use your best stock for the door panels, as they'll show the most. And here's a tip I didn't know until after it was too late: Keep all your cathedrals facing in the same direction and your panels will be more pleasing to the eye.

For the four doors, you'll need six ⅝"-thick panels, two each of three sizes. You'll also need two ⅝"-thick panels for the lower carcase sides.

Unless you have access to a lot of wide stock, you'll also need to glue up ¾"-thick panels for the upper carcase sides, top, bottom and shelves, and the lower carcase bottom, shelf and top.

I glued up all my panels oversized. After the glue was dry, I took them out of the clamps, stickered them and set them aside. I cut each to its final dimension as it was

needed, after calculating its exact measurement from the dry-fit frames and carcase sides. I don't trust cut lists; no matter how religiously I stick to the plan, measurements change in execution.

Mortises & Tenons Galore

With the panels set aside, I moved on to all the pieces that would be joined with mortise-and-tenon joints. Initially, I'd planned to concentrate on one carcase at a time to more easily keep things organized. I quickly realized that's an inefficient work method, as the mortise-and-tenon setups are the same on both the top and bottom pieces of the project. Rather than create each setup twice on the machines, I prepared all my stock and cut the joints at the same time.

First, chuck a ¼" chisel and bit in the mortiser, and take the time to make sure the chisel is dead parallel to the machine's fence. I began with the leg mortises – the only pieces on which the mortises aren't centered. After choosing the best faces for the show sides of each, mark which leg is which. Mark out your mortises. On the inside back of the rear legs, they're set in 1" so the rail can accommodate the ⅝"-thick backboards. On the front and sides, they're ¼" back

from the show faces, so that the rails end up flush with the front of the leg faces. The top rails are flush with the top of the legs, so lay out 1½" mortises on the inside front of the two front legs, and 2½" mortises on the side, ¼" down from the top. The bottom rails are all 3", so your mortises will be 2½", 1¼" up from the bottom of the leg.

Cut the mortises for the back rail first with 1" distance between the chisel and the fence, then change the setup to ¼" spacing, and cut the remaining mortises in the legs. To make clean mortise cuts, most of the Popular Woodworking editors use the "leap-frog method." That is, skip a space with every hole, then clean up between the holes. Some woodworkers prefer to overlap each hole to get a clean cut. Try both methods on scrap pieces, and use whichever you prefer.

Assuming your stile stock is exactly ¾" thick, the setup should remain the same for the face frame and door mortises, but double check that the chisel is centered in your stock before making that first frame cut. And, make sure you always work with the same side against the fence – if you are off a little bit, you'll be equally off on every joint, and cleanup will be easier.

Lay out all the mortises on your face frame and door frames and make the cuts. (A sturdy 6" rule is my preferred tool for cleaning the detritus out of the bottom of each mortise.)

Now it's on to the tenons. I prefer to set up the full ¹³⁄₁₆"-wide dado stack at the table saw, and raise it to just shy of ¼". That way, I can make two passes on each end of my tenoned workpieces, and simply roll around each face to create the tenons, without having to change the setup at all for any of my 1¼"-long tenons.

With the tenons cut just a hair oversized in thickness, I test-fit each one individually in its mortise and used a shoulder plane to reach the final fit. Planing a slight chamfer at the end of the tenon will help it seat. (The fit should be a tight press fit. The tenon shouldn't move around in the mortise – nor should you need a mallet to get things together.)

Grooves for Floating Panels

With the mortise-and-tenon joints all dry-fit, it's time to cut the grooves that will accept the floating panels. Chuck a $^1/_4$" three-wing cutter into your router table, and raise it $^1/_4$" (you can use your already cut mortises to set the height – no measuring necessary). Set the fence to make a $^3/_8$"-deep cut.

Start with the legs – and double check to make sure you have the faces marked correctly. The floating panels are on each side of the carcase, so a groove is needed from mortise to mortise on the front face of both back legs, and on the back face of both front legs. Unless your ear protection blocks out all noise, you should be able to hear the difference in sound as the router cutters move from the hollow of the mortise into the groove cut (mark the starting and stopping point if you're worried about recognizing the sound differential). With the leg flat to the table and the mortise toward the bottom, push the leg against the fence so that the router bit is spinning in the empty mortise hole, then move the leg across the table, cutting a groove that stops in the other mortise, then pull the leg away. Repeat until all four leg grooves are cut, and set the legs aside.

Test the bit height on your $^3/_4$" stock before proceeding. It shouldn't need adjustment … but it never hurts to be sure. Grooves are needed on all frame pieces that will house a panel – that's the inside edges of all the door rails and stiles, and on both long edges of the medial rails for the upper doors. On the stiles, the groove goes from mortise to mortise. On the rails, in order to cut a

Shaker Stepback

NO.	ITEM	DIMENSIONS (INCHES)			MATERIAL	COMMENTS
		T	W	L		
Upper Section						
2	Face frame stiles	$^3/_4$	$1^3/_4$	$52^3/_4$	Cherry	
1	Upper face frame rail	$^3/_4$	$3^1/_2$	43	Cherry	TBE*
1	Lower face frame rail	$^3/_4$	2	43	Cherry	TBE
2	Side panels	$^3/_4$	12	$52^3/_4$	Cherry	
1	Top	$^3/_4$	$11^3/_8$	43	Cherry	
1	Bottom	$^3/_4$	$11^3/_8$	43	Cherry	
2	Shelves	$^3/_4$	$11^3/_8$	43	Cherry	
4	Door stiles	$^3/_4$	$2^1/_2$	$47^1/_4$	Cherry	
2	Door top rails	$^3/_4$	$2^1/_2$	$17^3/_4$	Cherry	TBE
2	Door center rails	$^3/_4$	2	$17^3/_4$	Cherry	TBE
2	Door bottom rails	$^3/_4$	$2^1/_2$	$17^3/_4$	Cherry	TBE
2	Upper door panels	$^5/_8$	$15^7/_8$	$17^3/_4$	Cherry	
2	Lower door panels	$^5/_8$	$15^7/_8$	$22^3/_4$	Cherry	
1	Front crown	$^7/_8$	4	$49^1/_2$	Cherry	Trim to fit
2	Side crown	$^7/_8$	4	$15^3/_4$	Cherry	Trim to fit
Varies	Backboards	$^5/_8$	varies	$52^3/_4$	Cherry	
Lower Section						
4	Feet	$1^3/_4$	$1^3/_4$	$7^1/_4$	Cherry	$1^1/_4$" dowel at top
4	Legs	$1^3/_4$	$1^3/_4$	28	Cherry	
2	Side panels	$^5/_8$	$13^7/_8$	$21^5/_8$	Cherry	
4	Side rails	$^3/_4$	3	$15^3/_4$	Cherry	TBE
1	Upper front rail	$^3/_4$	2	43	Cherry	TBE
1	Lower front rail	$^3/_4$	3	43	Cherry	TBE
1	Upper back rail	$^3/_4$	2	$42^1/_2$	Poplar	
1	Lower back rail	$^3/_4$	$2^1/_2$	43	Poplar	TBE
1	Center stile	$^3/_4$	2	$24^1/_2$	Cherry	TBE
2	Door panels	$^5/_8$	$14^7/_8$	$17^5/_8$	Cherry	
4	Door stiles	$^3/_4$	$2^1/_2$	22	Cherry	
4	Door rails	$^3/_4$	$2^1/_2$	$16^3/_4$	Cherry	TBE
2	Middle shelf cleats	$^3/_4$	$15^1/_2$	2	Cherry	
2	Bottom shelf cleats	$^3/_4$	$14^1/_2$	1	Cherry	
1	Top	$^3/_4$	$18^3/_4$	47	Cherry	
1	Shelf	$^3/_4$	$14^1/_2$	$42^1/_2$	Cherry	
1	Bottom	$^3/_4$	$15^1/_4$	$42^1/_2$	Cherry	
Varies	Backboards	$^5/_8$	random	27	Cherry	
* TBE=Tenon both ends, $1^1/_4$"						

Many mortises. The majority of joints in this project are mortise and tenon. Take the time to set the hollow-chisel mortiser to cut dead-on centered mortises, 1¼" deep – it will save you a lot of frustration and time later.

Table-saw tenons. The full dado stack on our table saw is ¹³⁄₁₆" and the tenons are 1¼" long, so I made the first cut on each face with the workpiece tight to the fence, then slid it to the left for a second pass. The blades are raised just shy of ¼" so I was able to simply roll the end of each ¾" workpiece to cut the tenons with one setup.

A sea of panels. I wanted to glue up all the panels at the same time – but I ran out of clamps and space. Above are the six door panels and two lower side panels.

full ³⁄₈" deep across the rail, you'll be nipping the inside edge of the tenon. That's OK – but be careful to cut away as little as possible so that the joint retains maximum strength.

Raised Panels

Now dry-fit the sides and doors and take the final measurements for all the panels. Add ⁵⁄₈" to both the height and width of each; with ³⁄₈" hidden in the groove on all sides, you build in an ¹⁄₈" on either side for your panel. Retrieve the door and side panels from your stickered stack; cut them to final size at the table saw.

Now, set up a fence-extension jig on your saw – a stable flat panel attached to your rip fence will work, but that jig will be stationary and you'll have to carefully move your workpiece across the spinning blade. It's safer to make a jig that fits over the fence and slides along it. That way,

you can clamp the workpiece to the jig and move the unit instead.

For any stock thickness, set the blade angle to 12°, and set the fence so there's ³⁄₁₆" between the fence and the inside saw tooth as the tooth clears the bottom of the throat plate. Raise the blade enough so that the stock fits between the blade and the fence (approximately 2³⁄₄"). This ensures the blade will clear the stock completely as the cut is made. Make sure you use a zero-clearance throat plate; otherwise, the thin offcuts will get caught and kick back.

Cut across the grain first, at the top and bottom edges. Any tear-out will be cut away on your second two cuts, which are with the grain. Clamp your workpiece firmly to the fence extension and slide it smoothly across the blade. Now repeat until all six panels are raised, and sand away the mill marks. These panels

will fit snug in the ³⁄₈"-deep grooves, and allow for seasonal expansion and contraction. And if you prefer a more country look to a Shaker style? Face the raised panels to the outside of the piece and you're there.

Shapely Feet

At some point before you do any glue up, you'll want to turn your feet at the lathe and create a tenon at the end to join to the leg. (Of course, you could also add 6" to your leg length, and turn the foot on the leg stock. However, I decided I'd rather muck up a 6" length of wood than a 34" piece, so I made the feet as separate pieces.) I first milled each foot blank square, then turned them round and shaped each foot, following the pattern at right.

Even if each foot is slightly different (you can't tell unless they're right next to one another), be careful to turn the

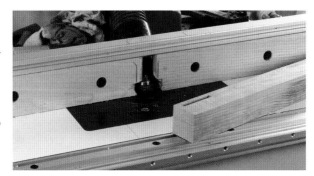

A home for floating panels. To cut $3/8$"-deep grooves for the floating panels, set up a $1/4$" three-wing cutter (also known as a slot cutter), using your mortises to set the cutter height. The groove will run from mortise to mortise.

Raised panels. Set up a fence-extension jig on the table saw, set the blade at a 12° angle, set the distance between the fence and blade at $3/16$"and raise the blade until it just clears the workpiece as the cut is made. This jig, built by Senior Editor Glen D. Huey, slides along the rail, so the workpiece can be clamped in place.

tenoned ends as close in size as possible. To achieve this, I set my calipers to $3/4$" and held them against the tenon as I cut the waste away with a wide parting tool. As soon as I reached a $3/4$" diameter, the calipers slid over the piece. I then turned the rest of the tenon to match.

Why make those tenons the same? Well, you have to fit the tenons into drilled holes that are centered in the bottom of each leg, and I wanted to use but one drill bit and achieve a tight fit.

I clamped each leg perpendicular to the floor, and drilled $3/4$"-diameter x $1 1/4$"-deep holes centered in the bottom of each leg. Be careful to keep your drill straight (or set up a drill press for greater accuracy). With the holes drilled, I set the feet aside until the rest of the bottom carcase was done.

Time for Glue Up

Dry-fit all your panels to the grooves inside the door frames and the bottom case sides, and make any necessary

adjustments. Once everything fits snug, get your clamps ready and work with one glue-up at a time (I started with the lower doors and side panels, as they involved fewer pieces).

Use an acid brush to apply a thin layer of yellow glue on the walls of your mortises and the tenon faces, slip the rails in place, then slide the panel in place and cap it off with the opposite stile (keep a damp rag handy to wipe away any squeeze-out). Clamp until the glue is dry. (Again, add glue only to the mortise-and-tenon joints; the panels should float.) The upper doors are a bit tricky to glue up, with two panels plus the medial rail in each. I'm sure my contortions were amusing to watch. I recommend getting a friend to help wrangle things in place.

While you're waiting for the lower sides to dry, glue up the upper face frame, check it for square, clamp and set it aside. Once the lower side panels are set, complete the lower carcase's mortise-and-tenon joints by gluing the lower back

rail, the front rails and the center stile in place. (The upper back rail is notched around the legs at both ends, so it's easier to use pocket screws for that joint, though you can cut a mortise-and-tenon joint if you prefer.)

Now it's on to the upper section. Cut your sides, top, bottom and shelves to final size. The $3/4$"-thick top, bottom and shelves are housed in $1/4$"-deep grooves cut into the side pieces. So set up the dado stack again at the table saw but use only enough blades and chippers to create a $3/4$"-wide cut (and be sure to run a few test pieces first). Raise the stack to $1/4$". Mark the cuts on one of the case sides and set the fence off that piece, making the cuts in both sides before moving the fence for the next location. Make sure your cuts are on the inside faces of your sides. Note in the illustration that the top and bottom pieces are not at the ends; they're set in to add rigidity, and the bottom protrudes $1/4$" above the face-frame bottom and thus functions as a door stop.

Before you take off the dado stack, run a $3/4$"-deep x $7/16$"-wide rabbet up the back of each side; these will house the backboards.

Now lay one side piece flat on your workbench (groove-side up) and fit the top, bottom and shelves into place. Set the other side piece on top, and use a dead-blow mallet to fully seat the pieces in the grooves. (This is a big workpiece – you might want to grab a helper.) If the

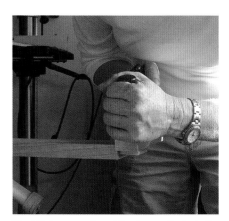

Final fit. I purposely cut the tenons just a hair oversized. I reached the final fit by testing each tenon in its mortise, then shaving each cheek as needed with a shoulder plane. And, I planed a slight chamfer on the tenon ends to make them easier to fit.

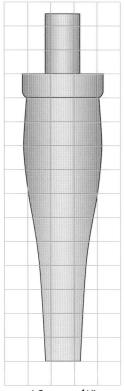

1 Square = 1/2"

FOOT LAYOUT

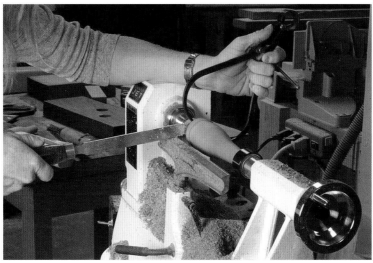

Custom feet. I shaped my 6" feet on the lathe and turned a 3/4" x 1 1/4" tenon at the top of each. While the feet needn't be identical, the tenons should be close in size. I held calipers set to 3/4" against the piece as I used a parting tool to make the cut. When I reached 3/4", the calipers slipped over the tenon and I was done.

Foot holes. Before the bottom carcase is glued up, drill holes to receive the tenons on the turned feet. I used a 3/4" Forstner bit to drill 1 1/4"-deep. Match your bit and depth to the size of the tenons on your feet.

pieces fit together snug, you could pull them back out, add a little glue and refit them. But after struggling to get them in place once, I didn't want to go through that exercise again (and it was a lot of exercise). Instead, I chose to toenail the shelves in place from the bottom face at both the front and back edges.

At this point, I also pegged all the mortise-and-tenon joints, and pegged the shelves in the upper carase into the sides, using 1/4" white oak pegs (for more on pegging, see "Square Pegs, Round Holes" in the techniques section at popu-larwoodworking.com).

Now fit your doors to the face frame, and mark then cut the hinge mortises. Keep the door fit tight – you'll do the final fitting once the entire carcase is together (things could move when you add the backboards later – trust me). You might as well fit the lower doors and hinges at the same time.

Now, flip the upper carcase on its back and glue the face frame in place, adding enough clamps to pull it tight along each side. If things work out cor-rectly, you'll have a slight overhang on both sides, which, after the glue dries,

you can flush to the face frame with a trim router or handplane.

Backboards

Is that dado stack still in your table saw? Good. Mill enough 5/8"-thick stock for your backboards for both the top and bottom, and run 5/16" x 3/8" rabbets on opposing edges for shiplaps (and don't forget to calculate the rabbets as you're measuring the width of your rough stock). The outside pieces get only one rabbet each.

I used random-width boards pulled from an old stash of sappy cherry. Because the backboards will be on view with the doors open as I watch TV, I didn't want to use a less attractive sec-ondary wood. So I used less-attractive pieces of primary wood. With the rabbets cut, change the table saw set-up back to a rip blade, and rip the outside backboards to final width (the humidity was low here when I built this, so I used dimes as spac-ers).

Screw the backboards in place, with one screw at the top and bottom of every board set just off the overlapping edge. (That screw holds the joint tight, but allows for slight movement of the under-lapped piece. Your last board needs two screws at the top and bottom to keep it secure.) Now do the final fit on your doors, taking passes with a handplane or on the jointer (take a 1" cut on the trailing end first, then reverse the piece to avoid tear-out). I aimed for a 1/16" gap all around (on some sides, I even hit it). After marking locations for any

Supplies

Lee Valley
800-267-8735 or leevalley.com

4 pr. • 3" x 1 11/16" narrow extruded brass fixed-pin butt hinges #00D02.04, $22.00 per pair

Rockler
800-279-4441 or rockler.com

4 • 1 1/8" cherry Shaker pegs #78469, $9.49 per pair

Prices correct at time of publication.

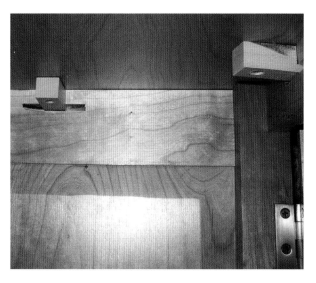

Buttoned down. The top of the bottom section is attached to the side and front rails with buttons. I used a biscuit joiner to cut two ½"-deep x 1¼"-wide slots on each side, and three along the front. I simply screwed through the back rail into the top's bottom to secure it at the back.

necessary wire and air-circulation holes in the backboards, take the doors and backboards off, drill any needed holes at the drill press, then set the doors and backboards aside for finishing. Drill any cord/air holes at the drill press with a Forstner bit.

Complete the Bottom

Flip the lower carcase and choose your foot position. Line up the grain of the foot with its matching leg so the look is pleasing. One of my holes was a bit off straight, so I used a rasp to take down one side of my tenon until I could adjust the angle accordingly. Once everything

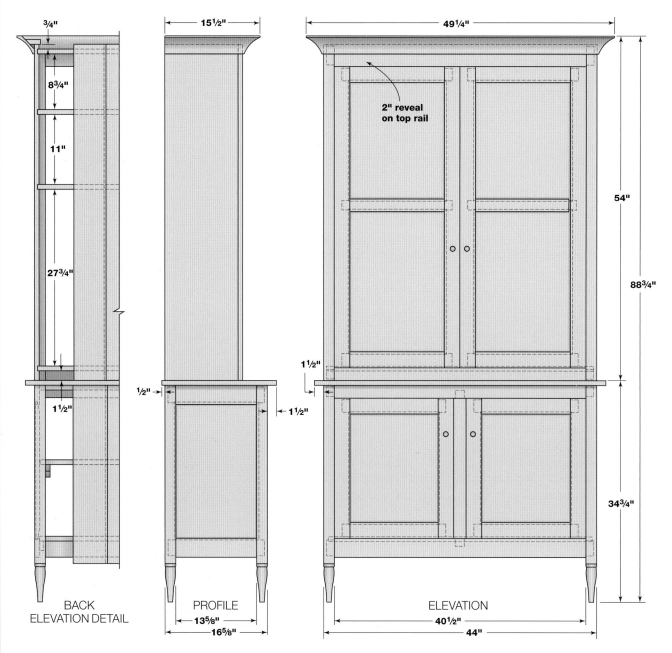

3/4"

8¾"

11"

27¾"

1½"

BACK
ELEVATION DETAIL

15½"

½"

1½"

13⅝"

16⅝"

49¼"

2" reveal
on top rail

54"

88¾"

1½"

34¾"

ELEVATION

40½"

44"

Cutting crown. The crown is cut by running $^7/_8$" x 4" stock at an angle over the table saw. Raise the blade to $^7/_{16}$" then center your stock to the blade. Clamp a long straightedge to the table to guide the stock, then lower the blade and make a series of passes as you gradually raise the blade until you reach $^7/_{16}$" (or your desired depth).

Gap for ventilation

Cut shelves and top rail to fit around legs.

12"

2½"

BOTTOM
CASE
SECTION

fits to your satisfaction, drip a little yellow glue in the holes and seat the feet. You don't need clamps here (unless you're using them to pull something in line). If the fits are good, simply flip the piece upright and the weight will keep the feet in place as the glue dries.

With the backboards and doors off, now's the time to fit the cleats that support the bottom and shelf in the lower section, and cut button slots in the top rail to attach the top. The bottom is notched around the legs and the back edge is rabbeted to fit neatly over the back rail. But because I need airflow in the bottom section for A/V equipment, I fit the shelf to the inside corner of each leg and to the front center stile where it serves as a door stop. I left a gap at the back and sides to run wires and for air circulation.

To complete the bottom section, use a biscuit cutter to cut slots in the front and side rails for buttons, and notch the upper back rail around the rear legs and use pocket screws to hold it in place. For added strength, countersink a screw through the front edge at each end into the leg, too. Cut the top to final size, and attach it with buttons at the front and sides. Countersink screws underneath through the back rail into the bottom of the lower section.

The Crowning Touches
Set up your table saw to cut crown moulding, and sand it smooth before fitting. (For instruction on cutting cove moulding on the table saw, see Senior

Editor Glen D. Huey's video under the techniques section at popular woodworking.com/video).

Often, the crown is connected with a flat piece to the top edge of the sides and face frame. But my face frame and sides weren't high enough, so instead, I cut blocks with 45° angles (on two faces for the corner pieces), glued those to the inside of the crown and added brads to the top of the carcase for a bit of additional strength.

The Finish
I sanded each piece to #180 as I went along, so once the construction was complete, I was ready for the finish. Because I didn't have two decades to wait for a nice warm patina to develop (we shot the opening picture just 20 minutes after the handles were in place), I added warmth with two sprayed coats of amber shellac

and a top coat of dull-rubbed-effect, pre-catalyzed lacquer.

Because I couldn't afford five sets of hand-forged iron hinges but wanted an aged look to the hardware, I de-lacquered then added patina to brass hinges with gun bluing.

Oh yes – the handles. I tried to turn them, but ran out of time and talent. Thank goodness for our local woodworking store and its Shaker pull supply. The handles were sprayed separately, set in a scrap of plywood. You see, I didn't know where I wanted to place them until the entire piece was assembled and the A/V components were in place. A friend helped me hoist the upper piece atop the lower cabinet, where it's held in place simply by gravity. I then marked my pull locations, drilled $^3/_8$" holes with a Forstner bit and glued the pulls in place.

Blocked in place. I intended for the top of the carcase to match the top of the crown, so I could attach the crown with a piece that tied into both. That didn't happen. So instead, I cut blocks with a 45° angle on the front, and glued them to the top of the carcase and the inside face of the crown – one at each front and back corner and three more along the front. You can also see the shiplapped back in this picture. Each piece is secured top and bottom at the corner by a screw.

White Water Cupboard

BY GLEN D. HUEY

Shaker stepback cupboards aren't abundant. In fact, there are only a few examples in the many published books on Shaker furniture. Unless you have a sharp eye for Shaker furniture, or are excited about painted furniture with a heavily worn surface, I doubt you would give a second look to the original cupboard on which this project is based. However, the fact that the original is part of the White Water Shaker Village collection propels this piece, in my opinion, toward the top of Shaker cupboards. A reproduction of this cupboard is a must. And in the process, we can turn the clock back to see the cupboard in its earlier days.

Inspiration From the Original

The original Shaker stepback, with its missing crown moulding and other absent features, required detective work before construction began. As we move through the project, we'll examine some missing features and try to reach conclusions that bring this piece back to an earlier day.

The first question is: What about feet? The cupboard at White Water has a three-sided frame that rests on the floor. Was that the original design? Or were the feet worn away or removed?

Also, what happened to the crown moulding? It's obvious there was a moulding, but it is long since gone. What was the profile?

Other features to look at are the unique drawer construction and the use of a half-dovetail sliding joint to secure the shelves to the case sides – even with this complex but strong joint, the builder nailed in the shelves.

Face (Frame) Facts

Before we get to the detective work, we need to build the cases and face frames. The frames for both sections use mortise-and-tenon joints. Mill your parts to size according to the materials schedule, but leave an extra $1/8$" in width on the stiles. After the frames are fit to the cases you'll use a router and flush-trim bit for a perfect fit.

Locate and mark the mortise locations for $1/4$"-thick tenons. Wherever possible, each joint should have a $1\frac{1}{4}$"-long tenon. With the face-frame material at $7/8$" in thickness, a $5/16$" face shoulder produces a centered tenon. An edge shoulder of a matching size ensures a stout joint.

There are two frame joints where the matching edge shoulder is not used: on the bottom rail of the lower section where the tenon would end up $3/8$" wide, and on the bottom rail of the upper section where the tenon would be $5/8$" in width.

As always, cut your mortises first then cut your tenons to fit the mortises. Set up and cut all the mortises on your face-frame parts. It's best to cut the mortise then reverse the position of the workpiece and make a second pass at each mortise. Yes, the resulting mortise may be wider than $1/4$", but the joint will be centered on the stock, and that's most important.

Cut your tenons using your favorite method, then test-fit all your joints. When your tenons fit snug and can be slid together with a little muscle, it's time to assemble the face frames. Work methodically through the assembly. Apply glue to both the mortises and the tenons to achieve the most strength. Clamp the frames and allow the glue to dry.

To assemble the face frames correctly, you'll need to work in a specific order. Plan the steps and have plenty of clamps handy.

Inspired by an original cupboard at the White Water Shaker community (above), our revitalized Shaker stepback (left) blends nicely into the surroundings of the North Family dwelling.

The bottom of the lower section is joined to the sides with half-blind dovetails, as is the top of the upper section.

Two routers, two bits and a guide bushing take the guesswork out of creating the half-dovetailed sliding joints.

Freaky Dovetail Joints

Dovetails abound in the carcases. Both sections have half-blind dovetailed corners and shelves attached with half-dovetailed sliding joints.

On the upper section the case top is dovetailed to the sides; on the lower section, the case bottom has the dovetails.

The pins of the half-blind dovetails are positioned in the sides with the tails in the mating pieces. Also, there is a 3/4" difference in widths between the upper case sides and the top, and the lower case sides and the bottom. Those offsets capture the backboards.

The half-dovetail sliding joint is easy with two router setups. You can work with a single router, but you'll need to change the bits multiple times or position the fence in the exact same location each time.

The setups are this: One router has a 3/4"-diameter, 14°-dovetail bit coupled with a 5 1/64" outside-diameter template

White Water Cupboard

NO.	ITEM	T	W	L	MATERIAL	COMMENTS
Base						
2	Sides	7/8	18	34 1/4	Poplar	
1	Bottom	7/8	17 1/4	48 3/8	Poplar	Dovetailed to sides
2	Shelves	7/8	17 1/4	48 3/8	Poplar	Sliding dovetail ends
1	Top	7/8	20	50 3/4	Poplar	
1	Base frame front	5/8	3 7/8	49 5/8	Poplar	Miter both ends
2	Base frame ends	5/8	3 7/8	19 1/8	Poplar	Miter one end
6	Drawer guides	5/8	1 1/2	17	Poplar	
1	Back	1/2	48 3/8	34 1/4	Poplar	Tongue-and-groove
6	Profiled feet	3/4	5 1/2	7 1/4	Poplar	
2	Rear feet	3/4	5 1/2	3 1/2	Poplar	
4	Foot plates	3/8	5	5	Oak	
Base Face Frame						
2	Stiles	7/8	3 7/8	34 1/4	Poplar	
1	Top rail	7/8	1 5/8	43 7/8	Poplar	1 1/4" TBE*
1	Middle rail	7/8	1 3/4	43 7/8	Poplar	1 1/4" TBE
1	Bottom rail	7/8	1	43 7/8	Poplar	1 1/4" TBE
1	Vertical divider	7/8	4 7/8	27 3/8	Poplar	1" TBE
2	Drawer dividers	7/8	1 1/2	7 1/8	Poplar	1 1/4" TBE
Base Door Parts						
4	Stiles	7/8	3 1/4	25 1/4	Poplar	
2	Top rails	7/8	3 1/4	18 1/4	Poplar	Through-tenons
2	Bottom rails	7/8	3 1/2	18 1/4	Poplar	Through-tenons
2	Panels	1/4	12 3/8	19 1/8	Poplar	
Base Drawer boxes						
2	Outside fronts	7/8	13 3/4	17	Poplar	
1	Center front	7/8	10 5/8	17	Poplar	
Top						
2	Sides	7/8	9 1/8	44 1/2	Poplar	
1	Top	7/8	8 3/8	47 3/8	Poplar	Dovetailed to sides
3	Shelves	7/8	8 3/8	47 3/8	Poplar	Sliding dovetail ends
1	Back	1/2	47 3/8	44 1/2	Poplar	Tongue-and-groove
1	Crown front	3/4	3	55	Poplar	
1	Crown end	3/4	3	24	Poplar	
Top Face Frame						
2	Stiles	7/8	3 7/8	44 1/2	Poplar	
1	Top rail	7/8	5 1/2	42 7/8	Poplar	1 1/4" TBE
1	Bottom rail	7/8	1 1/4	42 7/8	Poplar	1 1/4" TBE
1	Vertical divider	7/8	4 1/8	33 7/8	Poplar	1" TBE
Top Door Parts						
4	Stiles	7/8	3 1/4	31 7/8	Poplar	
4	Rails	7/8	3 1/4	18 1/8	Poplar	Through-tenons
2	Panels	1/4	12 1/4	26	Poplar	

* TBE = tenon both ends

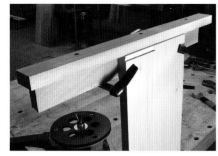

This shop-made jig not only dials-in a perfect sliding dovetail, it allows you to pull any warp out of your shelves.

It's not often you find plate grooves behind blind doors. It's a bigger wonder as to why two different grooves were plowed. Maybe it's for plates and bowls?

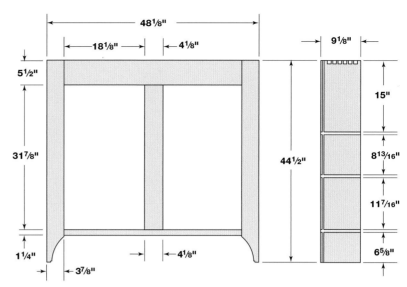

UPPER FACE FRAME & CABINET DETAIL

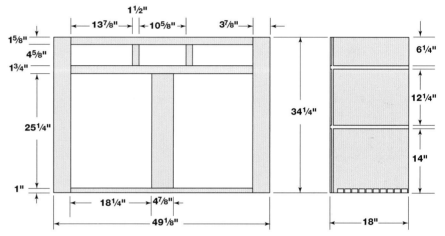

LOWER FACE FRAME & CABINET DETAIL

guide bushing. The second router has a ⅝"-diameter pattern bit with a top-mount bearing.

Begin by marking lines across the sides at both the top and bottom edges of the dados. Position and clamp a ¾" fence at the top edge of a shelf location. Always work with the fence set to the left of the area to be routed. If these guidelines aren't followed, you can form the half-dovetail on the wrong edge.

Begin with the dovetail router bit setup. Set the bit to cut ½" deep into the case side, then hold the guide bushing tight to your fence as you make a pass. The cut should be close to, but not beyond, the lower shelf layout line.

Grab your second router, set up with the bit tweaked to cut at the same depth, then make a second pass making sure to hold the bearing tight to your fence. This cut completes the socket. Move to the next shelf location and repeat the process.

Before moving on, cut the grooves in the side pieces for the backboards. The grooves are ⅜" in from the back edge of the case sides; each is ⅜" wide x ½" deep. A dado stack makes this quick work.

Jig Up the Slide

Now it's time to cut the mating shape on the horizontal shelves. To hoist these large panels onto your router table is quite a task. But with a simple shop-made jig, you won't need to. Instead of taking the panel to the router, you'll take the router to the work.

Build a jig to create the sliding half-dovetail with two straight pieces of 2½"-wide and ¾"-thick scrap that are 24" long. Screw the pieces together to form a "T" with one leg of the top piece set at ⅞".

For the jig to work, you'll have to size that top leg according to your router setup. This time use a ¾" outside-diameter template guide bushing with the same dovetail router bit. (The matching diameters allow the router bit to cut where the bushing rubs.) Clamp the jig on a test piece, then make a pass to create the half-dovetail profile as shown below.

Check the test piece in a socket. If the test piece is too wide, take a light table saw cut off the working edge of the jig, make another test cut and check the fit. Continue to take light passes off the jig to sneak up on the correct fit.

If your test piece is too narrow to fill the half-dovetailed slot, you'll have to remove thickness from the bottom piece of the jig, or remove and replace the top piece at a new location. Once the fit is correct – the workpiece slides into the slot without slop – the jig is ready to go.

Clamp the jig in position, then run the router bit to shape the profile on both ends of each shelf. (Use the jig and clamps to pull out any warp in your shelves.)

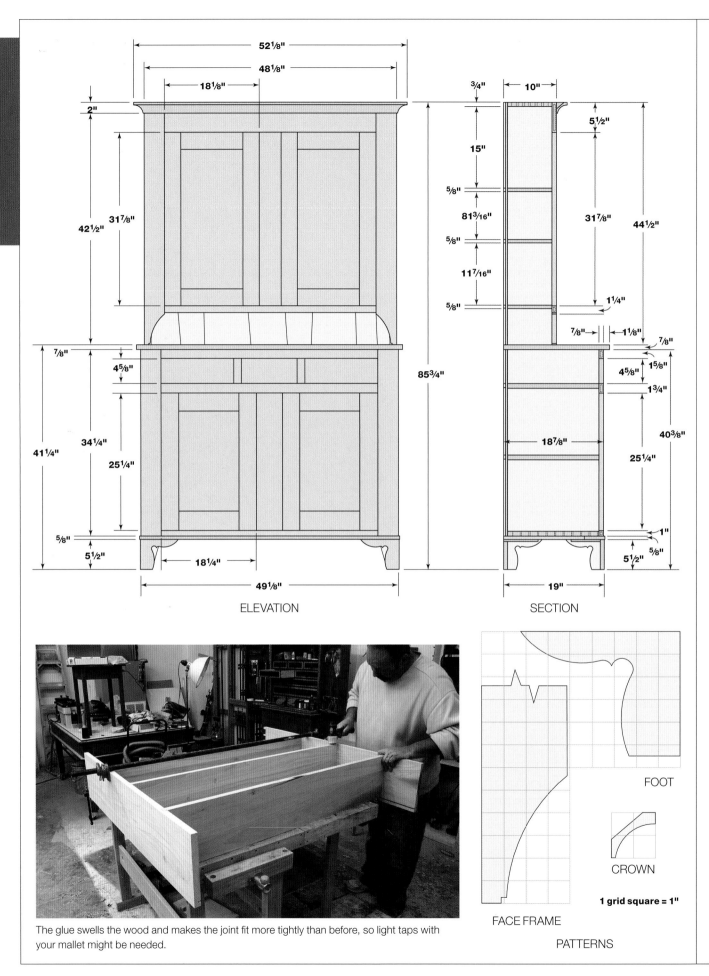

ELEVATION

SECTION

The glue swells the wood and makes the joint fit more tightly than before, so light taps with your mallet might be needed.

FOOT

CROWN

1 grid square = 1"

FACE FRAME

PATTERNS

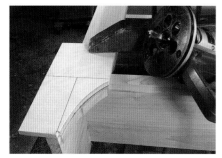

You could complete the face frame stile detail before the frame is attached to the box, but there's added stability afterward. Here, a plywood pattern ensures a perfect match.

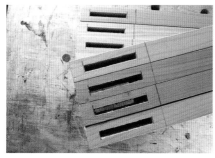

The door mortises are best accomplished by working down from both edges of the stiles. And be sure to keep the slot centered for the best results.

Because this dado cut is not a through cut, it's OK to use your fence as a stop when using the miter gauge, too.

I usually grab my Shinto rasp to fine-tune my tenon fit, but with the amount of work left to do, I found a bullnose plane did the work that much more quickly.

With #120-grit sandpaper, knock off the sharp edges around the panel area. This area is difficult to sand after the panels are in place, and the softened edges help age the cupboard's appearance.

Each shelf in the upper case receives two plate grooves on the top face (the lower section's shelf is not grooved). The grooves are 2" and 4¼" from the back edge of the shelf and extend from end to end. Use a router and a core box router bit.

Build the Boxes & Peg the Frames

Assemble the boxes by swabbing glue in the sockets (and a small amount on the shelf ends), then slide the pieces together.

After the shelves are installed, butter the dovetail pins with glue, then tap those joints together.

When the glue is dry, fit the face frames to their boxes. It's important to align the middle rail of the lower section with the drawer support. A thin bead of glue secures the frame to the boxes. Position the frames, add clamps then allow the glue to dry.

Drive square pegs into the face frames. Doing this after the glue sets provides additional strength so there is less of a chance to split the frame pieces.

To match the original cupboard, evenly space four pegs in each rail and outside stile.

Before adding the pegs, trim the stiles to the case with a flush-trim router bit with a bottom-mount bearing. The uppermost stile's peg is located behind the cove moulding. As is done on the original cupboard, don't forget to drive a couple nails into the shelves.

The detail work on the upper section face-frame stiles is router work. To create the design, make a plywood pattern of the curve – the pattern keeps the look consistent from side to side – then make the cut using a router with a pattern bit. Square the inside corner with a chisel.

Through-tenon Doors

Construction of the four doors is identical, so after you mill the parts to size, gather your stiles and mark them for ¼"-thick tenons with ½" edge shoulders.

With through-mortises, work from both edges of your stile as you mortise so you don't blow out the exit edge. Transfer your layout lines to both edges of the stiles and make sure you work within those confines.

Work past the halfway point of each mortise, then flip the stile edge for edge to clear the mortise.

Most 10" table saws have a maximum 3⅛" depth of cut. The door stiles on this piece are 3¼" in width. Because the through-mortise joinery on the doors exceeds the maximum cut, it's best to install your dado stack and sharpen your shoulder plane or bullnose plane.

Set a dado stack to its widest cut, raise the blade to just less than 5/16", position your fence to create a 3¼"-long tenon, then make the passes needed to clean away the waste.

The door's flat panels fit into a ⅜"-deep x ¼"-wide groove in the rails and stiles. Plow the grooves through the entire length of the stiles. (Doing so requires haunched tenons to fill in the small lengths of groove beyond the edge of the mortise. The haunches are formed with the dado stack as well.)

Fit each joint so the tenon fit is snug, but doesn't require a mallet to assemble.

Supplies

Horton Brasses Inc.
horton-brasses.com or 800-754-9127

4 • door catches; #SL-3, $16.00

4 • solid brass butt hinge; #PB-409, $21.50 pair

Woodcraft
woodcraft.com or 800-225-1153

3 • Shaker knobs;
  #125433, $9.99 (10 pack)

Prices correct at time of publication.

Achieving a tight top-to-bottom fit of your tenons takes time and wastes time. The holding power of the joint is the flat-grain connection – and that's not found on the edge shoulders. A small wedge can tighten up the appearance.

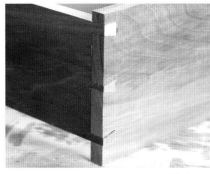

Drawer construction for the cupboard is in typical 18th-century fashion, but the drawer backs are below the sides by a ¼". Is this a boon or bust?

Small profiled pieces of wood hold the drawer guides from side-to-side movement while glue at the guide fronts and a few brads keep things tight to the dust board.

Dry-assemble the frames, then measure the openings for the panels. Measure across the opening, then add ⅝" (this builds in ⅛" of space for panel movement). Mill the four panels to size. Finish-sand the panels and knock off the sharp inside edges around the panel area before assembling the doors.

When ready, add a thin layer of glue to the tenons and in the mortises, then slip the joints together. Add clamps (keep clear of the through-tenons) and let the glue dry.

Chances are you'll have small top-to-bottom gaps in the tenon fit. If so, cut thin wedges milled to the same width as your mortise to fill them. This cleans up the look.

Fit and hang your doors.

A Drawer Build – D'oh!

I can't count the number of antique drawers I've studied, or the number of drawers I've built. I don't think I have ever seen drawers built as they are on the original White Water cupboard. The drawers use typical 18th-century construction methods, but the drawer backs are different – the backs are square at the top and bottom and are held a ¼" below the top edge of the drawer sides. At first glance, this looks odd, but there is a nice benefit to it.

The cupboard drawers are flush fitting with minimal gaps between the drawer fronts and the case. If you build with tight reveals, and the wood expands, you have stuck drawers. Drawer sides, stepped down from the fronts, allow the drawers to function, but this says "less-than-perfect craftsmanship" to me.

If you step down the drawer back in relation to the sides, you can fit the drawer front tight to the opening and slightly taper the top edge of the sides from front to back, all without any interference from the drawer back. I like it.

Build and fit your drawers. To keep the drawers traveling straight, you need drawer guides. To locate the guides, hold the drawer in position and mark along its edge.

Installation of the guides is easy. Spread glue on the first 5" of the guides (cross-grain construction precludes fully gluing the guides), place the pieces tight to the back face of the face frame, then tack each in position with brads. Also, add a couple brads near the back of the guide to keep it tight to the dust panel until the glue dries. (Don't use screws; unlike nails, they won't move with the seasons.)

Restriction of side-to-side movement is another interesting detail found on

If you flip the position of your miter gauge in the slot, you can guide one half of the foot pairing for its 45°-bevel cut. It's similar to using a panel-cutting sled.

the original cupboard. The furniture maker added small keepers cut from pieces of ½"-thick stock to both sides of each guide. Create a small bevel on the end of your board, crosscut the length to ¾", then rip pieces to width. (These are small pieces. Use a zero-clearance insert and a push stick, or cut them with a handsaw.) I couldn't tell how the pieces were attached. I used glue and tacked the pieces with a 23-gauge pin.

Swept Off Its Feet

The feet on the original are a mystery. There is no known photo showing any feet. The three-sided frame that today sits on the floor has no noticeable remnants of feet – no glue blocks or nail holes. In fact, nothing shows that feet were ever on this stepback. But the piece doesn't look right without something to stand on.

If you're a purist, skip the feet. If you look at the cupboard and think there's something missing, make the feet. Undecided? Make the feet separate and attach them with screws. If you change your mind, remove the feet.

Trace the foot pattern onto your stock, cut the profiles and sand the edges with a spindle sander. Arrange the feet into pairs. At the table saw, cut a 45° miter onto two sets of the pairs. Your miter gauge, with a short wooden fence attached, is the tool to use. Place the top of the foot (the long side) against the fence, then push the foot through the blade to bevel one half of your pair. To cut the opposing foot, reverse your miter gauge in the slot. Again, keep the top edge of the foot tight to the auxiliary fence, then push the piece through the

Make two passes with your blade set at 45° to form the slots for the splines. Add a fence extension and use a push stick to guide your foot through the blade.

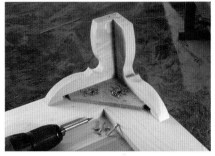

One of the easiest ways to join feet to furniture is with a plate added to the top edge of your foot pairs. Screw the plates down then add a single block at the miter for extra support.

blade while using a push stick to hold the stock tight to the tabletop and fence as shown below.

A 45° cut into a 45° angle forms a perfect slot for a spline to hold the pairs as one. Leave your table saw blade set at 45°, add an extension to your saw's fence and slide the fence into position. Make a cut into the bevel of each foot. Reposition the fence to make a second pass to increase the slot width to match a piece of ¼" plywood. Plywood is a great choice for splines because of its strength and stability.

Slip the front feet and splines together with glue. While the glue dries, dovetail the other profiled feet to the rear feet. Place the pins in the shaped feet with the tails in the rear feet.

Each foot unit receives a plate that's set in a ⅜"-deep rabbet at the top edge. Make that cut at a router table using a rabbet bit. The operation leaves a rounded corner. Square the corners or round the plates to fit. Afterward, glue and nail the plates to the feet.

The base frame's top edge is profiled with a ⅜"-roundover bit set to a ¼" depth of cut. The corners are mitered. I recommend a mitered half-lap. When complete, nail the frame to the case. The feet are then attached to the frame using screws through the top plates.

Tops, Mouldings & Backs

The lower section top is a simple plank of ¾"-thick stock. Cut a stop-rabbet on the underside of the back edge where the backboards attach. Align the top's rabbet with the grooves in both case sides.

The crown moulding is designed from

examples found on other Ohio Shaker pieces. The moulding is made using a table saw. Cut the cove while pushing the stock at an angle over the blade. (Raise the blade incrementally with each pass and make multiple passes.) The remaining cuts are made with the blade angled at 45° and the fence maneuvered to appropriate positions.

Miter the moulding at the corners and fit it in position. Use brads to attach the pieces and make sure to add glue to the short grain of the miters for a better hold.

The backboards on the original cupboard are unusual. Not only is the thickness ½" (rather than the usual ⅝"), the pieces are tongue-and-grooved

together. The joint is thin and fragile until installed.

Additionally, the upper section's back is comprised of non-rectangular pieces. It is an interesting assembly, but one that is difficult to copy without increasing the workload.

An Updated Finish

The finish schedule for the cupboard is involved, but easy to replicate. Sand the piece to #180-grit. Dye the piece with a water-based cherry aniline dye. A couple coats of 1½-pound shellac, sanded between coats with #400-grit sandpaper, allow the top coat of acrylic latex paint to be manipulated. Apply the paint, then rub through the paint at appropriate areas to simulate age. My mantra for aging paint is "less is best." Overdoing it is easy.

It's obvious that we've pulled our Shaker Cupboard back to an earlier day in its history. But the big question is: Did the detective work pay dividends? The feet are of a Shaker design and accurately scaled for this size cupboard. The moulding is in balance with the new base and the overall design is proportionally pleasing. Job done. There's no way you could walk past this cupboard without giving it a look-see.

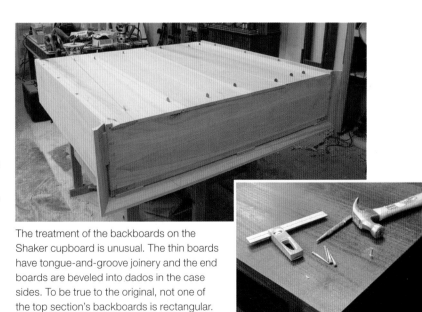

The treatment of the backboards on the Shaker cupboard is unusual. The thin boards have tongue-and-groove joinery and the end boards are beveled into dados in the case sides. To be true to the original, not one of the top section's backboards is rectangular.

It's best to attach the top after dye and shellac, but just before adding the paint to the cupboard.

The 'Wright' Counter

BY GLEN D. HUEY

If you joined the Shaker Hancock Bishopric in the early part of the 19th century, you may have had the opportunity to work with an outstanding craftsman named Grove Wright (1789-1861). Wright, along with his longtime apprentice, Thomas Damon, built the counter from which this piece was adapted.

In designing the counter, Wright chose an asymmetrical layout that differed greatly from the symmetry found outside the confines of the Shaker villages. Of particular note is the drawer arrangement. The counter front is divided into thirds. Four small drawers occupy one-third, while three wider and taller drawers fill the remaining two thirds. To my eye, this arrangement visually balances the two banks of drawers. The narrow section, busy with the four drawers, is equally weighted to that of the wider right-hand side with its three taller drawers. Also, this design, with no two drawer blades (also known as drawer dividers) meeting at the same location, allows each blade tenon to be long enough in length for added strength.

There are a couple other great attributes of this counter. Of the two known period counters, each has locks in the uppermost drawers. Locks indicate use in the Ministry – the one area in Shaker life where drawer locks were permitted.

A second feature on the original counters, and something I continued in this adaptation, are drawer sides and backs that taper from top to bottom. Tapered parts make it more difficult to execute the dovetails, but the resulting look is interesting because the narrow top edge of the drawer box catches your eye. Plus, cutting the dovetails is a fun and rewarding challenge.

Stock Up On 8/4 Material

On most post-and-frame furniture you expect the legs to be made from thicker stock. On this counter, thick stock is used for the vertical dividers and drawer blades, too.

The legs have a turned section at the foot, and stay true to Shaker design in that the turning is simple and straightforward. In fact, these legs could be shaped using hand tools. I, however, opted to use a lathe.

A simple saw cut at your layout line determines the shoulder and helps to keep it intact while turning.

Begin by marking a line around each leg at 7⁵⁄₈" up from the floor, then saw each corner prior to turning to prevent damaging the shoulders. From those shoulders down, each leg is rounded and tapered from full diameter at the top to 1¹⁄₄" at the floor.

Of the four legs, the two rear legs are mirrored in mortise layout. At the top and bottom of two adjacent square faces of each leg are ¹⁄₄"-wide x 1"-deep x 1³⁄₄"-long mortises. The two front legs have the mortises at the top and bottom, just as the rear legs do, and where the drawer blades meet the legs there are twin mortises. (When using a mortise machine, twin mortises are best created without changing your setup and simply reversing the legs in the machine.)

After the legs are mortised, create ³⁄₈"-deep grooves to accept the flat panels of the sides and back of the counter. Drop-cutting grooves using a table saw is not especially safe or easy, so use a router and ¹⁄₄" spiral-upcut bit, or a plow plane. Set a router guide fence to align your cut with the mortises, then lock it down and run the grooves from mortise to mortise.

Mill the vertical dividers to size, then add panel grooves to the back dividers. The front divider, with your layout matching the drawer blades, is mortised on the two opposite sides. Be sure to leave 1" of stock at the top and bottom for additional joinery, then mortise just as you did the front legs, reversing for the second mortise.

Joinery to attach the three vertical dividers to the top and bottom rails is unique in that a 1"-long tenon fits into

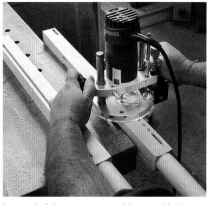

Instead of drop cuts at a table saw, it's best to use a plunge router and fence to make panel grooves.

the rails while the remaining material wraps behind the rails, except where the front divider meets the lower rail. I find it best to leave this step until the rails are complete to better fit the mortise-and-tenon joints.

Cut the rails to width and length. Lay out and mortise where the vertical dividers fit the top and bottom rails, including the center dividers on the ends. Because you have only ³⁄₄" on which to work, and it's OK if you cut through the end of your rails, make panel grooves in the rails and end dividers. Use a table saw or plane, but skip the router setup. Also, tenon all ends to fit the leg or rail mortises.

With the rails done, complete the vertical divider ends. There are a couple setups required to create your tenons. Make the cuts at your table saw, then fit each divider in position. Run through a dry-fit to make sure all your joints fit snug and correct.

Drawer blades attach to the legs with the extra holding power of the twin tenons. If you have cut the mortises as suggested, then your tenons are easily formed. As you cut one side of each tenon you can simply reverse the part in your jig to complete the tenons. If you mortised differently, you may have to make small adjustments.

Dry-fit your case front to check the fit of the tenons and make any necessary adjustments. You need to assemble the parts in a specific order. Fit the vertical divider into the top and bottom rails, then slip in the short drawer blades before you attach the left-front leg. Pull everything tight. Install the long blades into the vertical divider, then attach the right leg. With your dry-fit complete, lay out and mark the areas where the drawer runners tenon into the rails. Disassemble the front, then set up and cut a $\frac{1}{4}$" x 1" x $\frac{1}{2}$"-deep mortise at each marked location. Assemble the front a second time as you glue the joints. Clamp the assembly and set it aside as the glue dries.

Before the back of the counter is assembled, make your flat panels. These are easy. Mill your panels to $\frac{1}{2}$" in thickness, cut to the size of the openings plus $\frac{5}{8}$", then create a $\frac{3}{8}$"-wide x $\frac{1}{4}$"-deep rabbet on all four non-face edges. After

they're finish-sanded, the panels should slip snugly into the grooves. Glue the mortise-and-tenon joints but leave the panels to float freely as you assemble the case back. Allow the glue to dry before working the ends of the counter.

Assemble the end dividers to the rails and slide your panels into position. Then slip the assembly into the back unit making sure to glue only the joinery and again leave the panels free to move. Lastly, slip the front unit onto the case, add clamps and allow the glue to dry.

Get Inside the Case
The interior of the counter begins with the lower rail extension, which is set flush with the bottom rail's top edge. Cut the narrow piece to length and width, then fit the piece to your counter to locate and create the lower runner mortises. Glue the extension in place, and use a few spring clamps to hold things secure.

Drawer runners are 1$\frac{5}{8}$" wide with a $\frac{1}{4}$" x 1"-wide x $\frac{1}{2}$"-long tenon at the front. Each tenon is offset fully to one side. The opposite end of each runner is notched to fit around a leg or vertical

As the sole runner support, these dividers need strength. A screw through the back and a tenon in the rail gives the vertical dividers double the holding power.

Dry assembly is the best time to discover that your tenons are too tight – not after glue is spread and things become messy.

It's invaluable to test joinery setups using a scrap milled when your parts are milled. The twin tenons on the drawer blades can be fussy.

The 'Wright' Counter

NO.	ITEM	T	W	L	MATERIAL	COMMENTS
			DIMENSIONS (INCHES)			
4	Legs	1$\frac{3}{4}$	1$\frac{3}{4}$	32$\frac{1}{4}$	Maple	1" TBE*
4	Long rails	$\frac{3}{4}$	2$\frac{1}{4}$	44$\frac{1}{4}$	Maple	1" TBE
4	Short rails	$\frac{3}{4}$	2$\frac{1}{4}$	20$\frac{1}{2}$	Maple	1" TBE
3	Vertical dividers	1$\frac{3}{4}$	1$\frac{1}{2}$	21$\frac{1}{2}$	Maple	1" TBE
2	End dividers	$\frac{3}{4}$	1$\frac{1}{2}$	21$\frac{1}{2}$	Maple	1" Twin TBE
3	Drawer blades-short	1	1$\frac{3}{4}$	15$\frac{1}{8}$	Maple	1" Twin TBE
2	Drawer blades-long	1	1$\frac{3}{4}$	29$\frac{1}{2}$	Maple	1" Twin TBE
1	Panel-center back	$\frac{1}{2}$	13$\frac{3}{8}$	20$\frac{1}{8}$	Maple	
2	Panel-outer back	$\frac{1}{2}$	13$\frac{13}{16}$	20$\frac{1}{8}$	Maple	
4	Panels-end	$\frac{1}{2}$	9$\frac{1}{8}$	20$\frac{1}{8}$	Maple	
1	Rail extension	$\frac{3}{4}$	1	42$\frac{1}{4}$	Maple	
14	Runners	$\frac{3}{4}$	1$\frac{5}{8}$	19$\frac{7}{8}$	Pine	$\frac{1}{2}$ TOE**
14	Guides	$\frac{5}{8}$	$\frac{5}{8}$	18	Pine	
1	Top	$\frac{13}{16}$	27$\frac{7}{8}$	59	Cherry	1$\frac{1}{2}$ TBE
2	Breadboard ends	$\frac{13}{16}$	2	27$\frac{7}{8}$	Cherry	
4	Drawer fronts-short	$\frac{3}{4}$	4$\frac{3}{8}$	13$\frac{7}{8}$	Maple	
3	Drawer fronts-long	$\frac{3}{4}$	6$\frac{1}{8}$	28$\frac{1}{8}$	Maple	
10	Wooden clips	$\frac{3}{4}$	$\frac{7}{8}$	2$\frac{1}{4}$	Oak	To attach top to case
6	Pegs	$\frac{1}{4}$	$\frac{1}{4}$	1$\frac{1}{4}$	Oak	

* Tenon both ends; ** Tenon one end

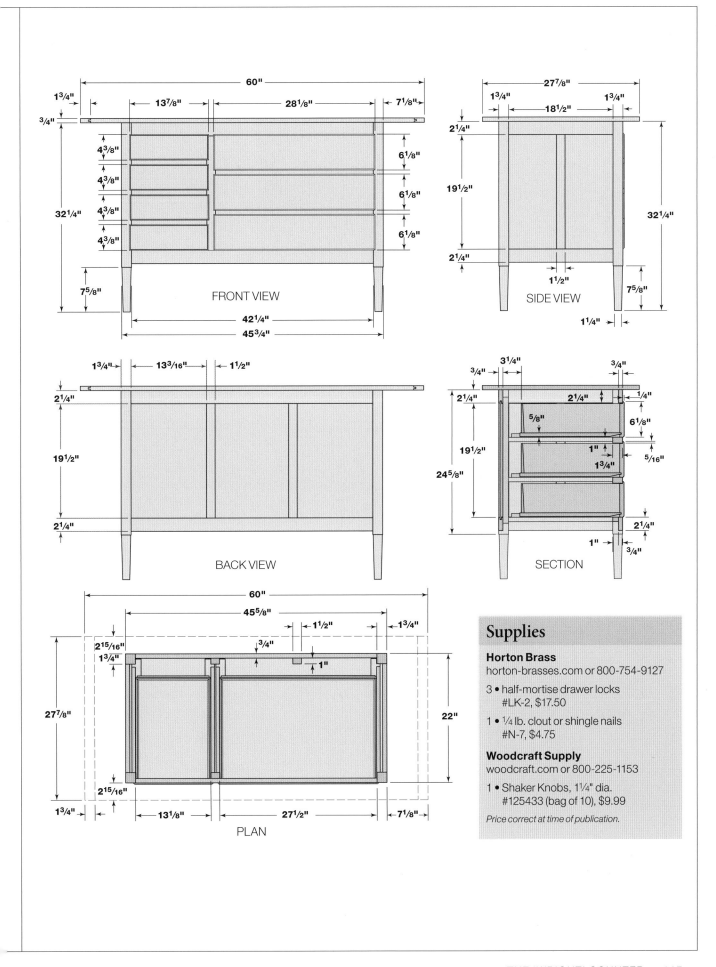

FRONT VIEW

SIDE VIEW

BACK VIEW

SECTION

PLAN

After the glue dries on the back assembly, work the panels and frame of the ends into the the back. The lighter front is easily lifted into position.

A thin bead of glue is all that's used to join the rail extension to your case. The L-shaped connection adds a lot of support across the counter's front.

divider, depending on its location. All notches are the same regardless of the runner location, so batch-cutting is OK. Make sure your notch is on the opposite edge of the tenons.

Each runner has its tenon glued into the blade mortise and a drop of glue is added at the notch before being nailed in place. The process is easy but takes time due to the fact that it is necessary to work one level at a time in order to have access to attach drawer guides. Install runners into the lowermost positions, then glue and tack in your drawer guides before moving to the next level.

The guides are 18" long, $5/8$" square stock. It's best to lay a straightedge from leg to leg (or divider to divider) to establish a line to which to set each guide. A

thin bead of glue is the holding power, but I add a few 23-gauge pins to acts as clamps as the glue sets. You could use springs clamps instead.

There is one tricky area where the lower set of runners fits on either side of the rear vertical divider. Nails driven to attach the two runners into the divider cross as they pass through the divider. Because of the counter's design, this happens only once.

More Than Just a Slab

Breadboard ends on the top are an important part of this project. The end overhang beyond the counter is substantial at 7". Without breadboards, there is a greater chance that the top would warp. Adding breadboard ends takes just a

few steps that yield great results not only structurally but aesthetically.

With your top milled to thickness, length and width, set your marking gauge for the tenon length, or $1\frac{1}{2}$". Mark the edges of the top and just onto both faces. To form a tenon at the end of my top, I use a straightedge (scrap plywood) to guide my router base. Measure the distance from the edge of the router-base to the edge of the router bit. Use that measurement from the marking gauge line to locate your straightedge. Lock the guide in position, set your depth of cut to $1/4$" then hog away the material. Repeat the steps for the bottom face of your top, then work the other end as well.

After your full-length tenons are formed, lay out for three individual ten-

Runners stretch from front to back inside the case; tenons are at the front with notches and nails at the back. Square each runner off the counter front.

Drawer guides do not need to fit tight to the back, so a steel rule or straightedge is a great way to align them. After adding a bead of glue, 23-gauge pins act as clamps.

ons evenly spaced over the width of your top. Set your first tenon in from the edge about 1". I made the tenons 3½" wide and set the middle tenon centered to the top, but these numbers can be adjusted. An important part of this joint is to incorporate a ¼"-long tenon that runs the entire length of the top. This technique builds strength and increases the likelihood that your top will stay flat.

Mill the material for your breadboard ends, then set up for and cut a ¼"-deep groove that matches the thickness of the tabletop tenon. When you achieve a snug fit, position the breadboard flush to the table's front edge and mark the location of each full tenon.

Between your layout lines, remove the waste to form each mortise. Make sure your mortises are deep enough to allow the breadboard to fit tight to the tabletop. Slip the pieces together, mark the center of each mortise-and-tenon joint, then drill a ¼" hole completely through the assembly at each mark.

Place a couple lines across the tabletop-to-breadboard joint to later help align your parts, then remove the breadboard from the tabletop – extra length on your breadboard makes this job easy. Because the tabletop experiences seasonal movement, the two outside holes need to be elongated before final assembly. With your drill bit in the hole, rock it from side to side to easily ream the hole.

Add glue to the center 8" or so on both the tabletop and breadboard, then slip the two together making sure to match your lines so the holes align. Put a drop of glue into the center hole then drive a ¼"-square wooden peg through the assembly. In the other holes, drive in a square peg and stop before setting the peg flush with your top. Add glue to the peg then drive the peg flush. The idea is to put glue only on the top ¼" of the peg. This allows the top to move freely.

After the glue sets, trim the breadboards flush with the top, round over the top and bottom edges with a ³⁄₁₆" roundover bit, then sand the top to #180-grit.

After I've completed the finish on the counter and top, I attach the top using wooden clips (also known as buttons). Slots are cut into the case, then clips are fit to the slots. Screws through the clips make the final connection.

Make Breadboard Ends

Breadboard ends not only help prevent a tabletop or other panel from cupping or warping over time, they also lend a refined look by covering the end grain and highlighting the pegged mortise-and-tenon joinery used to secure them in place.
— GH

A plywood straightedge guides my router in the first step to forming a tenon for the breadboard ends on the countertop. A 1 ½"-long tenon is the result.

The long tenons of your breadboard end hold pieces to the top, but it's the ¼" tenon that runs the width of the top that keeps things flat and level.

As you transfer tenon locations to the ends, add a little wiggle room (⅛" or less on either side). There is no need for tenons to fit tight side to side.

Holes in the outer tenons are elongated to keep pegs from splitting the top during seasonal movement.

How About Those Drawers?

Some authors of Shaker furniture books think these drawers are tapered because there was leftover clapboard siding from one of the buildings. However, because there are other furniture makers both inside and outside Shaker communities who did the same, I'm more inclined to believe that this was a technique chosen for its aesthetic effect. Of course you can make your drawers without all the tapering – but why not give it a shot?

Drawer fronts for the counter are sized to your openings plus ⅝" in length and ¼" in height. All edges are moulded with a ³⁄₁₆" thumbnail, then the top edge and both ends are rabbeted (⅜")to form lips. The bottom edge has no lip.

Other drawer parts, including the sides and backs, are milled to ½" in thickness, then cut to length and width based off your drawer fronts, drawer openings and counter depth.

After the parts are sized, it's time to make the tapered cut. Leave the parts square ⅞" from the bottom of the sides, then taper the balance leaving a ¼"-thick top edge. Set your band saw to cut between the marks, as shown in the photo below at left. Drawer backs have

Make Drawers with Tapered Sides

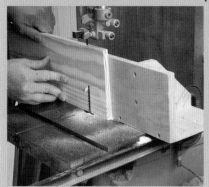

Tapered drawer sides and backs are quick work at a properly set up and tuned band saw. Tilt the table and use a fence for accurate cuts.

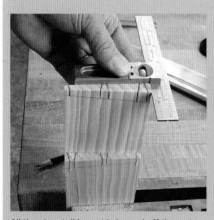

All the dovetail layout is based off the outside face of the drawer pieces. Here you see a back cut to create pins. Notice how each cut reaches layout lines transferred from the joining piece.

Half-blind dovetail pins on the drawer fronts need to be transferred to the drawer sides, but the drawer lip prevents the two from lining up. A scrap piece under the drawer side lifts it up to solve the problem.

Theories vary as to why some Shaker drawers were built using sides that taper from top to bottom. Whether they were made from leftover clapboards or purposely tapered stock, they offer refinement and enough of a challenge to make building them enjoyable.

— GH

A through-dovetail – generally the easiest dovetail joint – becomes a bit more of a challenge when both parts are tapered.

Because drawer-bottom grooves are cut on the tapered face, it's important to use a featherboard at the base of the drawer parts to hold them tight, flat and secure as you cut.

$\frac{1}{8}$" of flat surface, then are tapered to $\frac{1}{4}$" at the top. Smooth your band-sawn surface before beginning to cut dovetails.

Begin with the back-to-side dovetails. Transfer the side's profile onto your drawer back, orienting the parts correctly. Work off the squared face of the back to lay out and cut your dovetail pins. Chop away the waste.

Next, position the back to your drawer sides and transfer the pin layout – I marked all sides of each pin without bothering with a scribeline. Remove the waste to form your tails, then slip the joint together. As you complete the partial drawer box, slip the assembly into your case to check the fit.

Repeat the same steps to cut the pins and tails for the front-to-side joinery. (I found it best to elevate the drawer sides as I transferred my pin layouts to the drawer sides. The drawer lip held the pins from contacting the sides when they were flat on my bench.)

To cut the groove for the bottom panel, set up a router table with a three-wing cutter as shown at left. (Even with the flat surface on each drawer side, it's not easy to cut grooves at your table saw.) A well-placed featherboard keeps the sides tight and square to the cutter.

Glue and assemble your drawer boxes, then sand the units smooth on all faces. Bottoms are fit to the openings with beveled cuts that slide into the grooves. Nails driven through slots attach the bottoms to the drawer backs.

Locks were cut and fit into the top drawers as were small diamond-shaped holly escutcheons.

Finish Up

Of the two extant period Shaker counters, one is made from cherry and one from tiger maple. The cherry counter clearly has a cherry top. The maple counter's top appears to be well-aged pine, or it is much darker maple than that of the case. I wanted to make my top darker as well, so I decided to ebonize my cherry top.

I began with a mixture of ebony aniline dye. Not wanting to suffer the bluish cast found when using ebony dye, I remembered a product that Christopher Schwarz used to turn epoxy black: India ink. I mixed one part ink with 10 parts dye and the difference was noticeable. That's the solution I used to dye the top.

For the case, I sprayed a 50/50 mixture of Moser's golden amber maple and brown walnut aniline dye, applied boiled linseed oil to highlight the curl, then finished with several layers of shellac topped with a layer of pre-catalyzed lacquer for extra protection.

To keep from coloring the inlay, I taped around the escutcheons and sprayed a layer of lacquer from an aerosol can. When that was dry I taped off the inlay before starting the dye process. Knobs are installed after finishing is complete. Each is attached 4½" in from the drawer edge of the wider drawers, and centered in the smaller drawers. Drop a small amount of glue into the ½" holes, then drive the knob home.

One aspect of Shaker design that grabs me is the idea that you can easily mix and match pieces with other furniture in your home. Brother Wright's design and craftsmanship of this counter is classic Shaker. In fact, finished with an ebonized top, this counter, at least to my eye, takes on a contemporary look. Whether you ebonize the top or match hardwoods to your case, I'm sure it's the "Wright" counter to build.

With dovetailed drawers, an ebonized top with breadboard ends, and a tiger maple case dyed and stained to a deep amber, this Shaker design mixes easily with various styles.

3

Seating

Shaker-style Rocking Chair

BY OWEN REIN

The first thing to say about making chairs is they are hard to do. Chairs need to be strong because they get moved around a lot. There isn't always a lot of wood thickness to make the joints, and if you don't get them right, sooner or later the chair will break or fall apart. Aside from the structural demands, comfortable chairs need to conform to and support the human body in a balanced posture. Having taken care of all this, good chairs should be attractive because they stick out into a room and generally get looked at a lot.

Chairs don't design well on paper, especially post and rung chairs. The critical elements that make a well-balanced chair can't really be understood until you've sat on what you've made. For this reason I usually start my students off by suggesting that they plan on making half a dozen chairs rather than expecting to get everything right the first time. There are curves and bends that I don't even measure; I just know what feels good and where it should go. This comes only with practice.

I made my first rocking chair about 18 years ago working from measured drawings from the rocking chairs at Mt. Lebanon's Shaker community. I was not at all pleased with the way my first chair sat. So, through a process of trial and error that lasted about four years, I finally got to a point were I was well pleased.

If I haven't scared you off, and you would still like to try your hand at making a good rocking chair, I'll give you my best advice and the necessary information on how to make one of my Shaker-style rocking chairs.

Selecting the Wood

For the necessary strength in a chair, I use hardwoods with a good straight grain. White oak, hickory and sometimes ash. Maple would make a nice chair but it doesn't grow well here in Arkansas. The size of the growth rings make a difference, too. Slow growth wood is weak and brittle, and wood that grows too fast is sometimes hard to work and has a greater tendency to warp and check while drying. Because of this I don't like to use wood that has growth rings much smaller than $1/16$", or larger than $3/16$".

I always make my chair pieces from

Most woodworkers don't list a hatchet as part of their tools, but when I'm chopping out the shape for the top slat it's my best friend.

green wood and let them season before they are assembled. Along with other advantages in this process, it's important to assemble the chairs while the wood in the legs is a little green, but the spokes should be very dry. If done right the joints shrink tight and the spokes won't ever come loose. If green wood isn't convenient, dried wood can be used if properly glued.

Making the Pieces

I split out my green pieces from the log and shape them with a drawknife. If this is too rustic for you, you could use a table saw to cut pieces from milled lumber and shape the pieces on a lathe.

I start by making the back legs, starting with $1^5/8$" square by 48"-long stock, tapering the square pieces on the inside and front faces. Orient front and back on the legs so that the growth rings run side-to-side, not front-to-back. Start the taper 20" up from the bottom and end with the top at $1^1/8$" square. Then bevel the edges on the whole leg so that it is an even octagon in cross-section (this brings you halfway to being round, but still leaves you with sides).

Make the front legs about 24" long and $1^5/8$" square with the edges beveled to also form an octagonal shape.

Now prepare all the spokes. If you're working green wood, make the spokes longer than necessary and trim them to length later. The front seat spoke and the top and bottom spoke for the back need to be the thickest, about $1^1/8$" in diameter. The other seat spokes can be from 1" to

$7/8$", with the rest of the spokes finishing not less than $3/4$" in diameter. All these pieces have their long edges beveled to an octagon shape.

Care should be taken when making the two side rails for the back because they will receive a compound bend. Make these two pieces about $5/16$" x $1^1/8$" x 26". The extra length helps during bending. The growth rings should run parallel to the width (which will end up being the front and back faces of the rails). Selecting the wood for pieces that will be bent is important. The grain should be clear and straight with no small growth rings. Bevel these as octagons as well.

The jigs I use are fairly simple 2x material with blocks added to space and shape the pieces. Two sets of back rails are shown. The jigs for the back legs are even simpler.

The two back legs and the two side rails for the back are put in the bending jigs right after I make them. The green wood bends easily and I don't need to do any preparation other than follow the grain and keep the dimensions even. The back legs are placed in the bending jig so the growth rings are perpendicular to the sides. The top of the legs are bent back about 5"- 6". Use the scaled diagram to lay out and build a jig for the back side rails.

I mark the date on the pieces after they're in the jigs and set them aside for a month. Even after this time, the wood will be green enough to contract on the tenons and form a solid joint. If you use milled lumber, I would suggest steaming the pieces to be bent for about 20 minutes before putting them into the jigs.

Now turn to the other pieces. Cut the arms, the top slat and the two rockers. Again use the templates to shape the rockers and the top slat.

Making the Joints & Assembling the Frame

Start by taking the two extra thick spokes for the back (H) and taper the ends starting about 2½" from the end down until the end is a little more than ⅝" (this is done so the thick spokes will be more graceful where they meet the back legs).

Next, cut a ⅝"-round tenon on both ends of each of the other spokes. On all but one of the spokes these tenons are 1" long. The top spoke for the back panel has ¾"-long tenons to accommodate the taper in the back legs. Chamfer the ends of the tenons, bevel the shoulders and cut a "locking ring" (see photo next page) around the middle of the tenon. My favorite way of cutting these tenons is on a foot-operated reciprocating lathe.

Fitting the back together is tricky and needs to be done carefully because the joints are small and there isn't a lot of wood to work with.

First, drill ½" centered holes 4" from each end in the bottom spoke. Drill the holes as deep as you can without poking through the other side. With a ¼" mortising chisel cut out the corners and make the hole square (this is done to help keep the side rails from twisting).

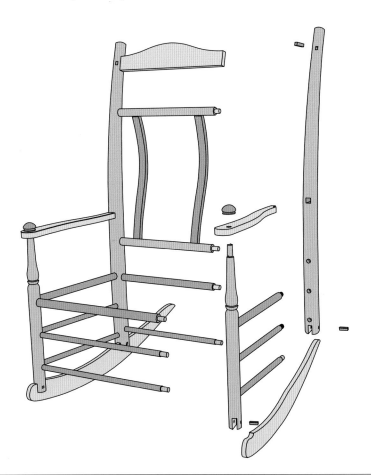

Shaker Style Rocking Chair

NO.	ITEM	T	DIMENSIONS (INCHES) W	L	MATERIAL
2	Back legs		1⅝ dia. x 48		W. Oak
2	Front legs		1⅝ dia. x 24		W. Oak
1	Seat front spoke		1⅛ dia. x 22		W. Oak
2	Seat side spokes		1 dia. x 18		W. Oak
1	Seat back spoke		1 dia. x 18		W. Oak
2	Front spokes		¾ dia. x 22		W. Oak
5	Side and rear spokes		¾ dia. x 18		W. Oak
2	Back top & bott. spokes		1⅛ dia. x 18		W. Oak
2	Back side rails	⅝	1⅛	26	W. Oak
2	Arms	¾	4	20	W. Oak
1	Top slat	⅜	3½	18	W. Oak
2	Rockers	⅝	5	34	W. Oak
2	Cookies		1¾ dia.		Walnut

Dimensions are rough-shaped sizes and include tenon

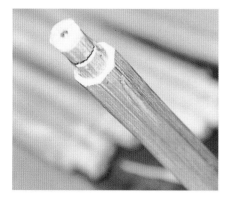

The tenon on each of the spokes includes a "locking ring." The depression cut around the circumference of the tenon allows the wood from the leg to expand into the ring as it dries, locking the tenon in place.

Take the side rails out of the bending jig. Adjust the curves to match and trim the tops if necessary. Measuring down from the tops, cut the rails to $19\frac{1}{2}$" long. Cut square tenons on the bottom end of each rail to fit the mortises cut into the bottom spoke. Mark each side rail and each mortise so that you will know which goes where.

Repeat this process with the top spoke and the top ends of the side rails, drilling the mortises in the top rail $3\frac{1}{2}$" from the ends.

After the joints are made I round off all the spokes with a half-round spoke-shave. The side rails I round off with a carving knife. With the seat spokes and the back it is important to do a good job rounding the pieces because sharp corners will cause increased wear on the weaving. I taper the spokes that go below the seat slightly towards the ends leaving small, even shoulders.

With my carving knife I flatten the sides of each round tenon perpendicular to the growth rings. When the spokes are driven into the holes drilled in the legs they are positioned so that these flats run up and down so that the round parts of the tenon exert most of the pressure towards the top and bottom of the leg, to avoid splitting the leg. Lastly, all the spokes that will be exposed are rubbed down with a handful of shavings to burnish the spokes.

Now take the two front legs and trim their bottoms flat. At this point I rough out the vase turning that goes above the seat. Mark 15" up from the bottom and cut a $\frac{1}{4}$"-deep saw cut all the way around the leg. While holding the leg in a draw-horse, I use a push knife to carve a valley about 1" wide with the saw cut at the bottom of the valley. Next, I use a draw-knife to taper the top end of the leg down to about $\frac{7}{8}$", trying to leave a pleasing "bulb" look above the valley.

Decide which leg will go on which side of the chair. Then, with the legs side by side, orient the grain so that the growth rings are at an angle to each other (not parallel or perpendicular) and the youngest growth rings are on the outside corners where the seat will be. This is done to help prevent splitting.

Measure up from the bottom $12\frac{1}{2}$" and make a mark for the top (seat) spoke. The middle spoke goes at 8" up from the bottom. The bottom spoke goes at $3\frac{1}{2}$" up from the bottom.

Cut the top off the leg about 23" up from the bottom, and for a $\frac{5}{8}$" round tenon about $1\frac{1}{2}$" long with a beveled shoulder. Chamfer the end, but don't flatten the sides.

Take the back legs out of their jig, adjust the bends to match if necessary, then trim their bottoms. On the insides of the legs measure up from the bottom and put a mark at 11" for the seat spoke. The bottom spoke goes at $3\frac{1}{8}$" up from the bottom. The bottom spoke of the back panel goes $5\frac{1}{2}$" above the seat at $16\frac{1}{2}$" up from the bottom. Don't mark for the top of the back panel. The center of the mortise for the top slat is at 42" up from the bottom. Here I chop out the 2"-long mortise for the top slat with a $\frac{1}{4}$" mortise chisel, cleaning up the sides with a 1" flat chisel. Make the mortise deep and square and straight, without going through the side of the leg.

To determine the proper drilling depth for the spokes in the legs, I use an adhesive bandage wrapped around the base of the drill bit as a depth stop. I use a drilling shelf to keep things straight, (see photo top right), though I still use my eyeballs to find the center of the leg. Drill $\frac{5}{8}$" holes as deep as you can for all the spokes. To determine where to drill for the top spoke of the back panel, assemble it without glue and snug the bottom spoke into its hole. I even drill the top spoke hole just a hair low to get a squeezing effect on the back panel assembly.

While drilling the mortises, holding the legs firmly in place is all important. I use a 6" wooden shelf where the legs are held against a back-stop by driving a wedge between the leg and a large wooden peg placed in a 1" hole drilled in the shelf. Scribing a perpendicular line on the shelf keeps the drill bit square with the leg. Keeping the drill bit level with the shelf keeps the holes in line with each other.

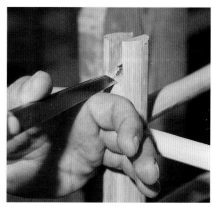

After drilling the starter hole and cutting out the waste, I clean up the rocker notch in the legs with a chisel.

When all the holes for the front and back spokes have been drilled (we haven't done anything for the side spokes yet) round off all four legs with the spoke-shave, trim the valley of the vase turning with the carving knife, then rub the legs down with wood shavings.

Shape the top slat and fashion tenons on its ends to fit the mortises chiseled in the back legs. Make sure the slat is good and smooth and that all corners are rounded.

Glue and assemble the back, taking a second to look it over for squareness. Put glue in the mortises, but not on the tenons. Likewise, glue and assemble the front and the back of the chair, making sure to keep the flats of the spoke tenons running parallel to the length of the legs. The tenons should fit tight. A heavy neoprene mallet knocks the pieces together quickly.

Now it's time to drill the holes for the side spokes. The centers for all but two of these holes are drilled $9/16"$ above the centers for the back and front spokes. The back holes for the two bottom side spokes go $9/16"$ below the bottom back spoke. I do it this way so that I'll have more wood for the rear rocker joint.

These side holes will not be at right angles to the front or rear spokes. Being that the seat is a trapezoid, the front angle will be less than 90 and the rear angle will be greater. A template of the seat makes a good drilling guide.

I drill the side holes the same way I do the front and back holes. The only difference is that this time when I put the leg on the drilling shelf, the leg on the other side is sticking up in the air in front of my face. If this is the front leg, I move it towards me 2" before securing the bottom leg. If it is the back leg I push it away from me 2".

When drilling the side holes, also drill $5/8"$ holes 1" up from the bottom of each leg for the beginning of the rocker joint. The back holes for the rocker joint need to be drilled at an angle to match the top of the rocker pattern. Drill the rocker joint holes all the way through the legs. Also, this is when to drill the holes in the back legs where the back end of the arm will go.

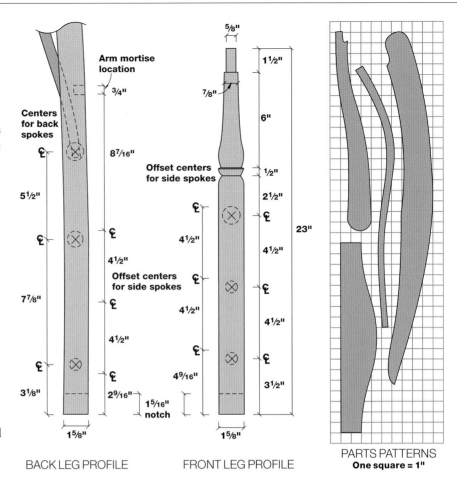

BACK LEG PROFILE   FRONT LEG PROFILE   PARTS PATTERNS
One square = 1"

Glue and assemble, and there you have the basic frame. Eye-ball the frame and if it's out of whack, you can usually improve the situation by pushing on the frame or using a rope and turn buckle.

Completing the Frame

The sides of the rocker joints are cut with a hand saw. The corners are then squared with the $1/4"$ mortising chisel, and the sides are trimmed with a carving knife. Use a scrap piece of $5/8"$ board to check the fit and alignment front to back. The fit should be snug without splitting the joint.

Next square up the mortises in the back legs for the arms with a $1/4"$ mortising chisel. This keeps the arms from twisting.

Now drill $5/16"$ holes and peg the top slat. I carve square-headed pegs out of walnut. Then cut the top of the back legs off where they look good and trim the ends with the carving knife.

Fitting the Arm

On one of the arm blanks draw the shape of the arm and cut it out. Use this arm as the pattern for the other arm. Drill a $5/8"$ hole in the front of the arm to receive the tenon on the top of the front leg. Smooth and shape the arm with a drawknife.

Fit the back tenon and bevel all

Drying Green Spokes

As mentioned earlier, using a combination of dried wood and green wood improves joint strength. While air-drying works well with the legs, to have the spokes dry enough to be captured by the shrinking green wood of the legs, they must be dried further. But it's important to dry the spokes correctly to avoid splitting, warping and checking.

In my shop, the spokes are stacked up on my counter so that each spoke will get plenty of air circulation around it. After the spokes have air dried like this for a month or more I take them home and bake them in the oven to get them "kiln" dried. With the spokes spaced out on the oven shelves I set the dial on warm (my oven door naturally stays ajar without a 2x4 against it). The oven is left on for a few hours and then turned off for a few hours. This cycle is repeated several times and sometimes I even leave the oven on overnight.

Spokes are easy to dry and there are lots of ways of doing it. In previous houses I stored the spokes in the space above the water heater and in a box on top of a gas refrigerator where I kept the air-dried spokes for a week. The key to drying spokes is to do it slowly, in stages, with lower temperatures and lots of air movement.

exposed corners of the arm with the carving knife. On the underside of the arm counter sink the hole to match the bevel on the shoulder of the front leg tenon.

Assemble the arm dry and mark the tenon at the top surface of the arm. I use a "cookie" to cap the front leg tenon. The cookies are made out of walnut and have a dome shape with a diameter of about $1\frac{3}{4}$". I rough them out on a lathe and finish them off with a carving knife. A $\frac{5}{8}$" hole is drilled in the bottom of each to fit the tenon. Check the depth of the hole in the cookie, then trim the top of the tenon if it is too long.

Remove the arm and make a saw cut to form the wedged tenon in the front leg. Make the cut perpendicular to the side spokes and cut down past the mark that you made earlier by about $\frac{1}{8}$" or so.

Now, out of some dry hardwood, make a wedge to fit this slot. Make sure it isn't too long or it'll hang up the cookie, not too thick or it may split the cookie, and not too thin or it won't spread the tenon enough to keep everything together tight.

Glue the mortises, assemble the arm with the wedge in place, then carefully drive the cookie home with the mallet. As the cookie covers the tenon it will force the wedge in place.

Scrape or whittle off any unsightly marks and put a coat of finish on the frame. I like using 100 percent Tung oil (make sure it says this on the label). It is non-toxic and can be left to soak in overnight before being rubbed down. Also this kind of finish is very easy to maintain.

Weaving the Seat

To weave the seat and back on my rocking chairs I use hickory bark or Shaker tape. I usually weave a two-twill herringbone pattern, or a variation thereof.

The procedure for weaving most materials is about the same. The warp is put on first, running front to back. The tension comes from weaving side to side so, to accommodate this, a little bit of slack needs to be cut in the warp. My general rule of thumb is when wrapping the warp, snug up each run without pulling it tight.

Also, never nail anything to the chair.

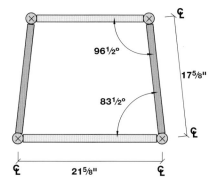

PLAN OF SEAT FRAME

Not only might you split a part of the chair, you might also split that which you want to nail to the chair. There is a much better way. Simply loop the material around the back spoke and tie it, or in the case of Shaker tape, loop it and stitch it.

When weaving the back panel, lay the warp in running top to bottom. Extra slack is needed in the warp to accommodate the curve in the back panel. Knowing how much slack to leave takes practice, and if you find that you didn't do the warp right while weaving, I wouldn't be ashamed to start over and do it again.

A few short pieces are added into the weave at the front corners of the seat to fill up the empty places left by the seat's trapezoidal shape.

Making the Rockers

Trace the rocker pattern onto a $\frac{5}{8}$" thick board trying to match the sweep of the

rocker and the sweep in the grain. Cut the rockers out with a band saw. With the two rockers held together with a vise or clamp, finish the edges with a rasp. Pay close attention to the bottom edge, running your hand back and forth along the length of the arc to make sure that there won't be any bumps in the rocker.

Bevel the corners with a carving knife and scrape the surfaces smooth. With the chair upside down, the final fitting of the rockers is done using chisels to make adjustments to the notch.

Glue the rockers in place. While the glue is setting up, cut four $\frac{3}{8}$" dowels about 2" long. I split these dowels out of scraps of straight-grain walnut. After roughing out the pieces with the carving knife, I drive them through a dowel reamer (a piece of plate steel with a wallered-out $\frac{3}{8}$" hole drilled in it) to get the exact size.

After the glue in the rocker joint is set, drill $\frac{3}{8}$" holes and glue the dowels in place. Saw the excess off.

More coats of Tung oil go on the frame of the chair, and before I call the chair done I give it one last coat of oil and wet sand the whole frame with 400 grit wet/dry sandpaper. This is the only sanding I do.

Making chairs is a lot different than making tables or cabinets. Accuracy is important in different ways. Good results don't come form a lot of fastidious measuring or planning. Good chairs are born of experience and a well-practiced system.

The arm shown with the wedge in place in the front-leg split tenon, waiting for a cookie. A finished version is shown behind.

At an early part of the weaving process, the herringbone pattern becomes evident.

Wedged-tenon Bench

BY JIM STUARD

With nothing more than wedged tenons and some good engineering, this is a phenomenally strong bench. The wedged tenons create a splayed dovetail effect that completely locks this bench together.

Begin construction by cutting out the four boards according to the Schedule of Materials. The extra length on the stretcher and legs is to accommodate a little extra length on the tenons for trimming.

After cutting and cleaning up the tenons, lay out and cut the through-mortises, which are angled to accommodate the wedged tenons. Cut the mortises to fit right over the tenons. To lay out the arc on the stretcher, drive a nail into the top of the arc at the center of the board. Then drive a nail into the starting point of both ends of the arc, as close to the edge of the board as possible. Take a strip of wood approximately $\frac{1}{8}$" x $\frac{1}{2}$" x 36" and bend it into an arc between the nails and trace a line on the stretcher. Remove the nails, cut out the arc and clean up the edge with a drawknife.

Now make the cutouts in the end panels. Lay them out according to the diagram, then cut them out with a coping saw. Make some relief cuts into the waste side to make cutting it out a little easier.

Once you have all the joinery fit, it's time to get ready to assemble the bench. This is a completely clamp-free glue up. The wedges driven into the tenons act as the "clamps" to hold the entire bench together. The wedges are cut at an angle wider than the 5° of the mortise because the wedge itself becomes compressed when driving into the tenon. This compression takes away some of the wedges' ability to spread the tenon. That's why you make wedges with a 7° taper. This yields a good spread on the tenon during assembly.

Now is the time to test a set of wedges in a joint. Using no glue, assemble a joint. Tap in a couple of wedges and see if they completely spread a joint apart before bottoming out in the tenon slot. If they leave a little room, cut a little off of the wedge's narrow end and taper it to fit the top of the slot accordingly. This gives a little more play to spread the tenon apart. Gently disassemble the dry-fit joint and proceed to glue up the bench

Glue up Your Panels. Taking some lumber from a friend's cherry tree, cut down, milled and air dried. I glued up two boards to make the top and ends for this bench. Some scraping of the joint is required after gluing. Try to arrange your boards so the joint between them is invisible.

Cutting Tenons. Cut the tenons to the actual width on the table saw. Set the blade to 1" high, defining the length of the tenons. After marking the depth with a gauge, cut the waste out from between the tenons. Set the saw to $\frac{7}{8}$" high for cutting the slots that accept the wedges used to hold the table together. See the diagram for the actual size of the outer parts of the tenon. Use a backing board on your miter gauge to hold the boards upright

and drive home the wedges with glue on them. It helps to wait a bit to clean up the squeezed-out glue. This lets it get a "skin" that keeps the mess to a minimum. Clean up with a chisel and a damp rag.

After cutting the tenon a little proud, mask off the tenon for sanding by taping around the entire tenon with two widths of masking tape. The tape keeps you from sanding a depression in the top around the tenon. Chisel and plane an angle on all four sides of the tenons and round them over with a sander. Remove the tape and sand the rest of the bench to 150 grit. Apply three coats of clear finish and rub out your finish with some steel wool and wool wax, a lubricant you can find at many woodworking stores.

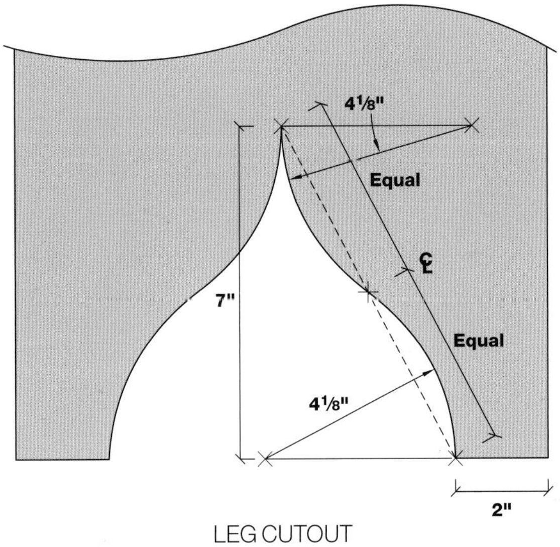

4 1/8"
Equal
℄
7"
Equal
4 1/8"
2"

LEG CUTOUT

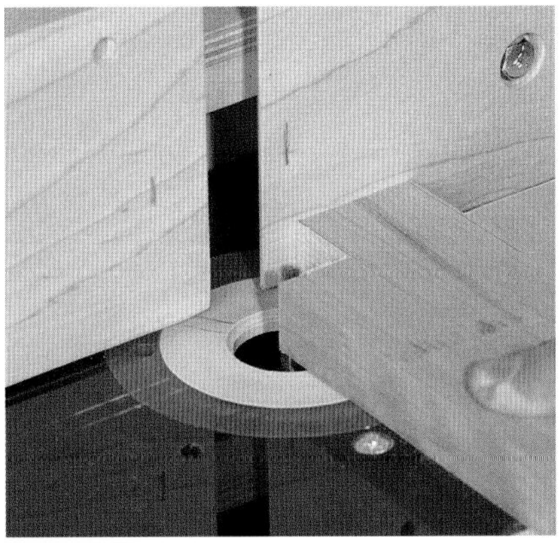

Routing a Shoulder. Next, set up the router table with a 1/4" straight bit to clean up the shoulders of the tenons. Mark on the router table fence where you need to stop and start each cut and gently push the tenon ends of the boards against the bit, missing the tenon.

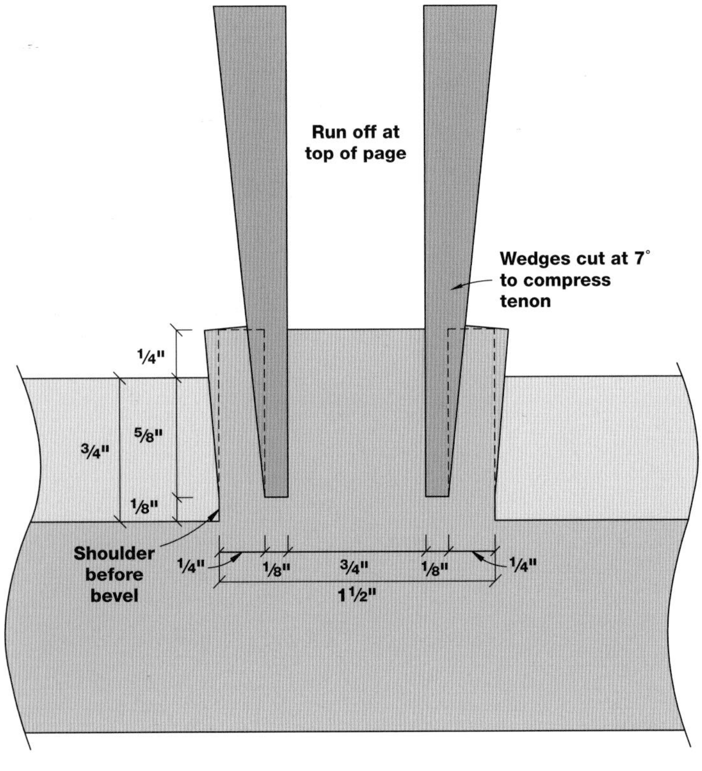

Run off at top of page
Wedges cut at 7° to compress tenon
1/4"
3/4"
5/8"
1/8"
Shoulder before bevel
1/4"
1/8"
3/4"
1/8"
1/4"
1 1/2"

WEDGE DETAIL

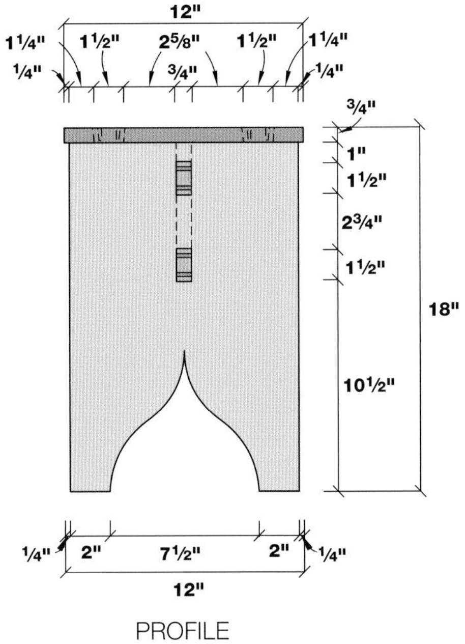

12"
1 1/4"
1 1/2"
2 5/8"
1 1/2"
1 1/4"
1/4"
3/4"
1/4"
3/4"
1"
1 1/2"
2 3/4"
1 1/2"
18"
10 1/2"
1/4"
2"
7 1/2"
2"
1/4"
12"

PROFILE

Wedged-tenon Bench

NO.	ITEM	DIMENSIONS (INCHES) T	W	L	MATERIAL
1	Top	3/4	12	36	Cherry
2	Ends*	3/4	11 1/2	18 1/4	Cherry
1	Stretcher**	3/4	6	28 1/4	Cherry
16	Wedges	3/4	1/2	3	Walnut

*1/4" added to length for trimming of tenon; **1/4" added to both ends for trimming of tenon

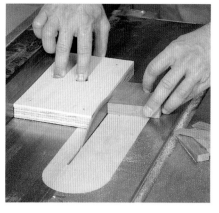

Wedges. The wedges are cut on the table saw using a simple jig (see diagram below). The stock is ¾" x 6" x 3". That means the grain direction is in the 3" dimension. Make a simple jig to hold the wedge stock while cutting on the saw.

Tapered Mortises. When you can press fit everything together, make a simple angle gauge to cut the 5° angle on the narrow widths of the mortises. The 5° angle widens the top of the mortise by about ⅛". Split this measurement and mark both sides of the mortise, with a ¹⁄₁₆" offset, for setting the angle gauge. Before chiseling the angle, take a small saw and cut the sides of the mortises to the marks, reducing tearout. Clamp the gauge in place and gently chisel out the angle on the mortise sides. The angle shouldn't go completely to the other side of the mortise. This leaves a softer bend for the tenon to make (see diagram), thereby reducing cracking – something you have to be careful about in a brittle wood such as cherry.

Trimming Tenons. When the glue is dry and cleaned up, make a template out of the cover from a steno pad. The front and back will do. Just tape them together and cut out a couple of holes for the tenons to come through. The more difficult set of tenons to reach are the ones below the top. Set your template up for those. Lay the template over the tenons and cut them flush with the template.

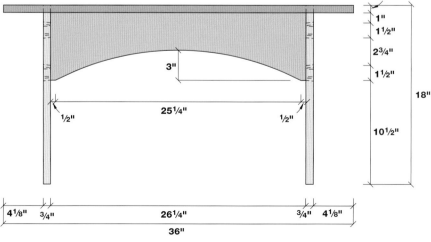

PLAN

1/4"
1¼"
1½"
2⅝"
¾"
2⅝"
1½"
1¼"
1/4"

12"

4⅛"   ¾"   26¾"   ¾"   4⅛"
36"

ELEVATION

3"
25¼"
½"   ½"

¾"
1"
1½"
2¾"
1½"
18"
10½"

4⅛"   ¾"   26¼"   ¾"   4⅛"
36"

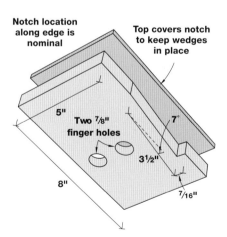

Notch location along edge is nominal

Top covers notch to keep wedges in place

5"   Two ⅞" finger holes   7°
8"   3½"
⁷⁄₁₆"

WEDGE-CUTTING JIG, SHOWN FROM BELOW

Shaker-inspired Bench

BY ROBERT W. LANG

here is an old Shaker hymn called "Simple Gifts" that begins with this line: "Tis the gift to be simple." This bench carries many of the qualities that the Shakers valued. The design is straightforward and driven by function, yet it's also graceful and elegant. The construction is obvious and building it doesn't require anything beyond simple tools and techniques.

The antique Shaker bench that inspired this piece actually led two lives. It was originally made without a back at the Hancock Shaker village. As it got older (and presumably the brothers or sisters using it also got older) wood was scabbed onto the back of the ends, and the backrest was added, making it more comfortable.

Made of pine, the original was longer – 94" –and likely was used with a dining table. I liked the look and simplicity of this piece, but I decided to make a shorter version for use in an entry hall or mud-room.

I used cherry, and happened upon a single board that was wide enough, and long enough, for the seat and the end pieces. If you're not as fortunate, you'll need to glue up stock for width, which is what I was planning to do on the way to the lumberyard.

Adapting the Design
The original seat was 1" thick, and the corbel supports were short pieces at each end. Because I would be using 3/4"-thick materials, I extended the seat supports to run all the way between the ends to brace the seat and strengthen the overall structure.

The second design change was to the ends – on the original the arched cutout that creates the legs of the bench wasn't centered on the end. Because the back was added, the cutout was pushed forward. I put the cutout at the mid-point of the ends and made it taller and elliptical.

Easy Layout, Strong Joinery
I stayed with the simple joinery of my example; a dado in the bottom of the seat to capture the ends and two more in the back rail to capture the back supports. Lap joints where the seat supports meet the ends complete the joinery.

After all the parts were cut to size, I routed the 3/4"-wide x 1/4"-deep dados in the bottom of the seat, and the back of the back rail. I made the T-square jig as shown at left to guide the router, and to locate all of the joints the same distance in from the ends.

With the dados cut, I made a test assembly of the two ends and the seat. When I prepared the stock, I planed everything to just more than 3/4". I made some final adjustments to the thickness of the ends with a hand plane to get a nice snug fit in the dados.

With these three pieces fit together, I turned them upside down on my bench. After making sure that the ends were square to the seat, I marked the seat sup-ports' locations working from the ends, as shown below left.

While I managed to avoid having to measure for the locations of the lap joints on the stretcher, I did need to measure for the depth of the cuts. Because the ends recess into the 1/4" dado in the seat, the lap joint cuts need to be 1/8" deeper than half the width of the support rails. The cuts in the rails and ends were marked at 1 7/8" using the end of my adjustable square.

Guiding Hand Tools
Like the dados in the seat, there are numerous ways to cut the lap joints. The seat supports are rather long, so I decided

This T-square jig locates the exact position of the router bit. The addition of an end stop on the bottom of the jig puts the cuts the same distance from the ends of both the seat and the back rail.

With the ends placed in the dados in the bottom of the seat, you can mark the location of the lap-joint cuts in the seat rail without measuring.

not to risk using the table saw, but cut them with a Japanese hand saw and guide-block as shown at left. With the guide block clamped on the edge of my layout lines, it was easy to keep the saw straight, and I had the long cuts made quickly.

I used a jigsaw to make the bottom cuts, but I could just as easily have used a coping saw. I used the same guide block to pare the sides of the joints with a chisel, as shown at left. I also used a rasp to fine-tune the fit. These joints are relatively easy to make, but you need to be careful – if you try to force them together, there is a good chance that the pieces could split, especially with cherry.

I like to sneak up on a good fit by testing the slots next to the adjacent slot rather than in them. If the wood should split, don't despair. You can usually glue the split pieces back together without losing any strength, or the repair ever being visible.

With the lap joints complete, I turned to the back supports. By making them as separate pieces, cutting the back taper

is very simple. I used my band saw and started the taper ¼" above the intersection with the seat, tapering to 1¾" at the top of the support. After making the cuts, remove the saw marks by running the pieces over the jointer, then cut the radius at the top of the ends with a jig saw or coping saw.

To make the ends a single piece, I simply glued the back supports to the ends. I used a butt joint, and had to be careful while clamping this up to keep everything aligned. You might want to add some biscuits to help keep the pieces in the same plane. Once the glue was dry, I cleaned up the joints with a card scraper, and I was then ready to cut the decorative curves.

I made a full-size pattern of the cutout in the ends, and the corbel at the end of the seat supports. I transferred the patterns to the pieces and then made the cuts with a jigsaw. I cleaned-up the cuts by sanding the curves with an oscillating spindle sander. Again, there are many ways to make these cuts and smooth the surfaces. A band saw or coping saw could

have made the cuts, and the curves could be smoothed with a spokeshave, a card scraper or a sanding block.

Edges with Character

I prefer to ease the sharp edges on a piece like this by hand with a block plane, and I did most of this before assembling the bench, being careful to avoid the areas in the vicinity of the joints. I could have used a router with a roundover or chamfer bit, but I enjoy the process of doing it by hand, and I like to vary the radius in different areas, adding character to the piece. With a router, I would have ended up with a sterile sameness on every edge.

The edges on the inside curves of the end cutouts were shaped with a spokeshave as shown in the photo below. After everything was put together, the edges near the joints were eased with a knife, a skew chisel and a rasp.

I did most of the sanding before assembly, sanding to #150 grit by hand with a sanding block. I avoided sanding in the areas of the joints to keep the joints from becoming sloppy. While

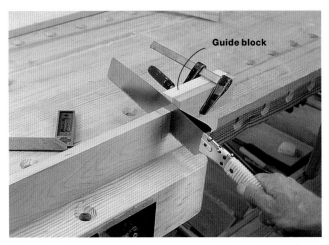

Clamp the guide block for the saw to just cover the pencil lines. By pressing the saw to the block as the cut is started, you establish a straight kerf.

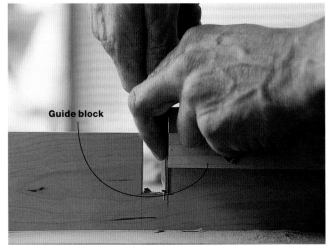

After the bottom of the joint has been cut, use the same guide block to guide the chisel to pare the sides of the joint.

Shaker-inspired Bench

NO.	ITEM	DIMENSIONS (INCHES)			MATERIAL	COMMENTS
		T	W	L		
2	Ends	¾	12¾	17½	Cherry	
2	Back supports	¾	2⅞	30	Cherry	Glue to ends after joints are cut
1	Back rail	¾	3½	54	Cherry	
2	Seat supports	¾	3½	53	Cherry	
1	Seat	¾	12¾	54	Cherry	

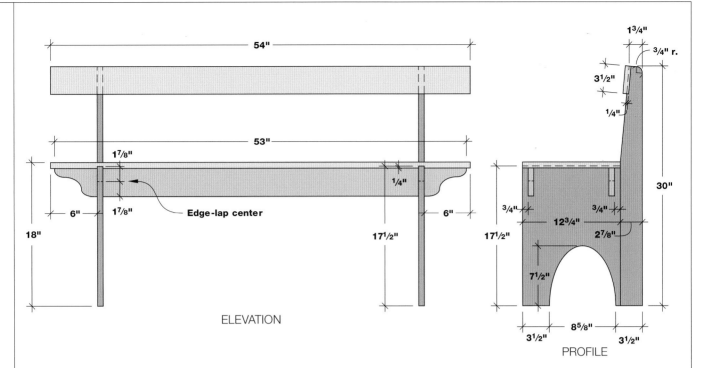

54"

1¾"

¾" r.

3½"

¼"

53"

1⅞"

¼"

30"

6" 1⅞"

Edge-lap center

6"

18"

17½"

ELEVATION

¾"   ¾"

12¾"

2⅞"

17½"

7½"

3½"   8⅝"   3½"

PROFILE

hand sanding can be tedious, it leaves a much better surface, particularly on narrow edges, than using a random-orbit or palm sander.

Because the lap joints have a good deal of mechanical strength, I didn't need to clamp them together. I did clamp a "speed square" in the corners to keep things from racking while the glue dried. After an hour, I put glue on the top of the end pieces, and the top of the support rails. Then I clamped the seat and back, and left the assembly overnight for the glue to dry.

A Bit of Insurance

In the photo of the original Shaker bench, the ends of the dowels or plugs are visible on the face of the back rail and on the front edges of the joints for the seat supports. I decided to reinforce these joints, as well as the dado in the seat, with #8 x 1¾" screws, covering the screw heads with contrasting plugs of black walnut.

Years ago I did repair work on wooden boats, and plugged screws were the way we held nearly everything together. Here are a couple of tricks from those days that speed the process considerably.

Most people cut plugs in a random pattern in a piece of scrap and then pry them out with a chisel. If you rip the scrap to roughly the outside diameter of the plug cutter, and use a fence on the

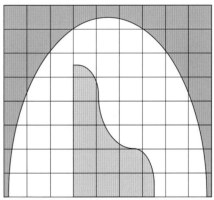

QUARTER-SIZE PATTERNS
One square = 1"

After the joints are cut and the back extension is glued on, position the paper pattern and mark the arched cutout.

The oscillating spindle sander is ideal for cleaning up the saw marks and sanding to the inside of the pencil line.

A spokeshave eases the edges the block plane couldn't reach.

drill press as shown on page 139, the plug cutter won't need to remove so much material, and it won't tend to wander.

The second benefit is that the plugs don't need to be pried loose with a chisel. Set the blade height on the table saw to 1/8" less than the strip of plugs, and set the fence so that the plugs are on the outside of the blade. Use a push stick to carefully make the cut, and you have a strip with the plugs still attached. You can easily break them off when you're ready to use them, as shown on page 139.

Flush-cutting handsaws can be used for trimming the plugs, but I prefer to use a chisel. Pay attention to which way the grain is running on the side of the plug, and make the cut with the edge of the chisel on the "downhill" side. I hold the chisel slightly above the surface, and one smack with a mallet removes most of the plug. A paring cut, pushed by hand, leaves the plug flush with the surface.

If I'm not sure which way the plug will break, I'll make the first cut higher up, so that the plug is entirely above the surface, and then make the final cut in the direction that the first cut broke, a shown below. This technique is faster than sawing, and a minimal amount of work with a scraper leaves the plug smooth and flush with the surface, as there are no saw marks to be sanded out.

A Fitting Finish

With the entire piece assembled, it was time to finish the work on the edges of the bench and to give everything a final sanding. I sanded all of the edges with #120-grit sandpaper, followed by #150. With the majority of the flat surfaces sanded to #150 grit before assembly, only some minor sanding was needed before the entire piece was hand sanded with #240-grit sandpaper.

Cherry is truly a beautiful wood, and it's my opinion that an oil finish brings out the best of its character and figure. I used a Danish oil finish, and wiped it on, working in the oil with a nylon abrasive pad, and keeping the surface wet for about 45 minutes.

After wiping the surface dry with a rag, I set the bench in the sun for a few

The lap joints should slide together with hand pressure and don't need to be clamped together. Speed squares clamped in the corners keep the assembly from racking while the glue dries.

hours, turning it every half hour and wiping off any oil that bled out. This exposure to the sun darkened the wood, giving a jump start to the patina that cherry develops as it ages.

The next morning I applied a second coat of oil, keeping the surface wet for 20 minutes before wiping it dry. I let the oil dry during a long weekend, and applied two coats of paste wax, worked in with a nylon pad and then buffed.

We tend to think that the furniture we sit on needs to be intricate in design and complicated to build. This Shaker bench proves otherwise.

Spend a little time preparing stock for plugs, and they will be easier to cut. The rabbet in the fence keeps chips from building up.

Keeping the plugs barely attached to the strip keeps them manageable. Break them off from the strip by hand.

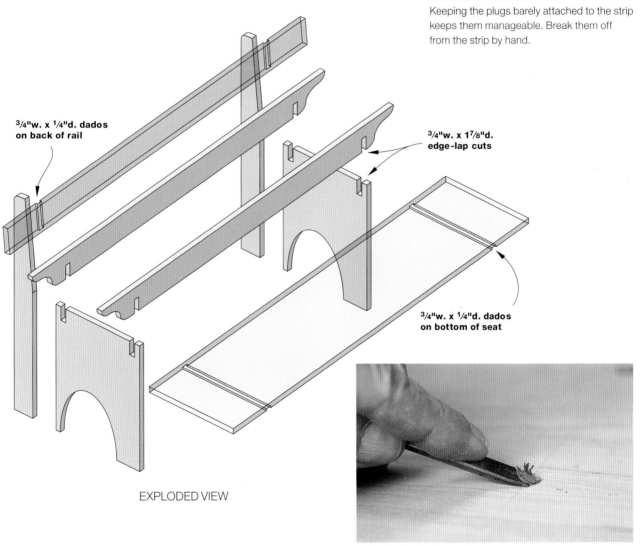

³/₄"w. x ¹/₄"d. dados on back of rail

³/₄"w. x 1⁷/₈"d. edge-lap cuts

³/₄"w. x ¹/₄"d. dados on bottom of seat

EXPLODED VIEW

It's faster to trim the plugs with a chisel than with a saw, and if you keep an eye on the grain direction they will be flush with the surface.

White Water Bench

BY CHRISTOPHER SCHWARZ

First I use a jack plane set to take a thick shaving to dress the long edges of the seat. I follow that up with a jointer plane, which straightens the edge and leaves a nicer surface. Finally, a smoothing plane prepares the edge for finishing.

Sometimes it's easier to take the tool to the work. Here I'm using a panel saw to cut the tapered shape on the end of an apron. The apron is resting on one of my two sawbenches, which are a handy workshop appliance.

The Shakers in the White Water community built these walnut benches so that visitors would have a place to sit while they observed the Shakers' worship services.

While going to a church just to watch might seem a bit odd to us moderns, I probably would be in the front row if I could travel back in time to the 1830s. Their worship services were marked by choreographed, rhythmic and practiced dances, and original and moving hymns.

Though I've never gotten to observe Shaker dancing in person, I have had the privilege of hearing their hymns reenacted on a few occasions. Many of the hymns are devoted to the daily tasks of life (such as sweeping), and are simply beautiful.

The White Water community in Hamilton County, Ohio, has one of the closed village's original benches in its possession; it's a 13'-long behemoth made from six pieces of walnut nailed together. I was permitted to measure the original and pore over its details to build two reproductions that Woodworking Magazine is donating to the Friends of White Water Shaker Village (whitewater-village.org).

The walnut for this bench was graciously donated by Dr. David Bryant, a local woodworker and turner with a band-saw mill. As a result, the bench shown in this article was built using wood that was cut about 10 miles from the original village.

We've scaled the 13'-long version down to a more home-friendly 6' long in the construction drawing. However, if you have a big family and would like a SketchUp drawing of the 13'-long version you can visit our web site and download it for free.

The original bench had tool marks that indicated it was built with hand tools using wood that had been processed (probably) by the Shakers' sawmill with a reciprocating blade (sort of like a giant jigsaw). In that spirit, I decided to use hand tools as much as possible for this project.

Processing the Stock

The original sitting bench was built using boards that were wide enough to be used without having to glue up several narrow boards into the necessary widths for the seat and the legs.

While finding walnut (or wood of any species) this wide can be a struggle these days, it's worth every effort. A seat made from a single wide board makes quite an impression on the viewer.

I roughly surfaced these boards (with some assistance) using a powered jointer and planer, then dressed them all by hand, first with a jack plane to get them flatter, and then with a jointer plane, which removed slight twists and cups. Then I ripped and crosscut the top and aprons to their final sizes.

Size and Shape the Aprons

There are several ways you could build this bench, and I have no way of knowing how the Shakers went about it originally. Here's how I decided to proceed: First I shaped the aprons, then I nailed and glued them to the underside of the seat. Then I notched the legs so they fit between the aprons and nailed them in place. If you're going to do it my way, the first step is to deal with the aprons.

Plane the aprons so they are flat and true using a jointer plane. Then mark the taper at both ends using the drawings as a guide. To cut the taper, I put each apron on my sawbenches and cut the taper with a panel saw filed with rip teeth. Then I cleaned up the sawn edge with a block plane.

Attach the Aprons to the Seat

The most critical joint in this project is the way the aprons attach to the underside of the seat. A good joint ensures the seat will stay rigid and will keep the legs in place as well. I was impressed by how tight this joint was on the original, even after 150 years or so.

To ensure this joint was tight, I took extra pains to dress the top edge of the apron so it was perfectly flat and square. Then I made sure that the apron mated with the seat without having to pull out any warping with clamps. This, by the way, is a challenge when you have 13'-long boards and an 8'-long workbench.

Then I glued the aprons to the seat. I used a modern yellow glue – our hide glue had gone missing that day. I let the glue cure overnight. Then I nailed the seat to the apron using 6d cut nails spaced every 8½", just like the original.

Once you've driven the nails, set them below the surface with a nail set. For cut nails, I use a homemade nail set made from an inexpensive punch. I filed its round tip to a rectangle, which is much more effective when setting rectangular-

It only takes a few strokes to clean up the sawn edge with a plane. Any sharp plane will do – planing downhill is always easy work.

head cut nails.

Then plane the edge of the seat and apron flush and smooth.

Shape & Notch the Legs

The legs are simple but effective. The two feet are formed by cutting a curve on the bottom edge. Then you notch out the top and nail the leg in place. To begin, lay out the curve on the bottom of the legs using a compass.

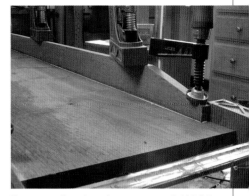

Some creative clamping ensures a tight joint. The clamp on the far right ensures that the apron will be flush to the edge of the seat at the ends. The F-style clamp keeps the tapered apron against the seat. Thank goodness for its swiveling clamping pad.

I laid out the nails using dividers (shown on the left). Then I drilled ³⁄₃₂" pilot holes and drove in the 6d nails and set them with a homemade nail set.

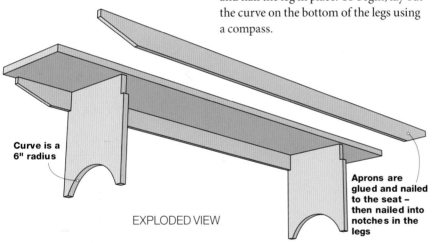

Curve is a 6" radius

EXPLODED VIEW

Aprons are glued and nailed to the seat – then nailed into notches in the legs

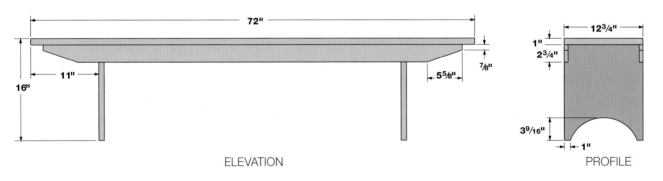

72"

16"   11"   5⅝"   ⅞"

ELEVATION

1"   2¾"   12¾"

3⁹⁄₁₆"   1"

PROFILE

White Water Bench

| NO. | PART | DIMENSIONS (INCHES) | | | MATERIAL |
		T	W	L	
1	Seat	1	12¾	72	Walnut
2	Aprons	⅝	2¾	68	Walnut
2	Legs	⅞	12¾	15	Walnut

Cut the curve using a bowsaw or some other frame saw, then fair the curve with rasps. The original craftsman stopped at this point. You can continue to refine the curve with sandpaper if you wish.

Now you can lay out the notches on the top of each leg. I think you should lay out and fit each leg individually. Don't just use the drawings to lay out your joints. Instead, place each leg where it will go on the underside of the seat/apron assembly and mark out the locations of the notches.

Then use a combination square to gauge how deep each notch should be. Again, don't trust your cutting list or the drawing. Take the measurement from the actual apron where the leg will go. This is one of the keys to tight joints in handwork.

Now saw out the notches on the top of each leg. If you have a full nest of saws, use a tenon saw to rip the long section of the notch and a carcase saw to crosscut the waste free. If you have only one saw, a crosscut carcase saw can do the whole job.

One common error is to make the notches a little too long. The result is that the bottom of the notch won't fit tight to the apron. To fix this, plane the top edge of the leg on a shooting board, which will tighten up the fit between the leg and the apron.

Now you can nail the legs in place. I clamped each leg tight to the apron and secured the leg to each apron with two 6d nails. Then I nailed the seat to the leg with five evenly spaced 6d nails. You can reinforce the legs with glue blocks.

Finishing Up

After setting all the nails, I finished up all the visible surfaces with a smoothing plane. However, the original craftsman didn't bother. The pencil lines from construction are still visible on the exterior surfaces.

Supplies

Tremont Nail

800-835-0121 or tremontnail.com
• 6d Fine Finish Standard cut nails #CE6, $11.10 for 1 lb.
Price correct at time of publication.

It's unclear what sort of finish was on the original – if it had a finish at all. The bench doesn't exhibit any evidence of a film finish, and it is water stained in some places, so I opted for a boiled linseed oil finish. Boiled linseed oil is appropriate to the period and it would become stained if exposed to water. But I hope that won't happen with this reproduction.

I applied four coats of boiled linseed oil and followed that up with wax. Then it was time to take a seat and wait for the dance to begin.

A sharp bowsaw makes quick work of this curve. The biggest challenge is keeping the blade level during the cut – the tendency is to tip the far end of the saw up. To train yourself, I recommend marking the curve on both faces of the leg and stopping every few stokes to gauge your progress.

A couple rasps make quick work of cleaning up the curve to your pencil line. Rasps are two-handed tools. Beware of your left hand. Until you build up callouses, you can cut yourself this way.

Here's the leg in place and balancing on the aprons. I'm marking the location of the notches. This is a remarkably accurate way to work.

This is fairly easy work with a backsaw and is a great way to improve your sawing skills. If the joint is too tight, you can clean up the notch with a wide paring chisel to get the leg to fit.

While some might say that 6d nails are a bit of overkill here, I don't think so. This joint keeps the legs from twisting and the bench from collapsing. So a little overkill is good.

4

Clocks &
More

Tall Clock

BY STEVE SHANESY

You'd never guess what the most inspiring aspect of building this clock was. Not the awesome curly maple or rich-looking finish, but something altogether plain – the clock's paper face.

Nice, but what's so special about it, you ask? It was hand-drawn and lettered using 100-year-old drawing instruments passed down from my great-grandfather, a draftsman, who laid out track beds for the railroads. The set, made in Manchester, England, by A. G. Thornton & Co., and lovingly stored in a velvet-and satin-lined walnut box, contains calipers, two delicately turned ivory handled inkers, and finely tooled and incredibly machined compasses.

After experimenting with these special tools I was ready to put pen to parchment. As I did so I was amazed at the tool's ability to guide the drawing tip, rendering the precise lines. In making my clock face I imagined for a brief moment looking over my great-grandfather's shoulder as he sat at his drawing board.

Using this old way of drawing was infinitely more simple to figure out than assembling the various parts that made

The bonnet, glazing compound, face, copper surround and cleats for attachment.

These are my great-grandfather's drawing instruments, which I used to hand letter the clock's face.

up the clock's works. Most parts were obvious as to their function: the works, pendulum, weights, chain, etc. But how they mounted, attached or were oriented to each other was a complete mystery. They arrived in a kit without the first hint of instruction, and left me scratching my head. Thank goodness building the clock's case was easier than figuring out the works. Easier, because I had

the help of three books referencing this famous clock made by Brother Benjamin, so determining overall dimensions was relatively easy, save for the fact none of them agreed exactly.

Lower Case

The original Shaker clock was built from poplar, but I had just enough curly maple to do the job. One board was even wide enough to make the 12"-wide front, which is where I began construction. To keep the look of a single-board front, cut the board to length then rip from each edge the "stiles" at the door opening. Next, cut out the door opening 30" up from the bottom, then 9" from the top. When done, mark the orientation of the pieces. Now glue the front together again, less the opening for the door.

Next, cut a ½" x ¾" rabbet along the inside back edge and top edge of the two side pieces. Mill the same rabbet on the top of the front piece, and on the back

These 90° clamps made gluing up the top case a lot easier. Getting things square was a real snap.

The homemade 10-minute cockbeading tool in use.

Tall Clock

NO.	ITEM	DIMENSIONS (INCHES)			MATERIAL	COMMENTS
		T	W	L		
Lower case						
1	Front	¾	12	65	Maple	
1	Door	¾	6⅞	25⅞	Maple	
2	Sides	¾	6¼	65	Maple	
1	Back	¾	11½	64¾	Plywood	
1	Top	¾	6¾	11½	Plywood	
1	Bottom	¾	5½	11½	Plywood	
Upper case						
2	Sides	¾	7½	15	Maple	
1	Back	¾	14	14¾	Maple	
1	Top	¾	7½	14	Plywood	
1	Front rail	⅜	1¼	13¾	Maple	
2	Door stiles	¾	2	14³⁄₁₆	Maple	
2	Door rails	¾	2	14⁹⁄₁₆	Maple	
1	Face panel	¼	13	12¹³⁄₁₆	Hardboard	
1	Face cover		13	12¹³⁄₁₆	Copper	
1	Buildup	¾	¾	14½	Maple	
Clockworks stand						
2	Ends	¾	2	4³⁄₁₆	Poplar	
2	Front/back	¼	4⁷⁄₁₆	5½	Plywood	
1	Top	¼	2	5½	Plywood	
1	Bottom	¼	2⅜	9	Plywood	
Mouldings						
Top chamfer: 36" of ¾" sq.						
Cove: 36" of 2⅛" sq.						
Base: 36" of ¾" x 3½"						
Base shoe: ½" x 1"						

edge of the top as well. While working on the top, also make the cutout to accommodate the swinging pendulum and the hanging chains from the works (see diagram). The front and sides are then glued up using a simple butt joint to take advantage of the long-grain to long-grain connection, while the top is glued and nailed in place. Before screwing in the back, fasten cleats to the front and sides (20" up from the bottom edge) to be used later to attach the bottom panel.

When the case is complete, make the two-part base using a $\frac{1}{2}$"-radius profile bit for the wider piece and $\frac{1}{4}$" for the smaller base shoe. Miter the front corners and cut a rabbet on the other end for the base back. The front and sides of the base sleeve over the lower case about 1" and are fastened from the inside of the case.

Upper Case

The upper case that shrouds the clock's works uses the same joints for the back and top as in the lower case. A $\frac{3}{8}$"-thick rail is haunch-tenoned and mortised into the sides at the bottom of the front to hold the sides square and in place. When glued up and still in the clamps, pin the tenons using $\frac{3}{16}$" dowel stock. After the upper case is assembled, add a filler strip to the front upper edge that's as long as the front is wide and $\frac{3}{4}$" square. This build-up accommodates the thickness of the door so that the top chamfered moulding is correctly positioned.

The upper door has a cockbead detail on its outside edge. To create the detail, take 10 minutes to make a simple scratch stock using a flat-head screw. Simply insert the screw in the end of a block that fits comfortably in your hand. Let the

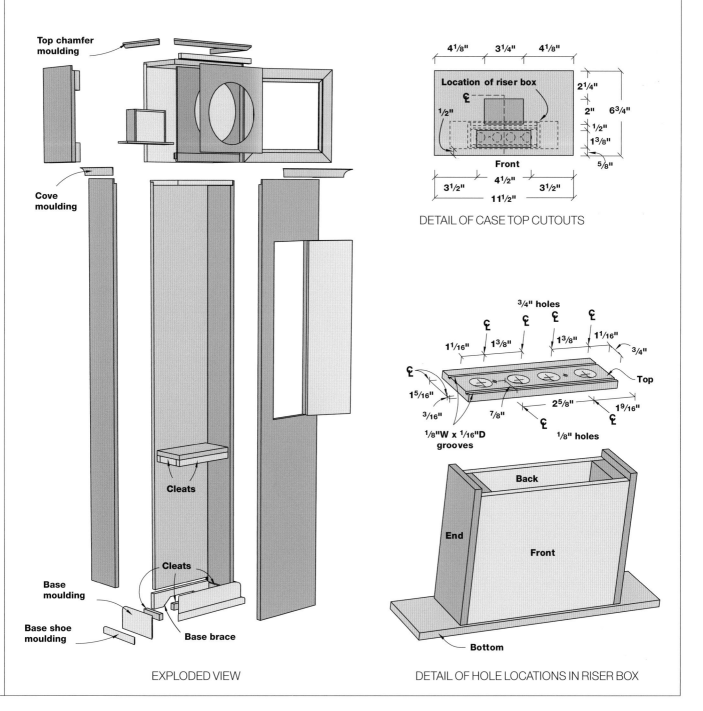

EXPLODED VIEW

DETAIL OF CASE TOP CUTOUTS

DETAIL OF HOLE LOCATIONS IN RISER BOX

Here you can see the cutouts to accommodate the swinging pendulum and the hanging chains from the works.

head project out about ¼". With a hacksaw, cut the projecting screw head in half from top to bottom. Dress the cutting edge (the face) with a file, and use a small triangular file to relieve the back.

Cut the cockbead on the milled stock for the door frame, then cut a ½"-square rabbet on the back inside edge of the stock to let in the glass. Now cut the parts to length and glue up.

Now, make the last mouldings you'll need. The chamfer at the top is easy. Run it, miter the corners and judiciously nail it in place. I used only a dab of polyurethane glue at the center of the moulding because its grain runs contrary to that of the sides.

The cove moulding is more difficult to produce and is made from a triangular-shaped length of wood using the table saw. By clamping an auxiliary fence at a severe, oblique angle to the blade, the part is then run with the blade just above the table, raising it slightly after each pass. Thank goodness only about three linear feet are required because this method requires a lot of sanding to remove the mill marks from the blade. When finished sanding, cut the miters and attach it just like the chamfer moulding.

You may be wondering how the top case attaches to the lower. It doesn't. It simply rests on top and lifts off to access the works (after removing the hands).

Clock Face

I used the clock face from the clock works package as a guide to lay out my paper face. Construction need not change if you use the painted aluminum face in the kit. In either case, fix the clock face to ¼" tempered hardboard using spray adhesive. Then drill a ⁵⁄₁₆" hole in the center of the face.

I'm sure Brother Youngs did not use copper sheet metal to surround the face outside the clock face proper, but I did. I made the round cutout using a router mounted on a circle-cutting jig. It's a

very simple process. When done, I used a random-orbit sander and 220-grit paper to put a satin-like sheen on the copper, followed by a coat of shellac to retard tarnishing. The hardboard and copper are mounted inside the upper case on cleats positioned to coincide with the mounting location of the works (see diagram).

The last bit of building is the small box on which the works sit. Its height is especially critical because that determines the height at which the stem protrudes through the hole in the face. Make the box using ¾"-solid poplar sides and ¼" Baltic birch top and bottom. Note that the bottom is wider and longer. Use the extra length to screw it down. Follow the diagram to position the holes in the top of the box where the chains run through.

Before the upper door can be hung, install the glass. I used glass from stock I salvaged from old houses. This old material has imperfections in the thickness which cause ever-so-slight distortions and adds to the authentic look of the piece. Regardless of the glass you use, install it using glazing points and glazing compound.

Now the upper door is ready to hang. The hinges in the clock kit don't require mortising so attach them directly. The lower door is the same. However, before hanging the door, run a ¼"-radius profile on the outside edges. Then attach the hinges to allow it to set ¼" proud of the

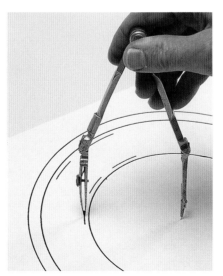 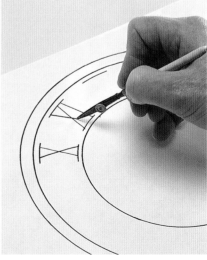

It's simple work to ink the lines for the paper face. After you make the three circles, use a compass to ink the top and bottom of the Roman numerals (right). Then ink the straight lines to fill in the numerals. It's not calligraphy, so you don't have to worry about curving lines far right).

Supplies

Klockit
800-556-2548 or klockit.com

1 • Hermle movement, multiple options,
select preference
#1161-853

casc.

It goes without saying that I was just itching to set up the works and check everything out. It's a good idea to do this before sanding and finishing anyway. Set it up and let it run overnight.

Final Touches

Thoroughly sand all the surfaces starting with 100 grit and progress up to 180 using a random-orbit sander. Break all the edges by hand with 120 grit. After removing the dust, color the wood using water-based aniline dye called Golden Amber Maple made by J.E. Moser (available through Woodworker's Supply, 800-645-9292 or woodworker.com). Because the water raises the grain, very carefully and lightly hand sand the flat surfaces with 360-grit paper. Be extremely cautious near edges. Don't sand through the color. Dust again, then apply a light coat of boiled linseed oil. As a penetrating finish, this step plays an important factor in making the curly figure on the wood pop. When done, rub down with a clean rag to remove any excess oil. Wait 24 hours to allow the oil to dry, then brush on four coats of amber shellac in a two-pound cut. Lightly sand between coats.

The unusual experiences of learning how to set up a mechanical-works clock along with creating the clock face from my heirloom drawing set added a new dimension to the satisfaction I always find at the conclusion of a project. I felt in touch with a distant branch of my family tree, rather than merely reproducing an artifact from the past. Some day, should my tall clock find its way into one of my children's homes, I hope my name, scrawled on the clock face, will imbue a similar sentiment.

Horology 101

I didn't know what "horology" meant when I received the big box full of clock parts for this project. Fortunately, I had a dictionary, so I quickly learned it means "the art of making time pieces." Too bad there wasn't a reference for identifying and assembling the clock parts. I'm still a long way from being an expert, but for this project at least, I think I can talk you through.

The "works" are the gears and movements that are sandwiched between a front and back plate. The works for this project are made by Hermle (see Supplies box). They are weight-driven, require resetting the chains every eight days, strike a bell once on the half hour and ring the hour with the number of rings for the hour struck.

The works have the stem for the hands facing front, of course, and the pendulum faces rear. The pendulum attaches to the works with a narrow, metal part called a leader.

The works require two weights suspended on two chains. One weight drives the time-keeping job of the works, the other provides the energy to make the chimes work. The weights use equal lengths of chain and so are reset at the same time.

When facing the works, the chains go over the sprockets with the weights on the outside of each sprocket. (When you set the chains on the sprockets make sure they are not twisted and are seated properly.) The weights are attached to the chains with an "S" hook.

Each lead weight goes inside a brass tube called a shell. Each tube has two end caps with holes where a rod with threaded ends go through, which keeps the whole thing together, with a nut on the bottom and hook on the top.

The hands of the clock fit on the stem, which consists of two parts, one inside the other. The hour hand goes on first and sleeves over the outside part of the stem. It is a tight press fit slipped on in the appropriate direction of the given hour. The minute hand, on the other hand (sorry!), has a square bushing and sleeves onto the inner part of the stem. It must be adjusted by turning the bushing that's pressed into the hand. A decorative brass nut holds the minute hand in place.

The pendulum helps regulate the speed of the clock. If it's running fast, you

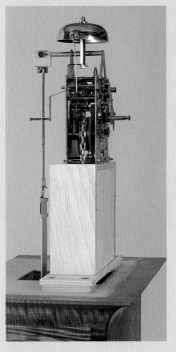

adjust the brass-colored circle down, making the travel of the swing longer. Moving it up shortens the travel, making the clock faster if it's running slow.

The beat of the clock – that's the rhythm of the tick/tock sound, is also important. Like your heart, it wants to be regular. Tap your finger to each tick/tock sound. The time between taps should be equal. Adjust the beat by moving the escapement ever so slightly. The escapement is the "C" shaped metal part in the center upper back of the works. It regulates the gear that's connected by a rod to the top of the leader from which the pendulum hangs.

The works are attached to the top of the box on which it mounts using two long, thin machine screws. They thread into tapped holes in the lower bars, which hold the front and back metal plates of the works together.

The works are mounted to a plywood box that rests on the lower case.

Isaac Youngs' Wall Clock

BY CHRISTOPHER SCHWARZ

It's difficult to open a book about Shaker furniture or to page through a woodworking catalog without coming face to face with a clock similar to this one. It seems that nearly every woodworking magazine and catalog has published plans for a clock with Isaac Newton Youngs' name on it.

So what possessed us to do the same thing?

Well, the goal of this project was to create a version of Youngs' clock that looked very much like the classic original but was built with joinery that a beginner would be comfortable with.

As I began drawing up our plans, I made an interesting discovery. Other plans for this clock that I consulted didn't look exactly like the original 1840 wall clock at the Hancock Shaker Village in Pittsfield, Mass. Many of these other plans made slight alterations to the size of the clock's case or the visual weight of the doors' rails and stiles.

In a few instances, these changes looked good. In others, however, it seemed that the designer – in seeking to make the project easier to build – made the clock a little chunky or squat. So John Hutchinson, Popular Woodworking's project illustrator, scanned in a photo of the original clock and scaled the parts using his computer-aided design software.

Suddenly the clock got a little taller, a little skinnier and the top door's stiles became narrower. After we "built" the project with CAD and compared it to the original, we knew we were on the right track.

Of course, we did make changes, but they are mostly invisible to the naked eye. To make the clock easy to build, the case is joined using rabbets and dados. The back piece is plywood, instead of solid wood. And the moulding on the top and bottom is a bead instead of a roundover. All the changes can easily be undone for those seeking Shaker purity.

Finding Rift-sawn Wood
Youngs built his original using mostly rift-sawn butternut. All of the grain in that clock is arrow-straight without any of the arching cathedrals that are common to this somewhat-uncommon wood.

To reproduce that look I sorted through a 4'-high stack of butternut at the lumberyard but came up empty-handed. Rift-sawn butternut, according to the guys at the lumberyard, is hard to come by. So I went with Plan B: rift-sawn red oak, which is plentiful and inexpensive.

Three things are important when choosing wood for this project: Pick boards where the grain is dead straight, the growth rings are close together and the grain is rift-sawn – not flat-sawn or quartersawn. Flat-sawn oak exhibits the cathedrals you see on every red oak kitchen cabinet in every suburban subdivision. Quartersawn oak shows off the medullary rays of the wood as shiny bits of what we call "ray flake." (Ray flake isn't desirable on a Shaker piece.) Rift-sawn oak generally has tight grain lines but no cathedrals or ray flake.

How do you find rift-sawn wood? Some lumberyards sort the wood for you. But if they don't, you can pick out the rift-sawn stuff by looking at the end grain. In rift-sawn wood, the growth rings intersect the face of the board at an angle between 30° and 60°. If the angle is less than 30°, the board is flat-sawn. If it's more than 60°, the board is quartersawn. Look over a few boards with this in mind and the difference will be obvious.

I bought 50 board feet of 4/4 red oak for this project. While that's more than I needed, it ensured that I would be able to choose the wood for the rails, stiles and panel with extra care. (If you can't find rift-sawn oak, call Paxton Woodcrafters' Store at 800-325-9800; they can ship it to you via UPS at a fair price.)

As you joint and plane your wood to its final thickness, set aside the straightest, tightest-grained boards for the rails, stiles and panel. Not only will these "look right," they will be more stable and less likely to twist out of shape during machining.

The Clock's Carcase
Here's how the basic skeleton of the clock goes together: The interior top and bottom pieces are secured in shallow rabbets in the side pieces. The $1/2$"-thick divider that separates the doors rests in dados in the side pieces. The back fits in a rabbet cut in the sides. The exterior top and bottom are merely glued to the top and bottom of the assembled case.

It's a bit of a trick to cut notches in the divider so that its front edge runs the entire width of the case. And you'll employ that same trick to notch the exterior top piece around the half-round hanger piece. But it's simple stuff.

Once you've cut the parts for the carcase to the sizes shown in the cutting list, the first step is to cut the $1/4$"-deep x $3/4$"-wide rabbets on the ends of both side pieces. I like to perform this operation with a dado stack set in my table saw. As you can see in the photo at left, I've added a "sacrificial" wooden fence and a featherboard to my saw's rip fence. This setup allows me to cut right up against the rip fence without leaving a little waste piece on the end of the board. The featherboard keeps the work pressed to the saw's table.

To make the cut, place a side piece against the miter gauge with the end of the board touching the sacrificial fence. Move the work forward into the cut and

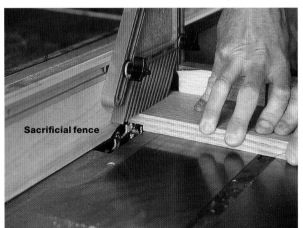

Sacrificial fence

With the sacrificial fence in place, this setup will allow you to cut the rabbet in one pass. This eliminates the need for multiple saw setups and you don't need to stand your work on edge to make the cut.

Don't change your saw's setup any more than you have to. By shifting the rip fence ¼", you can make the rabbets that hold the back piece by running the sides on edge.

A standoff block clamped to the fence as shown allows you to use the rip fence and miter gauge in tandem and reduces the chance of a nasty kickback.

keep firm downward pressure on the piece. Check your work with a dial caliper to make sure the height of the blades is correct. When you're satisfied, cut this rabbet on both ends of both side pieces.

To complete the joinery necessary on the side pieces, cut the ¼"-deep x ½"-wide rabbets on the sides that will hold the back. To cut this joint, keep the height of your dado stack the same that you had for your first cut. But shift the rip fence so that you expose only ½" of the dado stack's cutters. Then cut the

rabbets on the side with the parts run on edge as shown in the photo above.

Finally, cut the ¼"-deep x ½"-wide dado in the side pieces for the divider. Leave the height of the dado stack alone. In fact, lock the arbor of the saw in place. Then remove the dado stack and put enough chippers and wings on the arbor to make a ½"-wide cut. Also, remove the sacrificial fence from your rip fence.

Clamp a 1"-wide "standoff" block to your table saw's rip fence in the location shown in the photo below. Set your

rip fence at the 12" mark – this will put exactly 11" of space between your standoff block and the dado stack. That's right where you want the divider to be. Put a side piece against your miter gauge and against the standoff block. Cut the dado in the side piece and repeat the procedure for the other side. The joinery for your sides is now complete.

Tricky Notches
As you look at the cutting list for this project, you might notice that the divider

Isaac Youngs' Wall clock

NO.	ITEM	T	DIMENSIONS (INCHES) W	L	COMMENTS
Carcase					
2	Sides	¾	3½	31½	
2	Interior top & bottom	¾	3¼	9½	
1	Divider	½	4½*	10½	Notched
1	Back	½	10	31½	
1	Hanger	¾	5	3	
2	Exterior top & bottom	½	5**	11½	
1	Dial	½	9	10¼	
2	Cleats	¾	¾	10¼	
Upper Door					
2	Rails	¾	1¼	9½	½" TBE
2	Stiles	¾	1	11½	Includes ¼" horns
	Glazing moulding	⅜	½	48	
Lower Door					
2	Rails	¾	1¼	9	½" TBE
2	Stiles	¾	1¼	20½	Includes ¼" horns
1	Panel	½	8¾	18⅜	

* Finished size after machining will be 4¼"; ** Finished size after machining will be 4¾"; TBE = tenons both ends

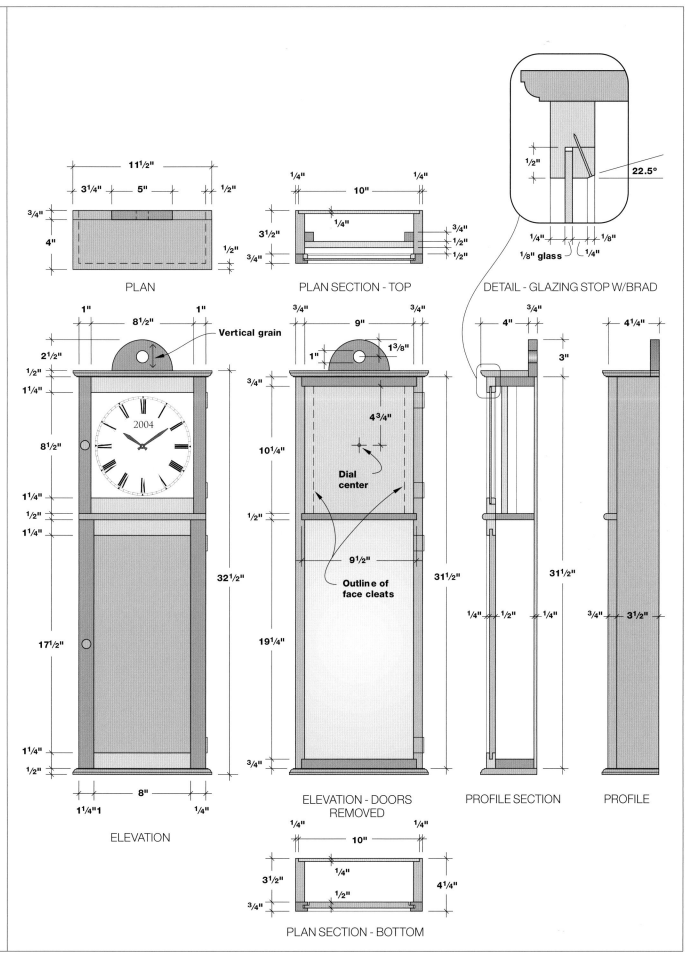

PLAN

PLAN SECTION - TOP

DETAIL - GLAZING STOP W/BRAD

1/8" glass

22.5°

Vertical grain

2004

Dial
center

Outline of
face cleats

Dial center

ELEVATION

ELEVATION - DOORS
REMOVED

PLAN SECTION - BOTTOM

PROFILE SECTION

PROFILE

is longer than the interior top and bottom pieces. It also runs the entire width of the clock's case and stands proud of the doors when they're closed. To make the divider do this, you need to notch the ends so they fit inside the dados and the front rounded-over edge then extends to the edges of the carcase.

This is actually easy. Here's the trick: First rout the 1/4"-radius roundover on a long edge of the divider, as shown in the drawing at right. Next, using your table saw, rip 1" of this detailed edge off of the divider. Crosscut the remaining piece to 9 1/2" long – the same length as the interior top and bottom pieces. Now glue the 1"-wide strip back to the divider.

If you do it this way you will have perfect notches on both ends and the grain will match all the way across the width of the board. (You'll use this same trick to

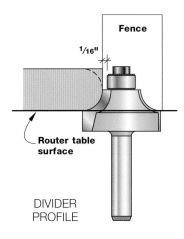

DIVIDER PROFILE

You could wait until the carcase is assembled to glue the detail back in place, but I find that you can get a tighter joint if you do this before the case is glued up. If your joint is smooth, you should be able to use painter's tape to position the detail to the remainder of the divider before clamping.

notch the exterior top around the hanger piece.)

Before you assemble the carcase, plane or sand the interior surfaces so they are ready to finish. If you are using sandpaper, sand up to #220-grit. Then perform a dry run without glue to make sure you have the clamps you need and your joints close tightly.

When you're satisfied, spread a thin film of glue in the rabbets and dados and put the interior top, bottom and divider in place. Clamp the second side in place and ensure all the parts of the carcase are flush at front and back.

Compare the diagonal measurements of the clamped-up case to ensure it's square and wait for at least 30 minutes for the glue to dry. Then take the case out of the clamps and secure the joints with nails. (Tip: If you drive the nails in at slightly different angles, you'll wedge the parts together.)

Adding the Top and Bottom

The exterior top and bottom pieces are merely glued to the completed carcase. But before you can do this, you need to do some machining to add the beaded detail on three edges and create a notch in the exterior top piece for the half-round hanger.

Begin by ripping a 3/2"-wide strip off the back edge of your exterior top piece. Take this narrow strip and crosscut 3 1/4" off each end. Now you can tape and glue these pieces back to the exterior top piece to create a notch in the center for the

hanger.

Next you can rout the beaded detail on the ends and front edge of the exterior top and bottom. Use the illustration below to set up your router table. First rout the bead on the ends and use a back-up block behind your work to control tear-out and add stability to this machining operation.

Once the ends are routed, cut the same detail on the front edge of both pieces. Before you attach these pieces, plane or sand the exterior of your carcase so it's ready for finishing.

With that done, you want to fit the exterior top and bottom pieces. These must fit tightly to the case, so it pays to clamp them in place without glue first. Note where any gaps are, then remove material with a block plane from any area that won't ever show to get the pieces to mate tightly. Don't rely on clamping pressure to close up gaps – you should be able to get a tight fit using hand pressure only.

I've found that the best way to attach each piece is to lay it on your bench, then spread a thin film of glue on the mating surface of the carcase and put the carcase in place. Before you clamp the two parts together, secure the pieces with a couple of nails.

Last Carcase Details

Cut the 5"-diameter half-round hanger to shape on your band saw and bore the 1" hole that's 1 3/8" from the top edge of the hanger. First glue it in place in the notch in the exterior top piece and secure it with screws through the back of the hanger.

To hold the dial in position, you need to nail in two 3/4" x 3/4" cleats in the top section of the case. When you position them, be sure to allow for the thickness of the dial (1/2" in this case), and the length of the stem of your clock's movement. Otherwise, the top door won't close.

Then cut the dial to fit the opening in the top and attach your movement to the rear. When you drill the hole for the stem of the movement, note that it is not in the center of the dial board. To center it in the upper door, you need to drill this hole 7/16" up from the centerpoint of the board.

I used a quartz movement to keep the clock simple and inexpensive. A

Using a folding rule – I like the ones where you can extend a 6"-long "finger" from the end – compare the diagonal measurements you make from corner to corner. If they're the same, your case is square. If not, place a clamp across the two corners that produced the longer measurement and apply a small amount of clamping pressure until the two measurements are identical.

mechanical movement with a pendulum is another option. If you choose this, be aware you'll have to cut a clearance hole for the pendulum in the divider.

You can download a file from our web site (search for August 2004 Magazine Extras) for the face of the clock if you want it to look like the one featured here. Otherwise, you can find 8" faces at a variety of supply houses or web sites.

Affix the paper face to the dial using a spray adhesive (I use 3M's Super 77 Multipurpose Spray Adhesive) and screw the dial to the cleats using four brass screws. Cut the plywood back to size, prepare it for finishing and screw it to the back of the case.

Building the Doors

Because the stiles and rails of these doors are narrow, there are some useful tricks to machining and assembling them.

The first trick is to cut the rabbets for the top door on wider pieces, then rip the rails and stiles free from these wider boards. This makes cutting the rabbets a much safer operation.

Second, I like to cut all my rails and stiles 1/16" wider than called for in the cutting list. Then I like to cut my stiles 1/2" longer than the finished size of the door. All this creates a door that is slightly oversized for its opening so that I can then trim the door to be square and perfectly sized after it's glued up. It takes a bit more time, but it saves frustration when doing the final fitting.

When you glue the strips onto the exterior top piece, tape them in place so they don't slide around as you add clamping pressure.

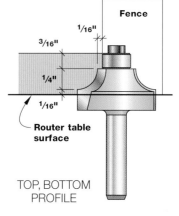

Fence

1/16"

3/16"

1/4"

1/16"

Router table surface

TOP, BOTTOM PROFILE

Begin by working on the upper door. Set up a dado stack set and sacrificial fence for your table saw much like you did to cut the rabbets for the carcase. Set the height of the blade and the position of your rip fence to make a 1/2" x 1/2" cut. After confirming your setup is correct, cut this rabbet on the inside edge of the rails and stiles for the upper door.

Before you switch over to your rip blade to cut the rails and stiles free of their wider boards, it's a good idea to go ahead and cut the rabbet on the ends of the rails. These end rabbets create the lap joint that joins the rails and stiles together for the upper door (see the illustration at right). This lap joint, when properly executed, is satisfactory for a small door. To cut this joint on the ends of the rail pieces, leave the saw's rip fence as it is and lower the sawblade so it makes a 1/4"-deep cut. Then make the cuts on the ends of the rail boards.

Set these boards aside for a moment and get your rails and panel for your lower door. This saw setup is exactly what you need to cut the stub tenons on the ends of the rails for the lower door and the rabbet on the backside of the panel so it will fit in the door's groove. Cut this joint on both faces of your lower rails. Then cut this rabbet on all four edges of your panel stock.

Finally, install a rip blade in your table saw and rip the rails and stiles of the upper door free to their final width plus $\frac{1}{16}$".

To complete the joinery on the lower door, you need to plow a $\frac{1}{4}$"-wide x $\frac{1}{2}$"-deep groove in the rails and stiles for the panel and for the stub tenons on the rails.

Keep the rip blade in your saw and set the fence $\frac{1}{4}$" away from the blade and set the height to $\frac{1}{2}$". Now plow the groove in two passes. The first pass has one face of the board against the fence; the second pass has the other face against the fence. Cutting the groove in two passes ensures it will be centered on the edge.

Next, prepare all your door parts for finishing. Don't worry about cleaning up the outside edges of the rails and stiles because they'll be trimmed after assembly. Clamping the upper door is a bit

trickier than most doors because of the lap joinery. First clamp the stiles against the rails like you would a traditional door. Don't forget to position the rails to accommodate the $\frac{1}{4}$"-long horns on the ends and don't use a lot of clamping pressure. Clamp each of the joints with a bar clamp positioned like you would compress a sandwich, as shown below right.

The lower door is easier to assemble. Paint glue in the grooves where the stub tenons will go (but not the panel), assemble the parts and clamp things up. Allow the glue to dry and remove the doors from the clamps.

Fitting & Fussing

Now it's time for the detail work. Your goal is to trim the doors so they fit on the carcase with a $\frac{1}{16}$"-wide gap between the doors and the carcase. This gap, called the "reveal," must be consistent. If it's not, other woodworkers will quickly notice.

Here's how I trim my doors, though there are many ways to do it: First true one stile on your jointer and rip the door to width, taking equal amounts of material from each stile. Then crosscut the door so it's just a hair longer than necessary. Finally, after installing the hinges, plane the top and bottom of the door to get that perfect $\frac{1}{16}$"-wide reveal.

The hinges are a snap to install because they require no mortise. If you

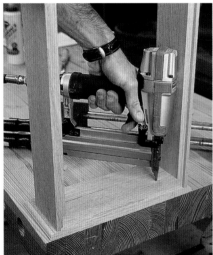
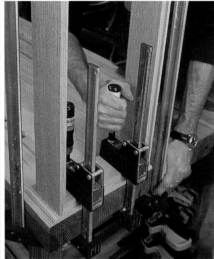

Whenever you can, use your bench to assist your clamping. It helps spread your clamping pressure over a wider area. Here you can see how a couple of well-placed nails keep everything in line as I apply the clamps.

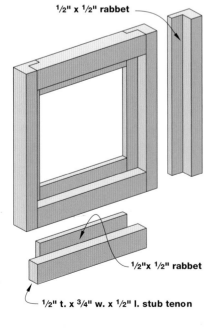

½" x ½" rabbet

½" x ½" rabbet

½" t. x ¾" w. x ½" l. stub tenon

UPPER DOOR JOINERY

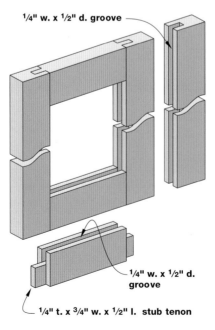

¼" w. x ½" d. groove

¼" w. x ½" d. groove

¼" t. x ¾" w. x ½" l. stub tenon

LOWER DOOR JOINERY

When working on narrow stock such as the door rails, it's safer to cut your joinery on a slightly wider board (this one is about 4" wide) and cut the part free when the joinery is complete.

lack confidence when installing hardware, here's a simple trick you can use: Screw the hinges in place on the carcase. Mix up some five-minute epoxy and put a few dabs on the hinge leaf that attaches to the door. Position the door right where you want it, tape it to the carcase with painter's tape and allow the epoxy to set. Open the door and drive in the hinge screws for the door.

After your project is finished, install the 1/8"-thick glass. The most handsome way to do this is with glazing moulding that you machine yourself. This moulding is simply 3/8"-thick x 1/2"-wide moulding with a chamfer machined on it. Because you'll finish the project before installing the moulding, now is the time to machine and sand it.

Install the Shaker knobs and the catches for the doors (I used a simple hook and screws), then disassemble the project for finishing. Break all the sharp edges with #120-grit sandpaper.

To give the piece an aged look, I chose to finish it with two coats of garnet shellac. Then I followed that up with two coats of a dull-sheen spray lacquer (shellac is very glossy). This finishing process mimics the look of the original clock quite well.

With the project finished, you can install the glass with a bead of silicone in the rabbet, then miter the glazing mould-

A Closer Look at Isaac Youngs

The Shaker faith arrived in the United States from northern England in the late 18th century. One of the earliest communities existed in New Lebanon, N.Y., and it was there that Isaac Newton Youngs made a name for himself in the early 19th century.

Born in 1793, Youngs joined the Shakers when he was just 14 years old. While the Shakers didn't permit watches (they were deemed "an unnecessary indulgence"), they did value clocks to support punctuality. Many clocks were kept in dining areas and common rooms.

Youngs would grow to become one of the group's chief clockmakers, building more than 20 of these projects over the course of his lifetime. His clocks clearly illustrate the Shaker principles of simplicity, purity and utility. Many follow what has come to be known as the Shaker style – namely, they are straightforward, functional and modest.

Along with his clockwork, Youngs delved into another passion while at the community – music. He helped develop the guidelines of small letteral notation that included material on the importance of melody, rhythm and meter. He knew it was important to teach this system of notation, to provide examples for students to study and to encourage a uniform system for the entire community. Youngs died in 1866.

At its peak in the mid-19th century, there were about 6,000 Shakers living in the United States. But after a long, slow decline in membership throughout the late 19th and 20th centuries, there now exists only one active village, located in Maine.

— Michael A. Rabkin

ing and secure it with silicone and brads as shown in the construction drawing.

The original clock is hung on a traditional Shaker peg. You could build yourself a "peg board" and array it with a number of Shaker-like accessories.

Another authentic option is to hang the clock on a single forged iron hook.

No matter how you hang it, whenever you check the time, you'll be reminded that it takes a little perseverence and (yes) time to get any project designed and built so it's just right.

You need to compress the joint vertically as well as join the pieces horizontally, so you need to clamp both simultaneously as shown.

Cringe if you want, but I like quartz movements. They're reliable, require little upkeep and are simple to install. I know this from installing and adjusting several mechanical movements in clocks over the years. Do whatever makes you happy on this point.

Clasic Tall Clock

BY ROBERT CASEY & GLEN D. HUEY

While attending an East Coast tool show, Editor Christopher Schwarz was handed a photograph of this clock. Recognizing the Shaker clock, Chris decided to talk with the builder, Bob Casey. Chris heard his tale and knew we had a story at hand.

Rather than have Casey come to our shop to work, or us travel to his home in Mattydale, N.Y., we decided to relate his story and build the clock from his drawings and instructions.

A Shaker tall clock was dominating Casey's mind one cold winter's day. He'd seen a clock that was exactly what he was looking to build. It was an 1811 clock built by Erastus Rude and was part of the collection at the Shaker Museum and Library in Old Chatham, N.Y.

With a phone call to Sharon Koomler, the museum's director, Casey was granted access to the clock for measurements. There's nothing like going straight to the original for sizes.

Casey was in the midst of assembling a cut list when he discovered that there were a few measurements he still needed. I would've missed a few measurements too if I'd been surrounded by fine Shaker craftsmanship and standing at the foot of the original tall clock.

Back to the museum to gather the missing figures, another lunch with friends, then on to the shop to build a clock.

A Slim Waist Starts it All
The clock begins at the waist, so cut the four pieces for the face frame and mill the waist sides at the same time. These pieces form the middle section of the clock.

In our shop, we're having a go at the Festool Domino, and the loose-tenon joinery for assembling the rails and stiles of the face frame was a perfect test.

When working with the Domino, I've found I like two "fixing holes" (a tight fit to the Dominos) into both ends of the rails and two long holes (slight gapping at each end) for the stiles. Add glue and assemble the face frame.

If you don't own a Domino you can use pocket screws, biscuits or a mortise-and-tenon joint (remember to add the extra length for the tenons to your cut list sizes).

Work on the waist sides is minimal. Cut a 7/16" x 3/4" rabbet along the back edge of each side using a two-step process at the table saw. Next, notch the rabbet from the bottom to the 3" mark. A line squared across the sides shows the amount of overlap when attaching the base.

The waist sides and face frame are joined to complete the waist. This edge joint is plenty strong with glue only.

The Size of the Waist Determines the Base
The material for the base sides and front panel requires a good grain match. This is a focal point of the clock. The fact that the grain changes directions from the waist to the base calls particular attention to this area.

Determining the length of the panels for the base is a matter of measuring the waist, adding the width of the spacers and cutting to the correct length.

The base panels are mitered at the corners. Therefore, take the width of the front of the waist, add 1 3/4" (the two side spacers at 7/8" thickness each) plus 1 1/2" (two times the thickness of the side panels) which gets you to the outside edge of the base front panel.

The same measuring steps are followed for the side panel lengths: the depth of the waist sides plus one 7/8"

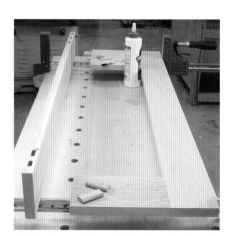

Cutting the mortises with the Domino is quick work. Select the best face for the waist frame of the clock.

Glue is all that's necessary for this assembly, but have enough clamps ready and work from end to end while applying pressure.

The left-tilt table saw is great for cutting the 45° miters for the base pieces. At a right-tilt saw, use a panel-cutting jig or sliding table attachment.

Classic Tall Clock

NO.	ITEM	DIMENSIONS (INCHES)			MATERIAL	COMMENTS
		T	W	L		
Waist						
2	Stiles	$3/_1$	$3^3/_1$	$46^5/_8$	Cherry	
1	Top rail	$3/_4$	$4^5/_8$	$7^1/_2$	Cherry	
1	Lower rail	$3/_4$	$8^3/_4$	$7^1/_2$	Cherry	
2	Sides	$3/_4$	$7^1/_2$	$46^5/_8$	Cherry	
1	Door	$3/_4$	$7^3/_4$	$33^7/_8$	Cherry	
1	Back brace	$3/_4$	2	$13^1/_2$	Poplar	
Base						
2	Sides	$3/_4$	$16^3/_4$	$9^7/_8$	Cherry	45° angle one end
1	Front	$3/_4$	$16^3/_4$	$18^1/_4$	Cherry	45° angle both ends
2	Side fillers	$7/_8$	2	$7^1/_2$	Poplar	
1	Front filler	$7/_8$	2	$16^3/_4$	Poplar	
1	Bottom	$3/_4$	$8^3/_4$	$17^1/_2$	Poplar	
4	Cove mouldings	$3/_4$	$2^1/_2$	22	Cherry	Two complete sets
Hood						
1	Front collar	$3/_4$	3	$19^1/_2$	Cherry	45° angle both ends
2	Side collars	$3/_4$	3	$10^1/_2$	Cherry	45° angle one end
2	Sides	$3/_4$	$8^1/_2$	$21^1/_4$	Cherry	
1	Arch rail	$5/_8$	$5^3/_4$	15	Cherry	
1	Hood rail	$3/_4$	$1^3/_8$	15	Cherry	
2	Side spacers	$5/_8$	$5^3/_4$	$8^1/_2$	Cherry	
1	Front gallery	$3/_4$	$5^3/_4$	$19^3/_8$	Cherry	45° angle both ends
2	Side gallery	$3/_4$	$5^3/_4$	$9^3/_8$	Cherry	45° angle one end
2	Arched bead	$3/_{32}$	2	16	Cherry	Trim to $1^1/_2$
2	Flat bead	$3/_{16}$	$1^1/_2$	16	Cherry	
1	Brace	$3/_4$	2	15	Poplar	
1	Top	$3/_4$	$10^5/_8$	$21^7/_8$	Cherry	
2	Wings	$1/_4$	$1^5/_8$	$21^3/_4$	Cherry	
2	Moulding	$13/_{16}$	1	23	Cherry	Under hood top
2	Half columns	$5/_8$	$1^1/_4$	17	Cherry	Turn to $15^9/_{16}$
2	Columns	1	1	17	Cherry	Turn to $15^9/_{16}$
Dial frame						
2	Stiles	$1/_2$	$2^1/_4$	$18^1/_2$	Cherry	
1	Rail	$1/_2$	$1^1/_2$	$15^1/_8$	Cherry	
1	Arch rail	$1/_2$	$6^3/_8$	$15^1/_8$	Cherry	
Door						
2	Stiles	$3/_4$	$2^7/_8$	$15^1/_8$	Cherry	
1	Rail	$3/_4$	$2^1/_4$	$10^3/_4$	Cherry	
1	Arch rail	$3/_4$	$5^1/_2$	$10^3/_4$	Cherry	
Movement support						
1	Seat board	$3/_4$	$4^1/_2$	$13^3/_8$	Poplar	
2	Seat board sides	$3/_4$	$3^1/_2$	10	Poplar	
1	Dial backer	$1/_2$	$13^3/_8$	17	Plywood	
2	Dial supports	$3/_4$	1	20	Poplar	
Back						
1	Backboard	$5/_8$	$14^3/_8$	80	Poplar	
1	Base wings	$5/_8$	$1^5/_8$	$14^1/_2$	Poplar	Makes two pieces
1	Hood wings	$5/_8$	3	21	Poplar	Makes two pieces

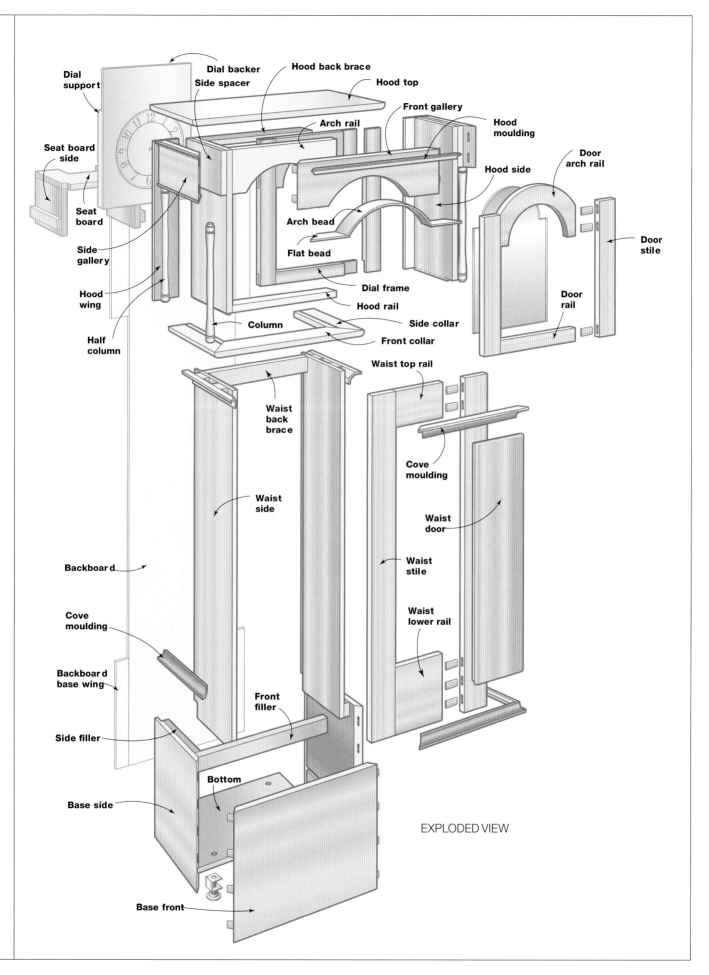

Dial support

Dial backer

Hood back brace

Hood top

Side spacer

Front gallery

Hood moulding

Arch rail

Door arch rail

Seat board side

Hood side

Arch bead

Door stile

Seat board

Flat bead

Side gallery

Dial frame

Hood rail

Door rail

Hood wing

Column

Side collar

Half column

Front collar

Waist top rail

Waist back brace

Cove moulding

Waist side

Waist door

Backboard

Waist stile

Cove moulding

Waist lower rail

Backboard base wing

Front filler

Side filler

Bottom

EXPLODED VIEW

Base side

Base front

Two clamps keep the joint locked in place. You'll need additional clamps if you attach the mitered corners with a spline. If you use splines, keep the splines back from the outside edge so the mouldings cover them.

Supplies

Horton Brasses Inc.
800-754-9127 or horton-brasses.com

2 • pair of clock hinges
#hdh-2, &10.75/pr.

2 • keyhole escutcheon
#h-66, &5.50

2 • keyhole pull
#h-560, $6.50

Merritt's Antiques Inc.
610-689-9541 or merritts.com

1 • Kieninger bell strike movement
#P1126C, $675

Clock Prints
513-926-1040 or
clockprints.zenfolio.com

1 • Shaker II clock face
#cl14, $22.15

Lee Valley Tools
800-871-8158 or leevalley.com

4 • 4" swivel leveller
#01S06.02, $2.40

1 • panel brackets,
pkg of 4
#01S04.05, $7.40

Woodcraft
800-225-1153 or woodcraft.com

1 • rare earth magnets, 9.5mm
pkg. of 10
#150950, $8.39

Prices correct at time of publication.

The levelers hold the clock plumb when it sits on a non-level floor. Adjusting the levelers through the bottom requires drilling access holes in the bottom of the base.

Attaching the waist properly to the base is important to the standing of the clock. If the waist isn't square to the base the clock will lean back or pitch forward. Bring the waist level before adding the screws.

spacer, then add ¾" for the thickness of the base front.

Square the ends of the glued-up panel. Then set the table saw blade to 45° and cut one base side that's ⅛" longer than the required length from each end of the board. Taking a cut from both ends keeps the grain running continuously around the entire base. Make the two cuts with a squared end against the fence.

Slide the fence toward the blade to the finished cut length and trim both panels. The second cutting provides a clean, accurate edge.

The middle panel needs to have the miters reversed in order to fit to the side pieces. Use a sliding table or panel-cutting jig at the saw for one end. Next, place that newly beveled cut against the fence (set to the appropriate dimension) and make a second cut to provide a perfect match to the beveled side panels. If you have a right-tilt saw the operation is different.

Next, install a dado stack at the table saw and dial in a width of ¾" set to cut ⅜" deep. Position the fence to cut a groove 2½" up from the bottom edge of the panels. All three pieces receive the groove for the bottom.

To complete the work on the base panels you need to cut a rabbet on the end of the sides for the clock's backboard. It's the same operation as the rabbet for the waist.

I returned to the Domino to see how it works with miters. I was surprised. Placing the fixing holes in the base front panel and the long holes in the side panel, allowed me to align the top edge easily. No spline to worry about. Add glue and the assembly is a snap.

Mill and fit the bottom into the groove. Make sure that you're able to remove the bottom because locating the holes for the adjustable levelers is next. Position the leveler against the base and bottom, mark the location then drill the ½" holes at the drill press. Slide the bottom into the groove then drive nails through the bottom and into the base sides to affix the bottom into the base.

Slip-fit the Waist and Base

Next, cut the fillers that fit around the inside top edge of the base. Because the grain direction matches all around the base, the fillers are glued in place and held with brads. These parts fill the area between the base and waist and add the support needed to firmly attach the two clock sections.

Position the base front down on the bench and slide the bottom of the waist assembly into the top of the base. Prop up the top of the waist to the same amount raised by the base and spacers. This aligns the notched area of the waist with the top edge of the base and squares the waist to the base. Install three screws along the interior front of the waist into the front spacer. Set two screws through the waist sides into the spacers. These screws are set in oversized holes to allow for wood movement and to deal with the cross-grain issues.

Cut and fit the back brace at the top of the waist setting the 2" face toward the back of the clock. The brace is used to hold the waist square, to add support and to attach the backboard with screws. Remember to hold the piece flush with the rabbet.

The cove moulding that eases the transition from the base to the waist, and from the waist to the hood, is next. Mill your lumber to size and set up the table saw to create the cove. Clamp an auxiliary fence to the saw on a 27° angle to the blade and 3⁄16" from the front edge of the blade when the blade is raised to 1⁄2" above the tabletop. Cut the moulding in several passes. (For more information on cutting cove moulding at the table saw see issue #117, October 2000.)

Sand the case to #180 grit and ease the sharp edges of the base prior to installing the moulding. Fit the cove to the sides and front. Use brads to attach the cove moulding.

The same cove moulding profile is used for the transition from the waist to the hood, but this moulding is nailed to the waist only. Flip the clock onto the bench to stand the piece on its top. Now you can fit and attach the moulding using the waist and benchtop for positioning. Don't forget to sand the edges and add glue at the corners. Brads hold this moulding, but to add strength install a few angle blocks as shown on page 166.

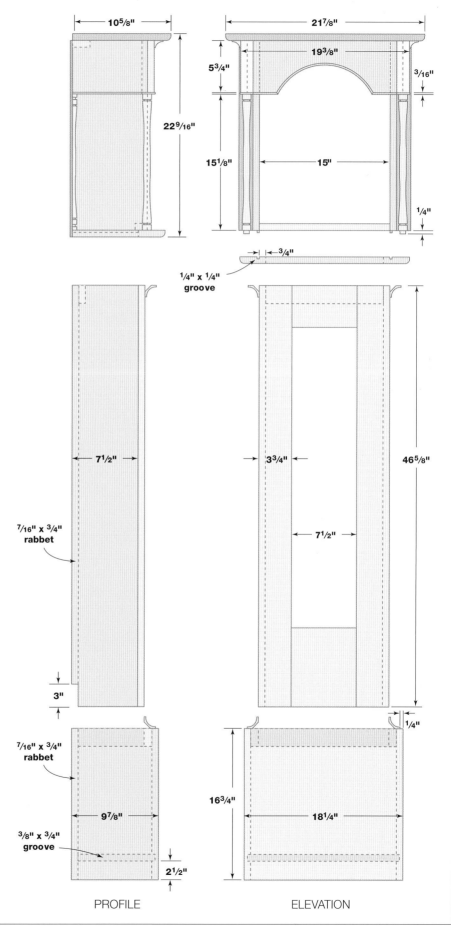

PROFILE

ELEVATION

Top it Off With the Hood

Building the hood begins with the collars. Mill the pieces for the front and side collars to size and miter the ends. Before joining the pieces with a spline or other method, make a ¼"- wide x ¼"- deep groove in each side collar, set ¾" in from the inside edge. The groove receives a matching tenon formed on the hood

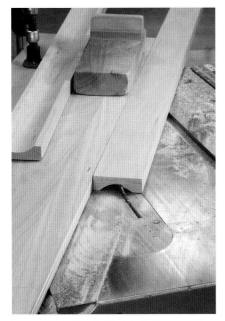

Incremental steps in blade height are used when cutting the cove. Then cut the 45° bevels on the long edges.

Scrap pieces cut with a 45° bevel, when glued in place, add support for the cove moulding and carry some of the load from the hood.

sides. Two passes at the table saw complete the groove. Assemble the U-shaped unit then route a ½" roundover profile along the bottom edge.

Mill the material for the hood sides. At the table saw cut a rabbet for the backboards along the back edge then cut a second rabbet leaving a ¼" x ¼" tongue on the bottom inside end of each hood side. Remove 1" of the tongue from the front edge of the sides.

To arrive at exact measurements for the hood rail and arch rail, set the hood sides into the grooves in the collar and measure between the two sides. Cut the two rails to size. Each rail is joined to the hood sides using a Domino – of course you can use other joining methods. The hood sides are not attached to the collar at this time. That step is completed after the finishing.

Lay out and cut the arch on the rail before any assembly of the hood. Find the center of the rail, move below the rail 3⅛" and draw the 6⅜" radius as shown on page 36. Save that offcut; you'll put it to use in short time. Sand the edge at the spindle sander. Create the joinery for the rails and hood sides and assemble the four pieces.

Next, mill the side spacers and gallery parts. Make the 45° cuts on one end of the side gallery pieces and both ends of the front gallery, fitting them to the hood and spacers. Assemble the gallery parts

with either a spline or Domino.

Slide the assembled gallery over the hood and check the fit of the side spacers. If everything fits, add glue to the spacers and attach them to the gallery. Use brads to hold the spacers in place.

Slide the assembly over the hood again. This time we have cross-grain construction; the grain of the gallery/spacers is horizontal while that of the hood sides is vertical. Attach the hood and gallery from inside the hood through oversized holes – two screws toward the front and two screws near the back of the hood sides. The larger holes compensate for any future wood movement.

The arch and the bottom edge of the gallery have a ³⁄₁₆" bead detail. The arch bead is the difficult piece. You can soak or steam a piece to get it to fit to the arch, but I elected to laminate two pieces, each ³⁄₃₂" thick (the thinner stock bends easily). The arched bead pieces are cut wider than the balance of the bead. If the pieces slide during the process you'll still have usable stock.

To make the laminations, add glue to the two mating surfaces then wrap with a couple pieces of tape to keep things from moving as you clamp. Set the pieces on the arch, add the cutoff to the stack and clamp tight. Allow the glue to dry completely. There will be a small amount of spring-back when the clamps are removed. Don't worry. The bend returns

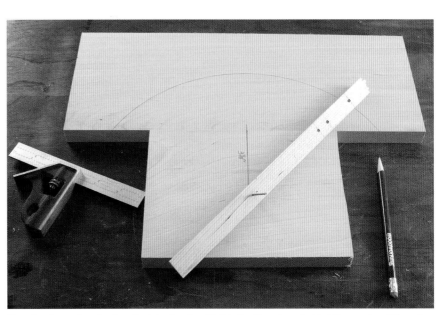

Drawing the arches for the clock is simple with this jig. The piece held at the center of the rail allows you to adjust the arch with each use.

and is held tight with glue and brads.

Joint one edge then cut the laminated bead to width. The band saw is the right machine. Set the fence to 1½" and trim with the jointed edge to the fence. Use sandpaper to form the bead detail on the outside edge. Trim the bead to get close to a fit then add glue to the bead and the arched area. Position the bead in the hood, keeping the interior edge flush. Then add clamps and allow the glue to set. Cut and fit the balance of the pieces that finish the bead, remembering to locate and drill the hole for the tenon on the columns.

That same hole is mirrored in the collar of the hood as well. Locate and drill the two holes at this time.

The work on the hood is complete with the addition of the top, the hood/back brace and the mouldings. The top is cut to size, routed on three edges with a ½" roundover bit and attached to the hood with screws through the top into the hood sides. The hood/back brace fits between the sides and is attached with glue and nails to the underside of the top. Finally, the mouldings are wrapped around the hood and attached with brads.

Next, turn the columns and fit to the hood. For online features including patterns and videos, go to popularwoodworking.com/aug07.

Framing the Dial

The dial frame fits inside the hood flush with the back face of the arched rail; it rests on the hood rail. The frame is attached to the hood with ½"-square x 2"-long glue blocks that are visible only from inside the hood. The frame is joined with half-lap joints.

Start with ½" material sized from the cut sheet then create the half-lap joints. Most of the joints are rabbets cut in two steps. The exception is for the dial frame arch rail. Because of its width you need to nibble the waste material from the stiles.

Cut the rails first. Set the blade height to ¼" and the fence to cut for the width of the stiles. Select the best face of the rails and position that face down so when the frame is viewed from the front, the stiles run from top to bottom and the rails appear to run between the stiles. Make the first of two cuts at each end

Taking the time to check the fit of the gallery assures a proper fit. After the gallery is assembled the spacers can be manipulated to specific thickness.

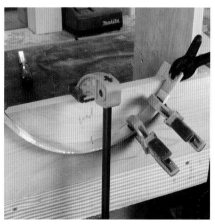

The offcut from the gallery front is an excellent caul for clamping the laminated bead into the profile. Small spring clamps close any gaps between the pieces.

Trim the bead to width at the band saw, but the majority of the work of matching to the flat bead is completed with chisels. Carefully angle the ends of the bead to fit those of the matching corner pieces.

Locate and trim the notch with a handsaw then cut 45° miters at the end. The holes for the columns are centered in the flat bead and held flush with the front edge of the hood side.

This moulding is created at the router table with a ½" cove bit. The bit is slightly raised with each pass, creating the irregular profile.

using the miter gauge while holding the stock against the fence.

Next, the stile cuts require two fence positions – one for the lower rail and the second for the wide arch rail. Set the fence for the width of the lower rail and make one cut at the bottom end of each stile keeping the stiles face up. Change the fence to the width of the arch rail and make another cut at the top end of

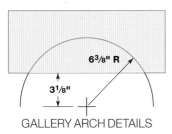

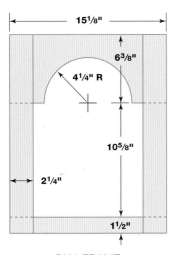

DIAL FRAME

The joints for the frame are half-lap and are rabbet cuts created in two steps. Check the setting by placing two cut pieces together. The faces are flush if the depth of cut is correct. Make any adjustments then finish the remaining cuts.

each stile. Nibble away the material for the wide arch rail with repeated passes over the blade. Don't exert pressure on the piece (which would bend it into the blade). Remove any saw marks with a chisel or scraper.

The remaining cuts, those that complete the half laps in the rail and stiles, are made with the stock held vertical with a tenon jig.

Draw the $4\frac{1}{4}$" radius on the arch rail, cut it at the band saw and sand the edge. Add glue to the joints. Spring clamps hold the joints tight, but also add a clamp across the frame to pull the stile edges tight to the rails and one to pull the rails tight to the stiles. Set aside to dry.

How About the Door?
The Domino makes this door easy. Mill the rails and stiles to size. The compass jig used to form the arch for the hood spacer is used again for the arch of the door. This time move below the stock 1" instead of $3\frac{1}{8}$" as before.

The lower door rail is flush with the bottom edge of the stiles and the arch door rail extends above the stile by $4\frac{1}{8}$". Position the pieces then draw the $4\frac{1}{8}$" inside radius and $6\frac{3}{8}$" outside radius arches on the stock. Also mark 1" in from the ends of the stiles for the location of the Dominos and cut the mortises. Cut the inside arch at the band saw, smooth any cut lines then assemble the door.

Next, cut the outside arch of the door frame. At the band saw you'll find a

small problem getting started with the cut. There is no direct access to the cut line, so nibble in a few times before turning the blade to cut the arch. Handwork cleans the cut.

Fitting the door to the hood requires some finesse. Once the door is in position make small adjustments to the frame until you achieve a consistent reveal around the door; I prefer a nickel gap.

The last construction necessary on the door is to cut a rabbet for the glass – that's a job for the router table and a $\frac{3}{8}$" rabbeting bit. Pay attention when cutting the arched rail. This is an area to climb cut to reduce tear-out. Once the rabbets are formed, square the corners with a chisel.

The interior sharp corners of the arch rail are eased for fitting the door glass. The glass is secured with Durham's Rock Hard Water Putty (waterputty.com) after the finishing is complete. Use a chisel to trim the corners.

The door for the waist is milled to size, has the edge routed with a $\frac{1}{4}$" roundover bit then the top, bottom and non-hinged edges have a $\frac{3}{8}$" x $\frac{1}{2}$" rabbet. The hinge side of the door receives a $\frac{1}{8}$" x $\frac{1}{2}$" rabbet.

Finally, install the hardware on both doors. The hood-hinge installation is straightforward: put the longer leaf of the hinge in the door frame. To install the hinges in the waist door you have to remove some of the $\frac{1}{8}$" lip. Mark the hinge area, remove the lip then use your chisels to set the hinge leaf flush to the door edge. The longer leaf extends into the case and is set flush with the waist stile edge. Both doors are held closed with rare-earth magnets.

Holding the Movement
We're using a Kienninger bell strike mechanical movement from Merritt's Antiques. The mechanical movement requires a seat board and a few other necessities. The seat board raises the movement into position and allows the dial backer to be attached. The paper dial is from Clockprints.

To create the seat board, use the pattern available online at popularwoodworking.com/aug07 then cut the two $\frac{3}{4}$" x 1" notches for the dial supports.

Fit the hood door. Once the outer arch is cut, the door is fit to the hood. Fit the door in position then fine-tune the fit to create an even reveal around the door.

Prep the door for glass. The inside corners are left rounded by the rabbeting bit and need to be squared with chisels. Cut the end grain using the force provided from a mallet while cutting the side grain with only hand pressure. Too much force can crack the face of the door.

To build the seat board assembly (the U-shaped member that slides between and attaches to the waist sides) connect the two seat board sides to the seat board. Hold the back edges flush to the seat board with a butt joint – two screws per side do the job. Then, attach the two dial supports to the assembly holding the bottom edges flush. Install two screws in each support. Once it's inside the case, slide the assembly to the correct position (based on your movement) and drive two screws per side through the seat board sides into the waist sides. The dial backer is held to the supports with four screws, one in each corner.

Hood catches keep the hood from tipping when removing or installing it onto the clock. Attach the hood catches to the sides of the seat board assembly holding them just above the collar. Secure with brads.

If you elect to use a quartz movement, attach the dial backer and paper dial directly to the back face of the dial frame.

The backboard for the clock runs vertical to the case. Mill a panel to the width of the waist and as long as the clock base, waist and hood. Figure the wing pieces, those that bump out and fill the additional width at the base as well as for the hood. Glue the pieces to the backboard. Once the clock is finished the back is attached to the braces and into the rabbeted sides with screws or nails.

Given the time, I'd finish the clock as Casey did – a few coats of oil and let nature take its course. But, to hasten the aged appearance, I used my favorite finish – aniline dye, glaze and shellac. The Dark Antique Sheraton dye is the basis on which to build the finish. To resemble the look of an antique clock, I've glazed the piece after the first layer of shellac, locked that layer with another two coats of shellac then added a topcoat of dull-rubbed effect lacquer. (For more on my finishing method see issue #161, April 2007).

Install the movement (download directions at popularwoodworking.com/aug07) and reinstall the hardware. Then you're ready to move the piece into the house for keeping time through the 21st century and beyond.

Positioning the movement. The seat board holds the movement in the correct orientation to the dial allows the weights to hang as needed. The cutout in the seat board is for the pendulum and the blocks attached to the sides keep the hood from tipping forward.

Classic Stepstool

BY JIM STUARD

ack when the Shakers started making furniture in the late 18th century, the only tools available to them were powered by people. No table saws, no electric jointers or planers. Your tool kit consisted largely of hand saws, chisels and planes. Your planer, jointer and table saw were usually a young apprentice who prepared stock by hand. The skilled woodworkers handled most joinery tasks.

Shakers eagerly sought out power tools and technology to help them do their work. But during the heyday of most Shaker communities, hand tools did most of the work.

Today there is a group of woodworkers who still pride themselves in building furniture this way. They call themselves "Neanderthals." And the way they communicate is, ironically, usually through the internet. We thought it would be interesting to build a project using only hand tools to get a feel for how early Shakers and electronic-age Neanderthals work. Admittedly, we copped out on one aspect of this project: We didn't surface the lumber from rough stock using hand tools. We rationalized this by figuring an apprentice would have done this work.

I think you'll enjoy unplugging your router for a few days to tackle this modest but satisfying project. And if you cannot give up your power tools, you can rest easy knowing that the early Shakers would have paid almost any price for that precision plunge router on your bench.

These stools were used in Shaker housing to get to the upper drawers in the enormous chests built for communal use. The stool was placed against the lower part of a chest for support. If you want to use this as a freestanding stool, add a hand rail.

the tools needed are as follows: clamps, a block plane, jack plane, a couple Japanese saws, two sharp chisels, a coping saw and a hand drill. For marking dovetails. I use a sharp knife, a square and a sliding t-bevel.

Begin construction by laying out the panels for the sides. Use a cardboard template to lay out the best yield from your panels. Because you aren't going to make these cuts with a table saw, you will have to make stopped cross-cuts and rips in the middle of the panels to cut out the

steps using hand saws. I've found the best way to do this is with Japanese saws.

Courtesy of Japan

There is a style of saw called an Azebiki-Nokogiri. In short, it's a saw with a curved blade for doing a "plunge" cut in the middle of a panel. The other saw I used was a Ryoba style. It's a two-edged

Clamp a straightedge to the back line of the stool, gently press the saw against it and rip the back edge (left). Use the ripping teeth on the back of the Ryoba.

After cutting the bottom, lay out the radius (below).

blade with rip teeth on one edge and crosscut teeth on the other. There are other Japanese saws designed for dovetailing, but I appreciate the utility of the two-sided blade.

Begin by laying out your cutting lines in pencil on the sides. The object is to first cut the back edge of the side, then cut the bottom edge square to that. Then

The 10-Cent Dovetail Jig

In the midst of laying out the dovetails for these stools, I decided I wanted a way to make the cuts for my tails as clean, accurate and quick as possible. There are 44 angled cuts for the dovetails alone. So I made this jig, and I think it will help the first-timers out there. Look at this jig as training wheels for cutting tails.

Basically, the jig is an "H" that fits over your work and guides your saw at the perfect angle. Flip the jig over, and it cuts the other way. Tails have never been easier to do. Begin by cutting two sides pieces $1/2$" x 3" x 4" from plywood. Then cut the spacer that goes between the two using falloff from your stool. This will ensure your jig sleeves tightly over your work. The spacer should be $3/4$" x $3/8$" x 4". I glued and nailed the spacer between the two sides and then cut one end at a 7- or 9-degree angle. I cheated and used a chop saw for this cut.

Then cut out a face piece ($1/2$" x 3" x 5") out of plywood. Glue and nail the face on the angled ends of the "H." Now use a Ryoba and a coping saw to cut the notches out of the face and fit the jig to your dovetailing stock with a rasp. When you've got a snug fit, try a couple of test cuts. Gently hold the Ryoba against the jig as you begin to make your cut. The guide will do the rest of the work.

It's pretty easy to hold the blade in position and cut down to the gauge marks. As a bonus, you can use the other end of the jig to make square cuts. With practice, you won't even have to trim the tails when fitting.

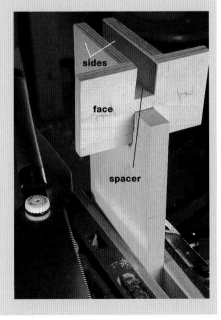

sides

face

spacer

lay out the steps from these two perpendicular lines.

Cutting a straight line isn't difficult, especially if you clamp a piece of wood to your work to serve as a guide. Simply clamp the guide to the work and begin making the cut with your Ryoba. Use your fingers to gently hold the blade against your guide. Take it slowly and your cut will be true.

Set up another straightedge and, using the finer crosscut teeth of the Ryoba, cut in about 4" from the front and back edges of the stool. Mark the center of the bottom and lay out a 9"-diameter semi-circle. Now cut the half circle on the sides using a compass saw. Clean up your cuts with sandpaper.

The best way to cut the steps is to make a plunge cut with the Azebiki saw and finish with the Ryoba, crosscutting against the grain and ripping with the grain. Again, clamping a piece of straight

After laying out the steps, start making the plunge cuts in the panel for each rise and run on the steps. Remember to use the larger ripping teeth for the long grain and the shorter crosscutting teeth for the cross grain. Start each cut by gently pressing the saw against the straightedge and use a rocking motion to use the entire length of the blade to make the cut.

wood to your work will ensure your cuts are straight.

There's nothing fast about this process. Slow and deliberate will do the trick. Once the sides are complete, cut the treads and risers to size. Clean them

When you've penetrated the other side of the panel, cut a slot large enough for the Ryoba. Finish the cuts into the inside and outside corners, but be sure to use the correct teeth for the direction you are cutting.

The results speak for themselves. With a kerf less than 1/16", it's possible to do some fine cutting. Notice the radiused cuts that resemble cuts from a table saw. These marks are from the Azebiki-Nokogiri saw.

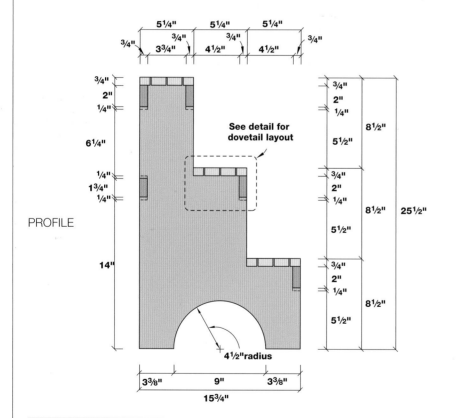

PROFILE

See detail for dovetail layout

5 1/4"   5 1/4"   5 1/4"
3/4"   3/4"   3/4"
3 3/4"   4 1/2"   4 1/2"

3/4"
2"
1/4"

6 1/4"

1/4"
1 3/4"
1/4"

14"

4 1/2" radius

3 3/8"   9"   3 3/8"
15 3/4"

3/4"
2"
1/4"

8 1/2"

5 1/2"

3/4"
2"
1/4"

8 1/2"   25 1/2"

5 1/2"

3/4"
2"
1/4"

8 1/2"

5 1/2"

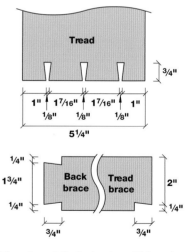

Tread

1"   1 7/16"   1 7/16"   1"
1/8"   1/8"   1/8"
5 1/4"

3/4"

1/4"
1 3/4"
1/4"

Back brace   Tread brace

2"
1/4"

3/4"   3/4"

7° angle on tails for hardwood (shown)
9° angle for softwoods

DOVETAIL LAYOUT DETAIL

Classic Stepstool

NO.	ITEM	DIMENSIONS (INCHES)			MATERIAL
		T	W	L	
2	Sides	3/4	15 3/4	25 1/2	Maple
3	Treads	3/4	5 1/4	16	Maple
5	Braces	3/4	2 1/4	16	Maple

After cleaning up the edges of the side panels, begin laying out the tails on the treads. Use the diagram to help. If you're going to use the training-wheels jig mentioned at left, don't lay out the sides of the tails on the top and bottom of the tread. Simply lay out the ⅛" spaces between the tails on the ends.Use the jig to define the tail shape. Braver souls will start with a marking gauge and then, using a sliding t-bevel set to 7 degrees, make knife cuts into the wood to mark the tails. If you can't see the cut lines, use a sharp pencil to put a little "make-up" on them.

up with a plane and make sure everything's square.

Dovetails

Start cutting the dovetail joints by laying out the tails on the treads and risers according to the diagram. On hardwood joints, the dovetail angles should be at a 1:8 ratio (7 degrees). On softwoods the ratio is 1:6 (9 degrees). Cut the tails, then number each joint for reference.

I built a couple little jigs to make cutting my tails easier. See the accompanying story for details.

Now use the tails to lay out the pins on the side pieces. Cut the tails by making the first cuts with the Ryoba and clean out the waste with a coping saw. Now try to fit the joints. If they are too tight, use a chisel to clean up the joint. If they are too loose, you can glue thin shavings into the joint to fill it out. Most people will never notice.

When cut correctly, the joints should tap together and be snug without beat-

Those of you using the training-wheels jig can now cut all of the tails on the treads and braces. You'll have to figure out which way the jig works best on each cut. If you're not sure, mark the tails with a pencil so there's no confusion. I like to use the rip side of the Ryoba to cut dovetails. This might rankle some of the hardcore Neanderthals out there, but I've found it's aggressive and the cut needs little or no trimming after.

Clamp a panel into a vise and use the tails on the tread ends and braces to mark the locations for the pins and brace notches. Use a knife to get a more accurate layout. Since they're easier to fit, I don't use a jig for the pins. Just lay them out from the tail marks, using a knife and sliding t-bevel set to 7 degrees. Fit the pins to the tails with a four-in-hand rasp, removing material from the pins until the tread can be lightly tapped onto the side. Use a backer block to do this so you don't split the tread.

ing on the stool. When you're satisfied with the fit, glue all the joints and mating edges together. Sand and apply three coats of your favorite finish. I used Watco, an oil and varnish blend.

After defining the tails, remove the little triangle of wood between them with a coping saw. The ⅛" gap is big enough for a small chisel to fit into for trimming.

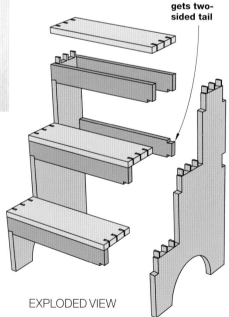

Back brace gets two-sided tail

EXPLODED VIEW

Traditional Hanging Shelves

BY TROY SEXTON

These shelves are quite popular with my two best customers: my wife and my daughter. We have them hanging in several rooms of our farmhouse where they hold plates and knickknacks.

Not surprisingly, these shelves are also popular with my paying customers. While many of them may dream of buying a custom corner cupboard, sometimes what they can best afford are the hanging shelves. So these small projects make everyone happy.

For the home woodworker, these shelves are a home run. These two traditional designs look great in most homes, and the woodworking part is so simple that almost anyone should be able to build these in a weekend.

Patterns and Dados

Both of these shelves are built using the same techniques and joints. The only significant difference is that the Shaker-style unit has three shelves and the 18th century "Whale Tail" project has four shelves and a more ornate profile that looks vaguely like a whale's tail. To me, it looks more like a goose.

Begin your project by selecting your lumber and planing it down to $\frac{1}{2}$" thick. Using the supplied patterns and the construction drawings, draw the profile on your side pieces and mark where the dados should go.

Now set up your dado stack in your table saw so it makes a $\frac{1}{2}$"-wide cut that's $\frac{3}{16}$" deep. As you can see in the photo, I made this cut using only the fence. I feel real comfortable with this cut; but if you're not, I recommend you use your miter gauge and a stop block attached to your fence to guide the work instead.

Cut the dados and then head for the band saw.

Cutting the Details

I use a band saw to shape the sides. Begin by making several "relief" cuts along the profile of your side. These allow you to remove the waste in chunks so your blade and workpiece are easier to maneuver through the cut.

Once you've completed both sides, sand the edges using a drum sander that's chucked into your drill press. I recommend you tape the two sides together

using double-sided tape and sand them simultaneously. It's faster and the sides end up identical.

Once that's complete, fit the shelves and sides together for a dry fit. Notice anything? The square edges of the shelves don't match the sides exactly.

Mark the shape of the sides onto the end of the shelves. Now, using a jointer with the fence beveled (or a hand plane), shape the front edge to match the side. You just want to get in the ballpark; sanding can take care of the rest of the contouring job.

Now cut the plate rail groove in the shelves. I used a router bit with a core box profile and a router table. The plate rail is $\frac{1}{8}$" deep and $1\frac{5}{8}$" in from the back edge.

Before you assemble the unit, finish sand all the surfaces except the outside of

the sides. Begin with 100-grit sandpaper and work your way up to 120, 150 and finish with 180.

Assembly and Finishing

Put a small bead of glue in each dado and put the shelves in place. Clamp the shelves between the sides and check your project to make sure it's square by measuring diagonally from corner to corner. If the measurements are equal, nail the sides to the shelves using a few 18-gauge brads.

If your measurements aren't equal, clamp the project diagonally from one corner to another. Clamp across the two corners that produced the longest measurement. Apply a little pressure to those corners and keep checking your diagonal measurements. When they are equal, nail the project together.

After an hour, take the project out of the clamps and sand the outside of the side pieces and putty your nail holes. Ease all the sharp edges of the project using 120-grit sandpaper. I dyed my project using a water-based aniline dye that I mixed myself from several custom colors. I recommend you use J. E. Moser's Golden Amber Maple dye for a similar effect. It's available from Woodworker's Supply at 800-645-9292 or woodworker. com.

Finally, add a couple coats of your favorite top-coat finish and sand between coats. Hang your shelf using some common picture hooks, available at any home center or from the source listed in the box below.

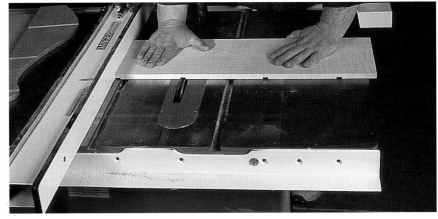

Cut the dados in the sides using a dado stack in your table saw. If you're a beginning woodworker, I recommend you perform this operation with a miter gauge to guide the work instead of the fence. I've made a lot of these shelves and am quite comfortable with this method.

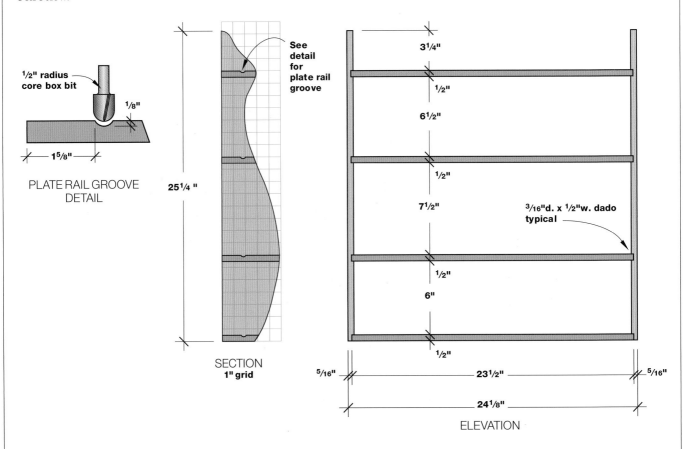

1/2" radius core box bit

1/8"

1 5/8"

PLATE RAIL GROOVE DETAIL

25 1/4 "

See detail for plate rail groove

SECTION
1" grid

3 1/4"

1/2"

6 1/2"

1/2"

7 1/2"

3/16"d. x 1/2"w. dado typical

1/2"

6"

1/2"

5/16"

23 1/2"

5/16"

24 1/8"

ELEVATION

Whale Tail Shelf

NO.	ITEM	DIMENSIONS (INCHES)			MATERIAL	COMMENTS
		T	W	L		
2	Sides	1/2	4 7/8	25 1/4	Maple	
1	Bottom shelf	1/2	3 1/8	23 1/2	Maple	in 3/16" x 1/2" dado
1	Middle shelf	1/2	4 7/8	23 1/2	Maple	in 3/16" x 1/2" dado
1	Middle shelf	1/2	3	23 1/2	Maple	in 3/16" x 1/2" dado
1	Top shelf	1/2	3	23 1/2	Maple	in 3/16" x 1/2" dado

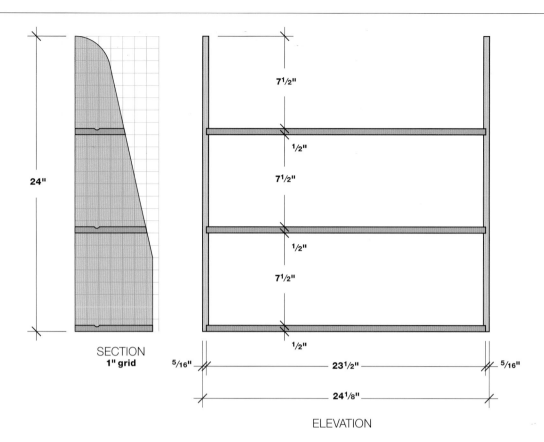

24"

SECTION
1" grid

7½"

½"

7½"

½"

7½"

½"

5/16"   23½"   5/16"

24⅛"

ELEVATION

Notice the relief cut I made in the sides. By removing the waste in smaller hunks (instead of all at once), the blade is more maneuverable.

Supplies

Lee Valley Tools
800-871-8158 or
leevalley.com

• Picture Hooks
  Item # 00D78.02, 50 picture hooks,
  $6.10 plus shipping

Prices correct at time of publication.

Shaker Hanging Shelf

NO.	ITEM	T	W	L	MATERIAL	COMMENTS
		DIMENSIONS (INCHES)				
2	Sides	½	6½	24	Cherry	
1	Bottom shelf	½	6½	23½	Cherry	in 3/16" x ½" dado
1	Middle shelf	½	6	23½	Cherry	in 3/16" x ½" dado
1	Top shelf	½	4¼	23½	Cherry	in 3/16" x ½" dado

Workbench

BY GLEN D. HUEY

When I started work at *Popular Woodworking Magazine* my workbench was a couple storage cabinets on wheels and a cut-off slab of solid-core door. The assembled bench design worked, but then again, it wasn't sturdy, solid or anywhere near going to be the bench that I used for an extended period of time. So it was decided that I should build a workbench. A Shaker-style workbench jumped to the forefront of the many design choices. I wanted a showy bench. One that when looked at in 100 years, most observers would wonder if it was for use or for show.

To create a Shaker design I knew that I needed to have doors and a stack of drawers under the benchtop. In keeping with traditional Shaker benches, I planned to paint the under-chassis. But the structural members, as well as the top, had to be tiger maple – of which over the years I had accumulated quite a stash of less-than-quality figured wood that would do nicely as a workbench top.

Stout Legs & Sturdy Mortises

Start the construction of the bench with the legs. Instead of searching for 16/4 stock that is milled to $3^{1}/_{2}$" square, look for material that can be glued to the required size. Rough-cut eight pieces of 8/4 stock that is $3^{3}/_{4}$" wide x 34" in length. Each leg is made from a pair of these blanks. Because you want a final size of $3^{1}/_{2}$", joint only one face of each piece to gain a smooth surface for a good glue joint.

Once the legs are assembled and the glue is dry, mill the pieces to the final dimensions, then begin the layout work to locate the mortises. I oriented the full faces of the legs to the front and rear, keeping each leg's glue line facing the ends of the bench.

The mortises for both ends and the back are identical. Each location receives a 1" x $4^{1}/_{4}$" mortise for a 5"-wide lower rail and a 1" x $2^{1}/_{4}$" mortise for the 3"-wide upper rail. The front legs receive an identical mortise for the 3" lower rail at the base of the leg – the rail beginning at $2^{1}/_{2}$" above the floor. The upper rail is $^{7}/_{8}$" thick and $2^{3}/_{4}$" wide. It's a dovetail joint (that's evidence of the furniture maker coming out in me).

There are many ways to cut the mortises. You can make a plywood pattern and use a plunge router and router bit, you can hog out the majority of the waste material with a Forstner bit at the drill press or you can slave through the work with a mortising chisel and a mallet. I elected to use a dedicated mortise machine. Whichever method you select, cut the mortises to a depth of $1^{1}/_{2}$".

Creating the Rails to a Strong Joint

Once the leg mortises are made, mill the material for your rails. That batch of material should also include the beams that stretch from front to back of the base and add support to the bench (see photo at right). The mortises for those beams are cut into the lower front and back rails. You also need to cut the mortises for the rear divider that runs between the rails of the back. A quick step back to the mortising stage then you're ready to cut tenons.

Install a dado stack in the table saw and raise the blade to $^{3}/_{8}$". Set the fence to act as a stop for a $1^{1}/_{2}$"-long tenon. Nibble away the waste material on the four surfaces of each rail exposing the tenon. Fine-tune the fit of each tenon into its respective mortise.

The front top rail is joined to the front leg posts with a dovetail joint. Cut the

Shaker craftsmen would employ the dovetail joint for the top rail. To maintain strength in the joint, set the socket back from the front edge.

dovetail socket into the top of the legs. Use a handsaw to define the edges of the socket then use chisels to remove the waste.

With the socket complete, fit the top rail to the legs. Slide the lower-front rail into the front legs, then add clamps to secure. Next, scribe the dovetail length onto the front top rail, lay the rail on top of the legs positioning the scribe line at the edge of the legs, and transfer the socket layout onto the rail ends. Saw away the waste material. Carefully fit the dovetail to the sockets to get a tight fit.

Pin down some strength. The added pins reinforce the joint. Because the size of the dowels match the size of the drill bits, the job couldn't be easier.

Workbench

NO.	ITEM	DIMENSIONS (INCHES)			MATERIAL	COMMENTS
		T	W	L		
4	Legs	3½	3½	33	Tiger maple	
1	Front lower rail	1¾	3	52	Tiger maple	1½" tenon both ends
1	Rear top rail	1¾	3	52	Tiger maple	1½" tenon both ends
1	Rear lower rail	1¾	5	52	Tiger maple	1½" tenon both ends
2	End top rail	1¾	3	17½	Tiger maple	1½" tenon both ends
2	End lower rail	1¾	5	17½	Tiger maple	1½" tenon both ends
1	Rear divider	1¾	3	25½	Tiger maple	1½" tenon both ends
2	Base beam	1¾	3	21	Poplar	1½" tenon both ends
1	Front top rail	7/8	2⅜	51	Tiger maple	1" dovetail both ends

Flat-panel Divider

NO.	ITEM	T	W	L	MATERIAL	COMMENTS
2	Stiles	¾	3	26½	Poplar	
2	Rails	¾	3	14½	Poplar	1¼" tenon both ends
1	Flat panel	¾	12⅝	21⅛	Poplar	

Beadboard Panels

NO.	ITEM	T	W	L	MATERIAL	COMMENTS
2	End panels	5/8	14⁷/₁₆	22⅜	Poplar	Assembled pieces
2	Rear panels	5/8	22¹⁵/₁₆	22⅜	Poplar	Assembled pieces

Panel Backing

NO.	ITEM	T	W	L	MATERIAL	COMMENTS
4	Horizontal end	5/8	5/8	14½	Poplar	
4	Vertical end	5/8	5/8	22½	Poplar	
2	Horizontal rear	5/8	5/8	50	Poplar	
4	Vertical rear	5/8	5/8	22½	Poplar	

Face Frame & Drawer Frames

NO.	ITEM	T	W	L	MATERIAL	COMMENTS
3	Vertical dividers	¾	1½	26⅝	Poplar	
4	Drawer dividers	¾	1⅛	33	Poplar	
1	Center divider	¾	1½	11¾	Poplar	
4	Rail extensions	¾	1¾	31½	Poplar	
8	Drawer runners	¾	2	16½	Poplar	½" tenon one end
2	Center runners	¾	3½	11¼	Poplar	½" tenon both ends
2	Rear dividers	¾	2¾	29½	Poplar	½" tenon both ends
4	Drawer guides	5/8	¾	15	Poplar	
2	Center guides	5/8	1½	15	Poplar	

Door Parts

NO.	ITEM	T	W	L	MATERIAL	COMMENTS
2	Stiles	¾	2¾	26½	Poplar	
1	Top rail	¾	2¾	11½	Poplar	1¼" tenon both ends
1	Bottom rail	¾	3	11½	Poplar	1¼" tenon both ends
1	Raised panel	5/8	9⅝	22⅜	Poplar	

Drawer Fronts (Other drawer parts taken from these sizes)

NO.	ITEM	T	W	L	MATERIAL	COMMENTS
2	Top row	¾	4⅛	14⅞	Poplar	
2	Second row	¾	5½	14⅞	Poplar	
1	Third row	¾	6⅝	30⅝	Poplar	
1	Fourth row	¾	6⅝	30⅝	Poplar	
2	Tray fronts	¾	2¾	13½	Poplar	
2	Tray sides	¾	2¾	16	Poplar	
2	Tray bottoms	⅜	12	14½	Plywood	

Misc. Parts

NO.	ITEM	T	W	L	MATERIAL	COMMENTS
2	Right ext. filler	5/8	2	17¼	Poplar	
2	Left ext. filler	1½	2	17¼	Poplar	
2	Attachment block	1¼	1½	14¼	Tiger maple/poplar	
1	Workbench top	2¾	27	84	Tiger maple	Laminated
1	Vise block	3⅜	1½	15½	Tiger maple	
31 lf	Retainer moulding	¾	¾		Tiger maple	

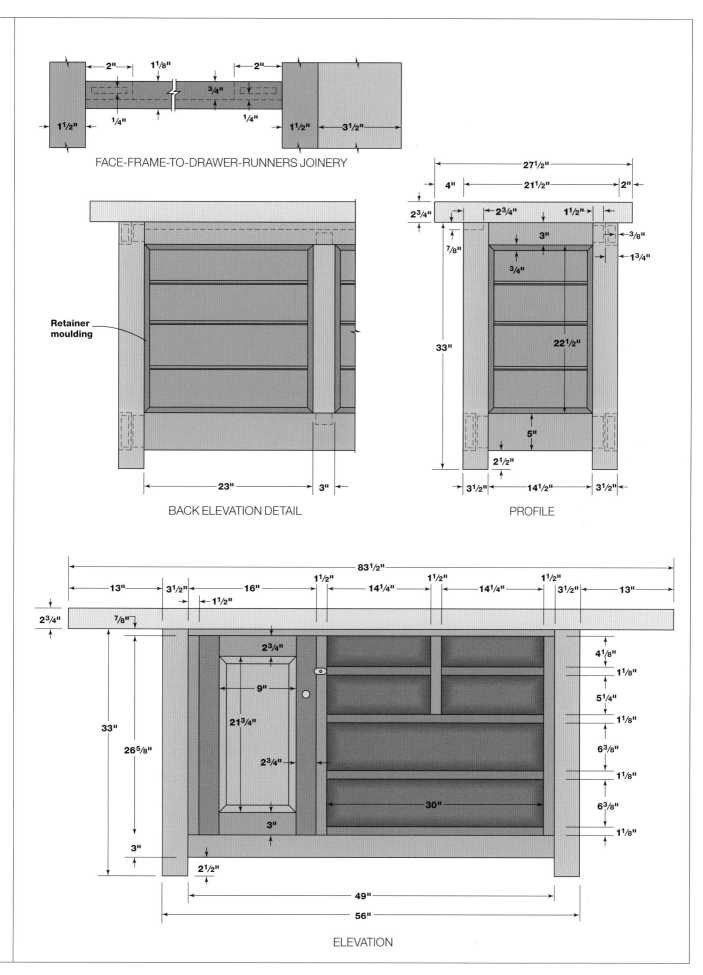

FACE-FRAME-TO-DRAWER-RUNNERS JOINERY

BACK ELEVATION DETAIL

PROFILE

Retainer
moulding

ELEVATION

All the rails are fit to the legs with mortise-and-tenon joinery. It's possible to simply add a benchtop at this point to have a well-built woodworking bench.

Assemble the Workbench Base

Work in stages. Sand the inner portions of the legs and the inside of each rail, then add glue to the mortise-and-tenon joints and assemble the back of the base. Add clamps to secure the assembly. Pin each joint with a ⅜"-diameter dowel. Use two pins in the wide rails and a single pin in the 3" rails.

Next assemble the bench base's front. I added a #8 x 1½" screw to reinforce each dovetail joint and pinned the lower rail of the front with a single dowel pin in each joint.

For the ends, glue the rails' tenons into the mortises and pin those joints as well. Don't forget the beams in the bottom of the base. Installing these parts makes the assembly of the base a bit tricky. It's necessary to slide all the joints together at the same time. When complete, the base structure of the workbench is standing strong.

Making Beaded Panels

To achieve a Shaker look on the exterior of the bench I decided to fill in the open areas between the ends and back with tongue-and-grooved pieces. To add a bit

of excitement I included a bead detail on each piece.

Cut the tongue-and-groove joints at the table saw. First mill the pieces necessary to fill each opening. Lay out the pieces edge to edge and mark the edges that get a groove and the mating edges that get a tongue. The starting piece has a groove only while the ending piece will have only the tongue. All remaining pieces have both a tongue and a groove.

Cut a ¼"-wide groove centered on the edge of the boards. To do this, set the blade height to ⅜" and the area between the fence and the blade at 3⁄16". Make a single pass over the blade, then reverse the board and make a second pass. The result is a ¼"-wide groove that's centered on the edge.

Making the matching tongue is also a job for the table saw. This time set the blade height to 3⁄16". Making the tongue is a two-step rabbet cut completed on both faces of the piece. Make the first pass with the board lying face down on the table saw surface. Cut both faces of the boards that get a tongue.

Now adjust the blade height to ⅜" and position the fence at 7⁄16". Cut the boards on edge to finish the tongue. This setup makes the cut so the fall off is not trapped between the blade and the fence, and the result is a ¼" tongue. Slight adjustments might be necessary to obtain an exact fit. The joint should slide together easily without the aid of a mallet or your palms. A joint that's too tight at this stage will present problems later, after paint is applied.

The bead detail is fashioned at the router table with a ¼" beading bit and is cut on the tongue portion of the joint.

The bead detail is placed on the tongue portion of the joint. Cutting the profile on the groove would weaken the joint considerably.

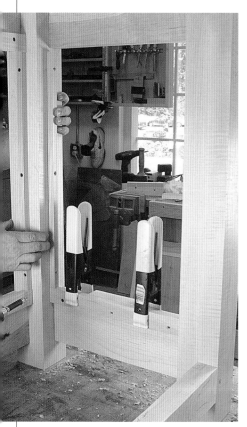

Sandwiching the panels. The panel backing, along with mouldings, hold the panels in position. The backings are screwed to the inside face of the rails as well as to the legs.

If the bead were cut onto the groove area the joint would fail due to material breakage.

Set the height of the beading cutter so the lower edge of the router bit bead profile is aligned with top edge of the tongue. Rout the detail into each piece that gets a tongue.

Holding the panels in place is accomplished with a combination of backing strips and mouldings. The backing strips are ⅝"-thick material that are attached with screws to the inside edge of the legs and vertical, back divider as well as the top and bottom rails. The strips surround the openings and hold the beaded panels in position. The retainer mouldings trap the panels and are added after the balance of the base is complete and the panels are painted.

A Flat-panel Divider

The first step to constructing the interior of the bench is to make the vertical flat panel that divides the drawer bank from the storage area fronted by a door. The

panel is created with rails, stiles and a floating panel.

Use mortise-and-tenon joints to build this panel. Cut the pieces to size according to the cut sheet. I use a mortiser to make the ¼"-wide x 2¼"-long x 1¼"-deep slots.

Next, cut a ¼"-wide x ⅜"-deep groove on the four pieces of the frame at the table saw (just as the groove on the beaded panels was created). The fence settings are different from the earlier setup due to the thicker stock of the frame.

Cut the matching tenons next. Set the table saw blade to a height of ¼" and set the fence to cut a 1¼"-long tenon. Make the cheek shoulder cuts on each end of the rails, then raise the blade to ⅜" and make an edge shoulder cut on the interior edge of the rails only.

The fence has to be adjusted to make the haunch cut in the outer edge of the rail. Move the fence toward the blade ⅜" and make a second edge-shoulder cut. You can see the haunch appear as the cut is made. The ⅜" offset in the fence matches the depth of the groove. The haunch will fill the plowed out groove.

To fit a flat panel to the frame you need to create a series of rabbets along each edge of the panel. The resulting tongue slips into the groove in the frame and is centered on the panel's edges. Set the blade height and fence both at ¼", then run each edge of one side of your panel over the blade. Flip the panel and run the second set of cuts with the settings the same.

Next, stand the panel on edge and raise the blade to clear the top edge of the previous cut. Adjust the fence to leave ½" between it and the blade. Make the cuts to create the tongue on the panel. Cut all four sides then reverse the panel to cut the remaining four sides allowing the tongue to emerge. Add glue to the mortise-and-tenon joints – but not on the floating panel and assemble the flat-panel divider.

Install the completed divider into the bench base with pocket screws. Two screws are set into the beam of the base and one additional screw is positioned into the top rail of the back. The divider is held to the front of the bench by the face frame, which defines the drawers and storage area.

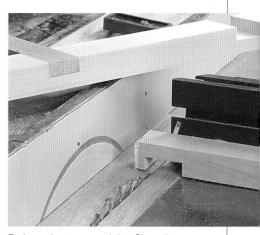

Perhaps the strongest joint. Given the narrow stock used for the face frame, the half-lap joint is stronger by far here than a mortise-and-tenon joint would be. This frame will be together a long time.

Putting on Your Best Face

The face frame for the workbench is built using a series of half-lap joints between the rails and stiles. This joint is strong, and because the face-frame pieces are narrow this joint offers more strength than a mortise-and-tenon could. The concept is to have the horizontal dividers pass behind the vertical dividers at each half-lap location. Pay attention to detail as you cut these joints.

Begin the half-lap joinery by milling the three vertical pieces, plus the divider that splits the top two rows of drawers and the four pieces that are drawer dividers. There is no top rail for the face frame – the top front rail of the base acts as the face frame's top rail.

Set the blade height to ⅜". After laying out the location of the drawer dividers according to the plan, use a miter gauge to guide the vertical pieces over the blade to remove the waste material. This requires a number of steps with each half-lap area being nibbled away. Find and cut the half-lap areas into the two drawer dividers for the center divider.

Making the cuts on the drawer divider ends is the easy cut. In fact, you can cut the half-laps at the ends of the drawer dividers and for the lower drawer divider into the three vertical dividers with the same setup.

Slide the fence toward the blade. Leave the appropriate length for the mating part of the joint, but don't change the blade height. Make the first pass over the

Matching the center divider to the face frame ensures the fit is correct. It's best to get exact measurements versus using a plan.

Clamping the face frame to the bench base does not require scads of clamps. Strategic placement and having a square frame guarantee an accurate glue-up.

blade to establish the length, then nibble away the remaining material. Test the joint for both width of cut and fit of the joint. A good half-lap joint finishes the same thickness as the material used in the joint.

To find the location of the half-lap joints in the center divider it's best to assemble the face frame and position the center divider flush with the top of the face frame assembly. There you can mark the areas that need to be removed for the drawer dividers as well as the overall length of the center divider. Then, it's back to the table saw to complete the joinery. Once the joints are made and fit, add the glue and clamps to assemble the face frame.

The face frame sets back 1" from the front edge of the base rails. Remember to position and glue the vertical divider on the left-hand side of the door. Attach the assembled unit to the base of the workbench with glue and clamps. Also, join the face frame and the flat panel divider with glue and a couple finish nails, which act as clamps while the glue sets. In addition, drive a screw through the bench's top rail into the ends of the vertical face frame pieces.

Support for the Drawers

The face frame divides up the drawer bank, but the drawers run on a web frame that attaches to the backside of the dividers. Each web frame is $\frac{3}{4}$" thick and the dividers are $1\frac{1}{8}$" wide. To work, the frames need to be held flush with the top edge of the dividers. Each frame has a

piece at the front called the extension and two runners.

The drawer web frames start with the drawer extension. The extensions run from side-to-side of the drawer opening, bridging the half-lap joints and have $\frac{1}{4}$"-wide x $1\frac{1}{2}$"-long x $\frac{1}{2}$"-deep mortises cut in each end of the rear edge for the runners' tenons.

The drawer frames are held in place with nails. Make sure the runners are level by starting at the bottom and measuring each location based off the front divider.

ners' tenons.

The runners begin as 2"-wide stock. Form a $\frac{1}{2}$"-long tenon on one end of each runner while the other end, the end nailed to the rear leg or flat-panel divider, is notched to use a $1\frac{1}{2}$" nail. Once the completed frames are in position, measure the location of the rear of the frames then add nails to secure the frames in place.

The lower frames are completed with the attachment of the runners to the extensions. Glue the tenons into the mortises and set the assemblies aside until dry.

However, the upper frames are different. Because the upper two rows of drawers are split, those frames also require a center runner that provides support on either side of the center vertical divider. The drawer extensions for those two rows need to have a third mortise to house the center runner. Position the runner in the center of the opening, not centered across the extension. Because of the center runners, it's necessary to install a rear divider that extends between the runners and fits into mortises placed in the runners. The center runner is attached to the rear divider with a mortise-and-tenon joint as well.

It's important to have plenty of clamps

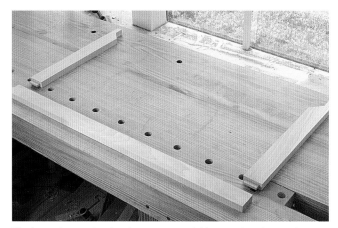

The lower frames for the drawers are quickly completed once the mortises and tenons are made. Assemble the frames and square the runners off the extension.

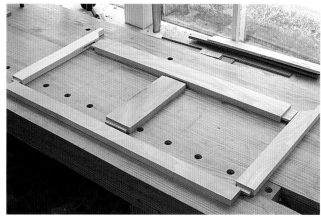

The frames for the upper drawers require three additional mortises as well as a rear divider and a center runner. And with mortises come tenons.

on hand or move through the installation of the frames in steps.

Drawers, Door & Trays

The door's frame is built just as the flat-panel divider was earlier. Use mortise-and-tenon joints with a haunch at the corners. The only difference is the door has a raised panel instead of a flat one. Create the raised panel at the table saw or with a raised panel cutter at the router table. Slip the panel into the groove as the door is assembled. Glue only the joints. The door is installed after the finish is applied.

Make the drawers using traditional dovetail joinery. The lipped fronts are rabbeted on three sides after the edges are rounded with a 3/8" roundover bit. The balance of the drawer parts are determined from the inside face of those fronts.

The 16"-long drawer sides are the same width as the inside of the fronts from the bottom edge to the start of the rabbet.

The drawer back is 3/4" less than the width of the drawer sides – the drawer bottom slides under the back and into grooves in the sides and front – and the length is equal to the inside face of the drawer front from rabbet to rabbet.

Use through-dovetails to join the drawer sides to the backs and half-blind dovetails to join the drawer fronts to the sides. The drawer bottoms are bevel cut at the table saw to slide into a 1/4" groove that is plowed into the drawer front and sides prior to assembling the drawer boxes.

Attaching the rail extensions to the face frame dividers requires many clamps. It's best to stage the process working one frame at a time. Once dry, level and nail the runners at the back.

The trays that fit into the storage area behind the door operate on full-extension drawer slides. The sides of the trays themselves are 2 3/4"-wide stock that is joined at the corners with through-dovetails. Remember to correctly size the box. The final width is dependent on the slides selected. The slides used on this project require a 1/2" of clearance per side, so the tray box is 1" narrower than its opening.

With the tray boxes built and assembled, use brads to attach a ledge around the interior of the box for supporting removable tray bottoms.

The full-extension slides need to be shimmed from behind so they are flush with the door opening. On the right-hand side, as you face the door, nail 5/8"-

thick x 2"-wide material to the flat-panel divider. The area on the left-hand side of the storage area requires 1 1/2"-thick stock to build out for the slides. Screw these to the legs.

The bottom tray is aligned with the top edge of the base rails – just high enough to bypass the rails as the tray is pulled out. The second tray is 12" above the first tray. In order to keep the trays level from front-to-back and side-to-side, use a pair of spacers to position the top tray assembly.

To finish the construction of the base of the bench, add two blocks at the top edge of the ends to provide a method to attach the top. The 1 1/4"-thick material is fit between the front and rear leg and glued in place.

A Showy Workbench Top

The top of a workbench is its important feature. This surface receives the most wear and should be solid (and showy) in my view. This bench has a tiger maple top that's 2¾" thick that begins as 3"-wide material. The top is a 32-piece lamination of hardwood that was ripped, milled and assembled into one heavy slab of lumber.

I ran each piece over the jointer to gain a straight, flat surface, then through the thickness planer to achieve a uniform thickness. From there, they were grouped and glued into three workable sections. Each of the three sections, when removed

The table saw allows you to fine-tune the fit of the drawer. Measurements for other drawer parts are based off the inside face of the drawer fronts.

The pull-out trays need to be level from front to back and from side to side. To ensure that happens, use spacers.

from the clamps, was once again jointed and planed to be straight, flat and uniform in thickness. Additionally the top was surfaced with a wide-belt sander to arrive at the final dimension.

The last step was to assemble the three sections. That left two joints that had to be worked by hand. Pay particular attention to the joint when gluing the final sections together. Any variations in the joint directly transfer to additional hand-work to straighten and level.

The vises selected for your bench are a reflection of your work habits. I like a quick-release vise for both my front and my end vise. Every vise is supplied with installation instructions that should be followed completely.

Drilling round holes for bench dogs – no square-cornered dogs for me – was

last on the list prior to beginning the finish. After hearing stories of woodworkers burning up drills or using the man-powered brace and bit and auger, I knew I had to find an easy method to drill my holes. Using the router to drill holes for adjustable shelf pins flashed through my thoughts. Could we apply that same method to the bench? Yes.

Use a ¾" up-cut spiral router bit (Woodcraft # 03K53 $55.99) to plunge-cut those holes. To keep the router positioned as the hole is cut, make a template that traps the base of the router (see photo below left). Clamp the template in place, position the router then plunge the holes. It's easy. To guarantee accurate hole locations, mark a centerline on the edge of the template and align that mark with the layout lines for your holes.

The top was laminated from 32 pieces of lumber. Work in stages, please. Trying to laminate all the pieces at once will be a glue-filled mess.

The stock for the top begins oversized to allow multiple trips to the jointer and planer. Having a level and true workbenchtop is paramount in bench making.

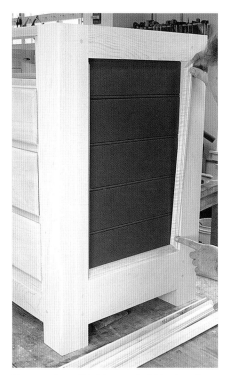

The panels on the base are held in place by the moulding that is installed in picture-frame fashion – the corners are mitered.

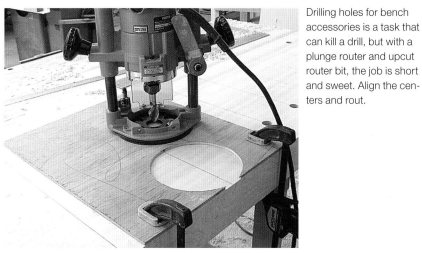

Drilling holes for bench accessories is a task that can kill a drill, but with a plunge router and upcut router bit, the job is short and sweet. Align the centers and rout.

A second rigging is needed to drill the holes in the top's front edge. These holes are for accessories that hold wide panels in place.

Drilling in the edge of the workbench top is another mystery to solve. I again used the router but the surface area was too narrow to plunge cut without concerns. To alleviate any problems, clamp a long guide to the base plate then clamp the guide to the top before plunging the cut. These front holes allow clamping of wide materials in the face vise. The top and base are attached with four 5" hex-head bolts with nuts and washers that are countersunk into the top and extend through the attachment blocks. The bench is now ready for finish.

Paint and Finish

All the panels and materials made in poplar are painted (Olde Century Colors "Cupboard Blue" acrylic latex). That includes the beaded panels, the face frame, the drawer fronts and the door. Paint two coats on all surfaces, sanding between coats. Once the painting was complete I could go back and add the moulding to lock in the beaded panels.

That moulding is installed with mitered corners.

The finish on the top and all the tiger maple framing is an oil/varnish mixture I've used for years. (See "Finishing Formulas" in April 2007, issue #161). Two coats were applied over everything. That's right, everything – including the painted parts of the workbench.

Hang the door using light-duty T-hinges along with a wooden knob and door catch.

I envision many years of building furniture on this bench. I wish I had built a quality workbench years back. Not that it would have improved my work, but maybe my work habits. No more scattering tools in the shop. I now have a workbench that has storage.

Two coats of an oil/varnish mixture is all the protection necessary for the bench. You don't want too much finish on the top. There's no need to have pieces sliding about.

Firewood Box

BY DAVID THIEL

If you haven't already stumbled on the concept of storing a larger cache of logs indoors, this Shaker reproduction will provide a stylish location for your wood stash.

Using pine, the piece is simple enough to complete in a weekend. First cut all of your pieces to length and plane them down to $3/4$" thickness. You'll almost certainly end up having to glue up some boards to attain the $20^3/4$" width. We opted to use biscuits to align the boards during the glue-up process.

Once the glue is dry, move to the next step – sizing the boards according to the Materials List. Because you're working with a fairly plain wood and design, the attention you give to grain figure and to matching wood color will make the piece more dramatic.

The next step is to lay out and cut the radius on the top front corner of each side. Use the profile view to locate the beginning and ending points of the radius. Use trammel points set at a $10^1/2$" radius to mark the corner, then use a jigsaw to cut both sides. Cut to the outside of the mark, allowing about $1/16$" overage to be sanded off. Clamp the two sides together for a final sanding to make sure the two radii match.

The next step involves cutting rabbets. We used two processes for this step. For the $3/4$" x $1/2$" rabbets we used the table saw, first running the $3/4$" dimension with the piece flat to the table, then the $1/2$" dimension with the piece on edge. Make sure your waste falls away from the fence to avoid binding between the fence and blade.

After making all the necessary $3/4$" x $1/2$" rabbets, set up a router with a $1/2$" x $1/2$" rabbeting bit with a pilot bearing. Use this setup to run the necessary rabbets to accept the back pieces.

If you haven't already done so, run the six back panels down to $1/2$" thick and cut to finished size. Then adjust the router setup to cut a $1/2$" x $1/4$" rabbet on opposing long edges of the back panels. These rabbets will give a shiplapped detail to the back of the box and also allow for expansion of the boards left to right.

The next setup for your router uses the rounded portion of a Roman ogee bit to run a cove profile on the radiused side edges.

The $1/4$" spacing shown on the back panels is accomplished by rabbeting a $1/4$" x $1/2$" rabbet on opposing long edges.

By using a portion of a Roman ogee bit, a delicate detail is added to the radiused edges of the sides. A cove bit with a guide bearing will also work.

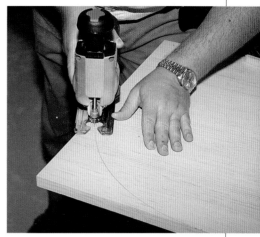
Use a jigsaw to cut the radius on the sides. Pay attention to tear-out by cutting from the inside of each piece.

The simple addition of a base shoe moulding helps make the piece more pleasing to the eye.

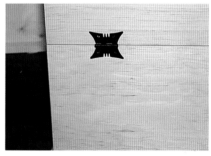
Wrought-iron hinges add to the Shaker style of the piece and complete the reproduction look.

I used a $1/8$" roundover bit to soften the perimeter edges of the door and front (don't round over the mating edges) as well as the front and sides of the top.

Before assembly, take the time to finish sand all the interior and any surfaces that will be difficult to sand after assembly. You will also want to sand off any glue or board-matching irregularities at this time.

Assemble the box using $1^1/4$" finish nails. Start by attaching the bottom between the two sides, flushing up the front edges of all three pieces. Use the top to help establish the spacing while nailing the sides. Next flush the top to the rear edge and nail it in place.

Now that you've established the box, nail the front into place across the bottom edge, check for square and nail up the sides.

The next step is to nail the back in place. You'll need to pay particular atten-tion to spacing the back pieces to maintain a uniform spacing on the shiplap joints.

To add another detail to the box we used a simple $3/4$" roundover bit to detail the top edge of the base trim pieces. We then mitered the front corners and tacked the trim into place.

Mark the locations for the hanging pegs, drill your holes and glue the pegs

RABBET DETAILS

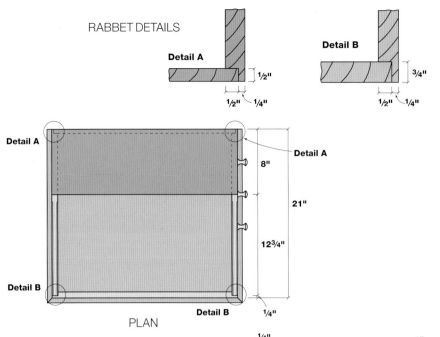

Detail A

1/2"

1/2" 1/4"

Detail B

3/4"

1/2" 1/4"

PLAN

Detail A

Detail A

8"

21"

12 3/4"

Detail B

Detail B

1/4"

into place. Be aware of glue squeeze-out or it will show when you put the finish on.

Now sand the entire piece to get it ready for finishing. We opted for a simple coat of clear lacquer to show the natural beauty of the sugar pine while sealing and protecting the wood.

Once the finish has hardened it's time to put on the hardware. To keep with the traditional styling of the firewood box, I went with wrought-iron butterfly hinges. The hardware shown was found at a local specialty hardware store, but you'll find similar pieces at the stores mentioned on the supplies list at the right.

Once the hardware's in place, the only detail left is stocking the box with wood. Then settle down for the evening in front of a cozy fire.

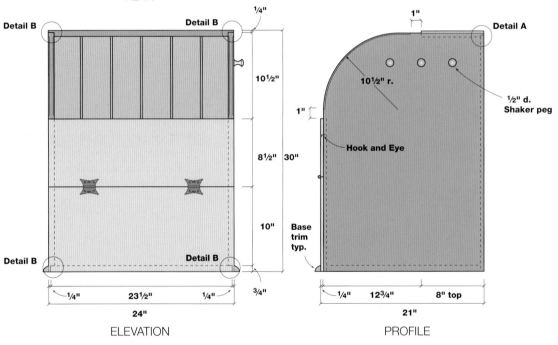

Detail B

Detail B

1/4"

10 1/2"

8 1/2" 30"

10"

Base trim typ.

Detail B

Detail B

1/4" 23 1/2" 1/4"

24"

3/4"

ELEVATION

1"

Detail A

10 1/2" r.

1"

Hook and Eye

1/2" d. Shaker peg

1/4" 12 3/4" 8" top

21"

PROFILE

1/2"

1/4"

LAPPED BACK DETAIL

Shaker Firewood Box

NO.	ITEM	DIMENSIONS (INCHES)		
		T	W	L
Low Bookcase				
2	Sides	3/4	20 3/4	29 3/4
1	Top	3/4	8	24
1	Front	3/4	10	24
1	Door	3/4	8 1/2	24
1	Bottom	3/4	20	23 1/2
4	Back panels	1/2	4 3/16	29 3/4
2	Back panels	1/2	3 7/16	29 3/4
2	Base trim	1/2	1	21 5/8
1	Base trim	1/2	1	24 1/4

Supplies

Woodworker's Supply Co.
800-645-9292 or woodworker.com

1 • pair, butterfly hinges, #110-708, $21.69/pair

1 • maple pegs, #119-354, $4.79/bag of 10

Prices correct at time of publication.

Distributed in Canada by Fraser Direct
100 Armstrong Avenue
Georgetown, Ontario L7G 5S4
Canada

Distributed in the U.K. and Europe by
F&W Media International, LTD
Brunel House, Ford Close
Newton Abbot
TQ12 4PU, UK
Tel: (+44) 1626 323200
Fax: (+44) 1626 323319
E-mail: enquiries@fwmedia.com

Distributed in Australia by Capricorn Link
P.O. Box 704
Windsor, NSW 2756
Australia

Visit our website at www.popularwoodworking.com
or our consumer website at www.shopwoodwork-
ing.com for more woodworking information projects.

Other fine Popular Woodworking Books
are available from your local bookstore
or direct from the publisher.

18   17   16   15   14   5   4   3   2   1

Acquisitions editor: David Thiel
Designer: Daniel T. Pessell
Production coordinator: Debbie Thomas

About the Authors

MEGAN FITZPATRICK

Megan is the editor of *Popular Woodworking Magazine*. She prefers using hand tools because they rarely make loud noises.

GLEN D. HUEY

Glen is the managing editor of *Popular Woodworking Magazine*. He is the author of a number of books on building furniture, and teaches and hosts DVDs about furniture building.

MALCOLM HUEY

Malcolm was a contributor to *Popular Woodworking Magazine* with articles, and more significantly with his son, Glen.

ROBERT W. LANG

Bob is executive editor with P*opular Woodworking Magazine* and has been a professional woodworker since the early 1970s. He is the author of several *Shop Drawings* books about furniture and interiors of the Arts & Crafts Movement of the early 1900s.

KERRY PIERCE

Kerry has been a frequent contributor to *Popular Woodworking Magazine* and is the author of a number of books on Shaker furniture.

CHRISTOPHER SCHWARZ

Chris is the former editor of *Popular Woodworking Magazine* and now serves as a contributing editor, covering the world of hand woodworking, as well as teaching and creating videos.

TROY SEXTON

Troy is a former contributing editor for *Popular Woodworking Magazine*, and continues as a professional woodworker.

STEVE SHANESY

Steve has worn many hats at *Popular Woodworking Magazine,* over the years, including editor and publisher. He has now officially retired and carries the title of woodworker-at-leisure.

JIM STUARD

Jim was associate editor of *Popular Woodworking Magazine* for a number of years and has now gone over the gentile world of fly fishing.

DAVID THIEL

David is a former senior editor of *Popular Woodworking Magazine* and is now works with books and videos under the *Popular Woodworking* brand.

Metric Conversion Chart

TO CONVERT	TO	MULTIPLY BY
Inches	Centimeters	2.54
Centimeters	Inches	0.4
Feet	Centimeters	30.5
Centimeters	Feet	0.03
Yards	Meters	0.9
Meters	Yards	1.1

Read This Important Safety Notice

To prevent accidents, keep safety in mind while you work. Use the safety guards installed on power equipment; they are for your protection.

When working on power equipment, keep fingers away from saw blades, wear safety goggles to prevent injuries from flying wood chips and sawdust, wear hearing protection and consider installing a dust vacuum to reduce the amount of airborne sawdust in your woodshop.

Don't wear loose clothing, such as neckties or shirts with loose sleeves, or jewelry, such as rings, necklaces or bracelets, when working on power equipment. Tie back long hair to prevent it from getting caught in your equipment.

People who are sensitive to certain chemicals should check the chemical content of any product before using it.

Due to the variability of local conditions, construction materials, skill levels, etc., neither the author nor Popular Woodworking Books assumes any responsibility for any accidents, injuries, damages or other losses incurred resulting from the material presented in this book.

The authors and editors who compiled this book have tried to make the contents as accurate and correct as possible. Plans, illustrations, photographs and text have been carefully checked. All instructions, plans and projects should be carefully read, studied and understood before beginning construction.

Prices listed for supplies and equipment were current at the time of publication and are subject to change.

Ideas. Instruction. Inspiration.

These and other great *Popular Woodworking* products are available at your local bookstore, woodworking store or online supplier.

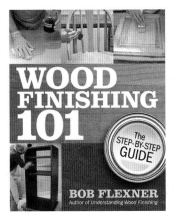

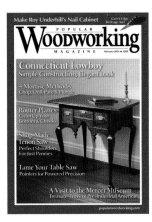

WOOD FINISHING 101
By Bob Flexner
Wood finishing doesn't have to be complicated or confusing. Wood Finishing 101 boils it down to simple step-by-step instructions and pictures on how to finish common woods using widely-available finishing materials. Bob Flexner has been writing about and teaching wood finishing for over 20 years.

paperback • 128 pages

WEEKEND WOODWORKER'S PROJECT COLLECTION
This book has 40 projects from which to choose and, depending on the level of your woodworking skills, any of them can be completed in one or two weekends. Projects include: a game box, jewelry box, several styles of bookcases and shelves, mirrors, picture frames and more.

paperback • 256 pages

POPULAR WOODWORKING MAGAZINE
Whether learning a new hobby or perfecting your craft, *Popular Woodworking Magazine* has expert information to teach the skill, not just the project. Find the latest issue on newsstands, or you can order online at popularwoodworking.com.

SHOPCLASS VIDEOS
From drafting, to dovetails and even how to carve a ball-and-claw foot, our Shop Class Videos let you see the lesson as if you were standing right there.

Available at shopwoodworking.com
DVD & Instant download

POPULAR WOODWORKING'S VIP PROGRAM

Get the Most Out of Woodworking!

Join the Woodworker's Bookshop VIP program today for the tools you need to advance your woodworking abilities. Your one-year paid renewal membership includes:

- *Popular Woodworking Magazine* (1 year/7 issue U.S. subscription — A $21.97 Value)
- *Popular Woodworking Magazine CD* — Get all issues of *Popular Woodworking Magazine* from 2006 to today on one CD (A $64.95 Value!)
- The Best of Shops & Workbenches CD — 62 articles on workbenches, shop furniture, shop organization and the essential jigs and fixtures published in *Popular Woodworking* and *Woodworking Magazine* ($15.00 Value!)
- 20% Members-Only Savings on 6-Month Subscription for Shop Class OnDemand

- 10% Members-Only Savings at Shopwoodworking.com
- 10% Members-Only Savings on FULL PRICE Registration for Woodworking In America Conference (Does Not Work with Early Bird Price)
- and more....

Visit **popularwoodworking.com** to see more woodworking information by the experts, learn about our digital subscription and sign up to receive our weekly newsletter at popularwoodworking.com/newsletters/

FOLLOW
POPULAR
WOODWORKING